MW00964507

MODERN MACROECONOMICS

THIRD EDITION

STUDY GUIDE

ROBIN BADE
MICHAEL PARKIN

The University of Western Ontario

PRENTICE HALL CANADA INC., SCARBOROUGH, ONTARIO

Canadian Cataloguing in Publication Data

Bade, Robin
    Study guide for Modern macroeconomics, third
edition

Supplement to: Parkin, Michael, 1939-   . Modern
macroeconomics. 3rd ed.
ISBN 0-13-591165-6

1. Macroeconomics. 2. Canada - Economic conditions -
1945-   . 3. Macroeconomics - Problems, exercises,
etc. 4. Canada - Economic conditions- 1945-   -
Problems, exercises, etc. I Parkin, Michael, 1939-   .
II Parkin, Michael, 1939   . Modern macroeconomics,
3rd ed.   III Title.

HB172.5P372 1992   339   C92-04804-9

© 1992, 1986, 1982 by Prentice-Hall Canada Inc.,
Scarborough, Ontario

ALL RIGHTS RESERVED.

No part of this book may be reproduced in any form
without permission in writing from the publisher.

Prentice Hall, Inc., Englewood Cliffs, *New Jersey*
Prentice-Hall International, Inc., *London*
Prentice-Hall of Australia, Pty., Ltd., *Sydney*
Prentice Hall of India Pvt., Ltd., *New Delhi*
Prentice-Hall of Japan, Inc., *Tokyo*
Prentice-Hall of Southeast Asia (Pte.) Ltd., *Singapore*
Editora Prentice-Hall do Brasil Ltda., *Rio de Janeiro*
Prentice-Hall Hispanoamericana, S.A., *Mexico*

ISBN 0-13-591165-6

ACQUISITIONS EDITOR: Marjorie Walker
SUPPLEMENTS EDITOR: Maryrose O'Neill
PRODUCTION ASSISTANT: Anita Boyle

1 2 3 4 5   AP   96 95 94 93 92

Printed in Canada by Alger Press Ltd.

Table of Contents

Part I *Introduction*

Chapter 1 What Is Macroeconomics? 1
Chapter 2 Monitoring Macroeconomic Activity 11
Chapter 3 Explaining Business Cycles, Growth, and Inflation 24

Part II *Aggregate Demand Fluctuations*

Chapter 4 Aggregate Expenditure and Income 38
Chapter 5 Aggregate Expenditure, Interest Rates, and Money 50
Chapter 6 Monetary and Fiscal Policy Influences on Aggregate Demand 63
Chapter 7 World Influences on Aggregate Demand 75

Part III *Fluctuations and Growth in Aggregate Supply*

Chapter 8 The Labor Market and Aggregate Supply 87
Chapter 9 Unemployment 97
Chapter 10 Capital, Technology, and Economic Growth 108

Part IV *Inflation, Deficits, and Debts*

Chapter 11 Inflation, Interest rates, and the Exchange Rate 118
Chapter 12 Inflation and the Business Cycle 128
Chapter 13 Public and Private Deficits and Debts 138

Part V *Macroeconomic Policy*

Chapter 14 Why Macroeconomists Disagree About Policy 148
Chapter 15 Stabilizing the Canadian Economy 159
Chapter 16 Stabilizing the World Economy 169

Part VI *Microfoundations of Aggregate Demand*

Chapter 17 Consumption and Saving 180
Chapter 18 Investment 190
Chapter 19 Money and Asset Holding 199

Part VII *The New Macroeconomics*

Chapter 20 New Classical Macroeconomics 209
Chapter 21 New Keynesian Macroeconomics 219

CHAPTER 1

What Is Macroeconomics?

Perspective and Focus

This chapter tells you what macroeconomics is about. It introduces you to the *subject matter* of macroeconomics by describing the questions that macroeconomics is designed to answer. These questions are about macroeconomic performance—about what determines six key macroeconomic variables. These questions are:

- What determines the rate of growth of real GDP?
- What causes fluctuations in the rate of economic growth and of unemployment?
- What determines the average level of prices and the rate at which they rise—the inflation rate?
- What determines interest rates?
- What determines the Canadian balance of payments with the rest of the world?
- What determines the value of the dollar abroad?

The first three questions are the central and most important questions for macroeconomics, but all six define its subject matter.

The chapter goes on to *describe* the facts about macroeconomic performance. It also describes the problem of stabilizing the economy.

The questions that macroeconomists try to answer have turned out to be hard ones, and the answers that they have found are still controversial. Because of this fact the chapter makes you aware of the variety of opinion and the nature of the controversy in macroeconomics today.

Learning Objectives

After studying this chapter, you will be able to:

- To explain what macroeconomics is all about
- To describe the changing pace of economic expansion and inflation in the Canadian and world economies
- To describe the problem of stabilizing the economy
- To describe the main schools of thought on how the economy works and how it might be stabilized

Increasing Your Productivity

How many times have you said to yourself "I worked hard for that exam and deserve a better grade"? The payoff from work depends partly on the number of hours we work. But it also depends on our *productivity*—on how effectively we use our work hours. You can increase your productivity in studying macroeconomics in a variety of ways. We give you our general advice on how to make your study effective in the preface of the textbook (on pages xvi and xvii) and in the preface to this *Study Guide*. Here we focus on the two most important additional things to pay attention to as you begin your study of Chapter 1: **reading graphs** and **being skeptical and curious**.

Reading Graphs

Graphs play an important part in macroeconomics. They convey a great deal of information to you and they enable you to convey a lot of information to your instructor. Don't just "look at" graphs—*read them*. When you read the text you know the order in which to proceed. You start at the top left-hand corner of the page and move rightward and downward. There is also a correct order in which to read a graph. Here it is:

1. Look at the *x*-axis and check that you understand the variable that is being measured along the axis and the units in which the variable is being measured.

2. Look at the *y*-axis and check that you understand the variable that is being measured along that axis and the units in which the variable is being measured.

3. Look at the curves in the graph *one at a time*. Be sure that you understand what each curve is telling you.

4. Look at any specially highlighted points and be sure that you understand why they are highlighted and what they are telling you.

5. Read the boxed notes.

6. Read the extended caption and as you do so look at the parts of the figure to which it draws your attention.

If you follow these rules each time you come to a diagram you will find that you make can read the text itself more quickly and with deeper and more lasting understanding.

Being Skeptical and Curious

Don't take any facts about macroeconomic performance on trust. Check them out. Also be curious and ask questions, such as okay, these may be the facts in Canada but what about in the United States or Europe or Japan? Are the facts the same there?

Appendix A (pages 622-624) and Appendix B (pages 625-631) provide you with a good deal of data about Canadian macroeconomic performance between 1926 and 1990 and the macroeconomic performance of France, Germany, Italy, Japan, the United Kingdom, and the United States from 1960 to 1990. Use these appendixes whenever you get a chance and check how general or how special any particular feature of Canadian macroeconomic performance is.

Self Test

Concept Review

1. Macroeconomics is the study of
   _____ _____
   _____.

2. The performance of the economy as a whole is called _____ _____
   _____.

3. Real _____ is a measure of the quantity of goods and services that all the individuals in the economy can buy with their income.

4. The unemployment rate is equal to the percentage of the _____ _____ that is either ____ __ ____ or seeking _____ or on temporary _____.

5. Inflation is a _____ of _____
   _____.

6. The recurring fluctuation in the pace of _____ _____ is called the business cycle.

7. Fiscal policy is variations in the levels of _____ _____ of
   _____ and _____ and _____
   to influence the state of the economy.

8. Monetary policy is variations in the ____
   _____ in _____ _____ to
   influence the state of the economy.

9. Direct controls are specific ____, ____, and _____ designed to modify the way people behave.

10. The goals of macroeconomic stabilization policy are called _____
    _____ _____.

11. _____ _____ is a body of macroeconomic theory based on the idea that the economy is a self-regulating mechanism, always tending in the direction of __ _____.

12. _____ _____ is a body of macroeconomic theory based on the idea that the economy does not possess a self-regulating mechanism, left to its own devices, it can get stuck with a high and _____ level of _____ and __ _____.

True or False

1. Macroeconomics is the study of aggregate economic activity.

2. The Canadian economy always grows, but it growth rate varies—sometimes it is rapid and sometimes it is slow, but it is always growing.

3. The unemployment rate is the percentage of the adult population that does not have jobs or are on temporary layoff from their regular jobs.

4. Inflation is a process in which money steadily loses its value in terms of the goods and services that it will buy.

5. An unexpected upturn in the inflation rate reduces the debts of borrowers and the wealth of lenders.

6. Macroeconomics studies what determines inflation, unemployment, real income growth, and interest rates. It does not study why the foreign exchange value of the dollar fluctuates.

7. Fluctuations in the pace of economic expansion is called the business cycle.

8. GDP fluctuates about trend GDP but because GDP exceeds trend GDP most of the time, trend GDP is positive.

9. Since World War II the Canadian business cycle has become less severe.

10. The Canadian economy has experienced three large and long expansions since 1950—one beginning in the 1952, one beginning in 1960, and one beginning in 1982.

11. The Canadian price level fell during the Great Depression but increased every year since World War II. As a result the Canadian inflation has gradually increased.

12. When disinflation occurred in Canada in the early 1980s, the Canadian price level continued to increase but at a slower rate.

13. Canadian inflation peaked during the mid-1970s at 25 percent a year. At the same time, inflation in the rest of the world was 13 percent a year.

14. Canada produces 5 percent of the world's total output and the United States produces 25 percent of it.

15. Since 1960, the growth rate of real GDP has been higher in Japan and the United States than in Canada. As a result, real income per person in the Canada is now less than that in Japan and the United States.

16. Since 1960, the real income gap between Canada and Central and South America has gradually gotten narrower.

17. Fiscal policy uses variations in interest rates to influence the state of the economy.

18. One of the targets of macroeconomic policy is mild fluctuations in the growth rate of real income and the unemployment rate.

19. To use wage and price controls in the hope of stabilizing of the economy is to use a direct control.

20. Monetary policy in conducted by government of Canada and the Bank of Canada, but when they can't agree the Bank of Canada takes control of monetary policy.

Multiple Choice

1. Which of the following people would be counted as being unemployed:
   (a) Mary who quit her job last week so she could spend her time looking after her ailing grandmother.
   (b) Tom who starts a new job next week. He has spent the last two months searching full time for a job.
   (c) Al teaches school in Newfoundland. He wants a teaching job in Alberta for next year and keeps watching the advertisements for teachers in Alberta.
   (d) Jerry has a part-time job and wants a full-time one. He keeps reading the local newspaper for such a position.
   (e) Martha is a novelist, who has written five best sellers. Martha needs a break and has just decided to sail around the world for the next year.

2. The percentage of the labor force that is either out of work and seeking jobs or on temporary layoff is known as the
   (a) discouraged worker effect.
   (b) added worker effect.
   (c) secondary worker effect.
   (d) problem of ratio.
   (e) unemployment rate.

3. Inflation
   (a) is a relative new phenomenon.
   (b) was not experienced in Canada until the 1970s.
   (c) became a problem when currencies ceased to be fixed in value to gold.
   (d) is not a problem until it become a hyperinflation.
   (e) none of the above.

4. Macroeconomics tries to explain
   (a) why some unemployed workers become discouraged.
   (b) why Canada has a deficit on its international balance of payments.
   (c) why real income growth in Canada has slowed in recent years.
   (d) (b) and (c).
   (e) all of the above.

5. The business cycle in Canada
   (a) reached a peak during the Korean War and the first OPEC oil shock.
   (b) reach a trough during World War II.
   (c) was at a trough when the second OPEC oil shock occurred.
   (d) was in an expansion phase for most of the 1980s.
   (e) none of the above.

6. Inflation in Canada
   (a) was low at the time of the Korean War and the first OPEC oil shock.
   (b) increased during the 1960s as the economy expanded.
   (c) was low when the second OPEC oil shock occurred.
   (d) increased during the 1980s as the economy expanded.
   (e) (b) and (c).

7. The growth rate of real GDP
   (a) was higher in Japan than in Canada during the 1960s.
   (b) slowed in Canada but not in Japan in the 1970s.
   (c) was higher in the "Big 4" European economies and in the United States than in Japan in the 1960s.

   (d) in Canada and Japan have gradually become equal since 1960.
   (e) (a) and (b).

8. Inflation, on the average, was lower in Canada than in the rest of the world during
   (a) the 1960s.
   (b) the 1970s.
   (c) the 1980s.
   (d) the 1960s and the 1970s but not in the 1980s.
   (e) (a), (b), and (c).

9. The business cycle in Canada in comparison with that in the rest of the world
   (a) peaked in the 1960s when the business cycle in the rest of the world hit a trough.
   (b) hit a trough in the 1980s when the business cycle in the rest of the world also hit a trough.
   (c) was in an expansion phase in the 1970s when the business cycle in the rest of the world was in a contractionary phase.
   (d) was in an expansion phase in the 1980s when the business cycle in the rest of the world was also in an expansionary phase.
   (e) (a) and (d).

10. A change in the level of government purchases of goods and services or taxes to influence the state of the economy is known as
    (a) monetary policy.
    (b) direct controls.
    (c) fiscal policy.
    (d) policy rules.
    (e) policy targets.

11. Global policies influence the values of a small number of aggregate variables, such as
    (a) the government's budget deficit and the money supply.
    (b) the money supply and the foreign exchange rate.
    (c) level of government purchases of goods and services and the international balance of payments.
    (d) overall level of taxes and the unemployment rate.
    (e) all of the above.

12. Which of the following is an example of a policy rule?
    (a) Cutting the money supply by 1 percent whenever the dollar depreciates by 0.5 percent.
    (b) A constitutional amendment requiring the budget to be balanced.
    (c) Increasing the growth rate of the money supply by 1 percent a year whenever the unemployment rate increases by 2 percent.
    (d) (a) and (c).
    (e) (a), (b), and (c).

13. Monetarists advocate that the government
    (a) adopt fixed rules for the behavior of the global macroeconomic variables.
    (b) adopt fixed rules for the behavior of the detailed macroeconomic variables.
    (c) use discretionary policy for the behavior of the global macroeconomic variables.
    (d) use discretionary policy for the behavior of the detailed macroeconomic variables.
    (e) (a) and (d).

14. Monetarists advocate that the government adopt fixed rules for the behavior of which of the following variables?
    (a) The money supply growth rate.
    (b) Government purchases.

    (c) The price of oil.
    (d) The average real wage rate.
    (e) (a) and (b).

15. Activists advocate that the government
    (a) adopt fixed rules for the behavior of the global variables.
    (b) adopt fixed rules for the behavior of the detailed variables.
    (c) use discretionary policy for the behavior of the global variables.
    (d) use discretionary policy for the behavior of the detailed variables.
    (e) (c) and (d).

16. Activists advocate that the government use discretionary policy to keep employment at its full employment level and inflation low and steady. Such actions are known as
    (a) rationalizing the economy.
    (b) fine tuning the economy.
    (c) isolating the economy.
    (d) dissecting the economy.
    (e) automating the economy.

17. The body of macroeconomic theory that is based on the idea that the economy is a self-regulating mechanism is known as
    (a) Keynesian macroeconomics.
    (b) classical macroeconomics.
    (c) monetarist macroeconomics.
    (d) new classical macroeconomics.
    (e) real business cycle macroeconomics.

18. Which of the following is a body of macroeconomic theory is based on the idea that if the economy left to its own devices it can get stuck with a high and persistent level of unemployment and lost output?
    (a) Monetarism.
    (b) New classical economics.
    (c) Classical economics.
    (d) Keynesian economics.
    (e) Real business cycle theory.

19. Classical macroeconomists perceive that the economy operates
    (a) like a self-regulating mechanism, always tending toward full employment.
    (b) with a fundamental design problem that can keep it away from full employment for long periods at a time.
    (c) like a self-destructive mechanism, always tending away from full employment.
    (d) under a specific rule designed to always operate at full employment.
    (e) none of the above.

20. The microeconomic foundations of macroeconomics is the model of the behavior of
    (a) individual households and individual firms.
    (b) individual firms but not individual households.
    (c) government enterprises and organizations.
    (d) foreign countries.
    (e) (a), and (c).

Short Answers Questions

1. Briefly summarize the difference(s) between Keynesian and classical macroeconomics.

2. Explain how monetary policy influences the state of the economy? Compare this influence with that of fiscal policy.

3. Do monetarists advocate rules or discretion in the conduct of macroeconomic policy?

4. Briefly describe the difference(s) between the new classical and new Keynesian research programs on macroeconomics.

5. Explain direct controls and how they can be used to stabilize the economy.

6. (a) Explain what macroeconomics studies.
   (b) What does macroeconomics seek to understand?

7. (a) What is real GDP?
   (b) What is the growth of real GDP?

8. (a) What are macroeconomic policy targets?
   (b) What do these policy targets include?

9. Briefly compare the business cycle in Canada with that in the rest of the world from 1960 to 1990.

10. Explain the disagreement between monetarists and activists about how the economy works and the policy options that should be used. Do they agree on any aspects of these?

Problem Solving

1. In Dream Land, there are 80 million workers and 10 million unemployed persons. Calculate the unemployment rate in Dream Land?

2. In 1982, actual real GDP was $3,166 billion and trend real GDP was $3,398 billion. Calculate the deviation of real GDP from trend?

3. Classify the following statements according to whether it deals with a detailed or global policy, a policy rule or discretion, and is probably a recommendation by a monetarist or activist.

(a) The proposed cut in capital gains tax rate is an important element of the long-term growth agenda.

(b) Fiscal policy typically provides a significant stimulus to the economy during recessions and early recovery.

(c) Effective job training programs to retrain workers are a key to increasing productivity and remaining internationally competitive.

(d) Investment in research and development and infra-structure, and the extension of research and development tax credit will help increase business productivity.

(e) The fundamental goal of Canada is the removal of all tariffs and the removal or reduction of nontariff trade barriers.

(f) Fundamental banking reform is critical to ensuring efficient operation of credit markets.

(g) The Bank of Canada has stated a policy goal of achieving, over time, price stability.

(h) Through most of the first half of 1991, the money supply stayed near the middle of its target.

✓ *Answers*

Concept Review

1) aggregate economic activity
2) aggregate economic activity
3) income
4) labor force, out of work, jobs, layoff
5) process, rising prices
6) economic expansion

7) government purchases, goods, services, taxes
8) money supply, interest rates
9) laws, rules, regulations
10) macroeconomic policy targets
11) classical macroeconomics
12) Keynesian macroeconomics

True or False

1) T 5) T 9) T 13) F 17) F
2) F 6) F 10) F 14) F 18) T
3) F 7) T 11) F 15) F 19) T
4) T 8) F 12) T 16) F 20) F

Multiple Choice

1) b 5) d 9) b 13) a 17) b
2) e 6) b 10) c 14) e 18) d
3) e 7) a 11) e 15) e 19) a
4) d 8) e 12) e 16) b 20) e

Short Answer Questions

1. Keynesian macroeconomics is a body of macroeconomic theory based on the idea that the economy does not possess a self-regulating mechanism and, left to its own devices, it can get stuck with a high and persistent level of unemployment and lost output.

   On the other hand, classical macroeconomics is a body of macroeconomic theory based on the idea that the economy is a self-regulating mechanism, always tending in the direction of full employment.

2. Monetary policy uses variations in the nation's money supply and in interest rates to influence the state of the economy, whereas fiscal policy uses variations in the levels of government purchases of goods and services and taxes to influence the state of the economy.

3. Monetarists advocate that governments have policies toward a limited number of global macroeconomic variables such as money supply growth, government expenditure, taxes, and the government deficit. They advocate the adoption of fixed rules for the behavior of these variables.

4. The three views are mainstream, new classical, and new Keynesian.

   The mainstream view is that a solid core of sensible macroeconomic theory exists that needs to be improved, but only at the edges.

   New classical macroeconomists believe that the classical view of the economy is a fruitful one and one that is likely to lead to better macroeconomic theory. Their goal is to explain such macroeconomic phenomenon as fluctuations in economic growth and unemployment as the "natural" consequences of a well functioning economy in which everyone is doing the best they can for themselves and in which markets work efficiently.

   New Keynesians believe that markets do not always work efficiently and that prices and wages are sticky, at least in the short run, so that the economy can get stuck a long way from full employment. Their research agenda is to explain fluctuations in economic growth and unemployment as the consequence of price and wage stickiness and other failings of the market economy.

5. Direct controls are specific laws, rules, and regulations designed to modify the way people behave. Direct controls stem from laws passed by the government and implemented by a wide variety of agencies.

   Examples of direct controls that influence the stability of the economy are wage and price controls that have sometimes been used in hope of keeping inflation in check.

6. (a) Macroeconomics is the study of aggregate economic activity.

   (b) Macroeconomics seeks to understand the determination of the unemployment rate, the level and rate of growth of real GDP, the general level of prices and the rate of inflation, the level of interest rates, the balance of transactions with the rest of the world, and the value of the dollar in terms of other currencies.

7. (a) Real GDP is a measure of the quantity of the goods and services that can be purchased with the income of all the individuals in the economy. It is a measure of living standards.

   (b) The growth in real GDP is a measure of the growth of people's real incomes. It is the pace of improvement in living standards.

8. (a) Macroeconomic policy targets are the goals of macroeconomic stabilization policy.

   (b) Macroeconomic policy targets include a high and sustained growth rate of real income, a low unemployment rate, mild fluctuations in the growth rate of real income and of the unemployment rate, and a low inflation rate.

9. From 1960 to 1981, the business cycle in the rest of the world lines up remarkably close with that in Canada. But there are some differences in the degree of recession and recovery. The rest of the world had a deeper recession in the early 1970s than did Canada. Further-more, Canada had a deeper recession in 1981 than did the rest of the world.

10. Figure 1.9 summarizes the answer to this question. Monetarists are classical economists and believe that the market operates like a self-regulating mechanism, always tending toward full employment. Activists are Keynesian in their belief that the economy has a fundamental design problem that can keep it away from full employment for long periods at a time. On policy issues, monetarists believe that a fixed rule governing the money supply growth rate and possibly other rules governing the size of the federal budget deficit are best for achieving macroeconomic stability, whereas activists believe that discretionary changes in interest rate, taxes, and government spending are essential components of any stabilization policy. Economist in each group favor stronger methods of achieving a balanced or more nearly balanced budget.

Problems

1. The unemployment rate is calculated by dividing the number of unemployed persons by the number of people in the labor force. The unemployment rate is 11.1 percent

2. (a) In 1982, the deviation was 6.8 percent.

   (b) The deviation of real GDP from trend GDP is calculated as (actual GDP − trend GDP) + trend GDP, expressed as a percentage.

3. (a) discretionary, activist
   (b) global, rule
   (c) detailed, activist
   (d) detailed, activist
   (e) detailed
   (f) global
   (g) global
   (h) monetarist, rule

CHAPTER 2

Monitoring Macroeconomic Activity

Perspective and Focus

A zillion things happen in the economy every day. This chapter tells you how economists organize their records of these events so they can keep track of the movements in the economy and develop theories that enable them to understand these events. The chapter makes three important distinctions. Those between

- Stocks and flows.
- Final expenditure and intermediate transactions.
- Income and expenditure.

In a nutshell, a stock is a value at a point in time while a flow is a rate per unit of time. The number of tapes or compact disks that you own are stocks—they are the numbers that you own at a given point in time. In contrast, the tapes or compact disks that you bought last week are flows—they are measured as the quantity bought per week.

Final expenditure is the purchase of a good or service by its final user. In contrast, an intermediate transaction is the purchase of a good or service to be used in the manufacture of some other good or service that eventually will be sold to its final user. For example, your purchase of tapes or compact disks are final expenditures. The purchases of plastic by EMI to use in the manufacture of tapes and compact disks are intermediate transactions.

But purchases of **new capital** equipment are final expenditures. If you buy a CD player or EMI buys a machine for pressing compact discs, the purchase is a final expenditure, not an intermediate transaction.

An income is a payment in return for the supply of the services of factors of production. In contrast, an expenditure is a payment in exchange for final goods and services. For example, the wages you receive for working in your college or university bookstore are an income. Your purchase of a textbook is an expenditure.

This chapter also introduces you to two sets of key identities that permeate macroeconomics. They are

- Aggregate expenditure equals aggregate income equals the value of aggregate output.
- Aggregate deficits across all sectors sum to zero.

Learning Objectives

After studying this chapter, you will be able to:

- Explain the distinction between flows and stocks
- Explain the distinction between expenditures on final goods and intermediate transactions
- Explain why aggregate income, expenditure, and product (or the value of output) are equal
- Explain the connection between the government budget deficit and the international trade deficit
- Define gross national product (GDP)
- Define nominal GDP and real GDP
- Explain what a balance sheet measures
- Define capital, wealth, and money
- Describe the main features of the debt explosion of the 1980s
- Explain how economic growth and inflation are measured

Increasing Your Productivity

Work hard to understand the important distinctions between (a) stocks and flows, (b) final expenditure and intermediate transactions, and (c) income and expenditure. For at least the next week or two, ask yourself every time you encounter a transaction whether you are looking at a stock or a flow, an intermediate transaction or a final expenditure, or an income or an expenditure.

You probably won't have any trouble understanding the distinction between income and expenditure when using examples such as your wages from working in the college or university bookstore in comparison with your expenditure on textbooks. But when it comes to looking at the Canadian national income accounts, somehow things seem to get complicated. Problems 2 and 3 (on page 54 of your textbook) are designed to help you sort out and apply the distinctions between income and expenditure. When working the problems just apply the test: Is the transaction a payment for the services of a factor of production such as land, labor, or capital (or the residual profit)? If it is, then it is an income. Is the transaction a payment for a final good or service—a consumer good or a capital good? If it is, then it is an expenditure.

Expenditure Equals Income Equals Value of Output

The key to understanding why aggregate expenditure equals aggregate income is an appreciation of the role played by inventories and profits. The change in value of the firms' inventories is considered part of aggregate expenditure. It is part of firms' investment. Thus if firms have produced something of value, even if it has not yet been sold to its final user, it is counted as expenditure on final goods and services.

Profit (or loss) is part of factor income. Aggregate income equals all the payments of wages and other factor incomes paid by firms to households plus the profit that firms have made but not yet paid out. A firm's profit equals its receipts from sales plus the change in the value of its unsold inventories minus the income it pays to factors of production. Thus profit plus income paid to factors of production equal receipts from sales of goods and services plus the change in the value of inventories. The sum of profit and the income paid to factors of production is factor incomes and the receipts from sales of goods and services plus the change in the value of inventories is expenditure on final goods and services. In aggregate, these are always equal.

Output can be valued either by what people are willing to pay for it or by what it costs to produce it. Since these two numbers are identical to each other, they are also equal to the value of output.

Leakages Equals Injections

Work hard at Tables 2.2, 2.3, and 2.4 and the associated Figures 2.2, 2.3, and 2.4 and be sure that you understand (a) what we mean by leakages and injections and (b) why they are always equal to each other.

Self Test

Concept Review

1. A variable that measures a rate per unit of time is called a ___, and a variable that is measured at a point in time is called a _____.

2. The stock of buildings, plant and equipment, houses, consumer durable goods, and inventories is called ____. The purchase of new capital is called _____, which is made up of ____ _____ and _____ _____.

3. The reduction in the value of the capital stock is _____. Total additions to the capital stock in a given period of time is ____ _____. The change in the capital stock is called __ _____ which is equal to ___ _____ minus _____.

4. The total sum of rent paid to the owners of land, wages paid to labor, interest paid to the owners of capital, and profit paid to the owners of firms is called _____. The purchases of final goods and services is called _____. The value of all final goods and services produced is called _____.

5. The goods and services bought by households, government, and foreigners are ___ _____ __ ____. Firm's purchases of new capital and their additions to inventory are___ goods, but their purchases of goods and services to be used by them in the production of goods and services are _____ _____. The increase in the value of a product when factors of production are used to transform it is called ____ ____.

6. _____ _____ is the value of the goods and services bought by households. The income that households do not spend on goods and services is called _____.

7. A flow out from the circular flow of income and expenditure is a _____, and a flow into the circular flow is an _____.

8. Government expenditure on final goods and services is called _____ _____ of goods and services, but the benefits and subsidies paid by the government are called _____ _____. _____ are total taxes paid minus transfer payments.

9. The flow of money from the rest of the world in exchange for Canadian produced goods and services is _____, the flow to the rest of the world in exchange for foreign produced goods and services is _____ . _____ _____ is exports _____ imports.

10. The government's budget deficit and the Canadian deficit with the rest of the world are called the _____ _____.

11. _____ _____ _____ is the total expenditure on final goods and services in a year by Canadian residents. Gross _____ product is the total expenditure in a year on goods and services produced in Canada. The total income received by Canadian residents in a year is _____ _____.

12. The value of the goods and services produced in year, measured in current prices, is called is _____. The value of the goods and services produced in year, measured in base year prices, is called is _____ _____.

13. Total income received by households is called _____ _____, and personal income minus personal taxes is called _____ _____ _____.

14. The _____ _____ is that part of the economy engaged in illegal activities.

15. A _____ _____ is a statement about what someone owns and owes. Some- thing that someone owns is an ___ and something that someone owes is a _____.

16. ___ assets are concrete, tangible objects, and _____ assets are pieces of paper that represent promises to pay.

17. Total liabilities minus total assets is called ____ or __ ___.

18. Anything generally acceptable in exchange for goods and services is called a ____ __ _____. Anything that is accepted as a medium of exchange is ___.

19. The rate of change of real GDP from one year to the next is called _____ _____.

20. The price level is measured by the ratio of nominal GDP to real GDP, multiplied by 100. It is called the __ _____. Other measures, the __ and the __ are ___ ____. These measure the cost of a particular ____ of goods and services as a percentage of the cost of the same basket in the base year.

True or False

1. The purchase of a new airplane by Air Canada is an expenditure on a final good, but the purchase of the food that Air Canada serves on its flights is not.

2. Depreciation is the reduction in the value of capital that results from its utilization or from the passage of time.

3. The Canadian governments' payment of unemployment compensation is part of its purchases of goods and services.

4. Consumer expenditure is a flow, and net investment is a stock.

5. The flow of money from Japan to Canada in exchange for Canadian produced goods and services is part of Canadian exports, and the flow of money from Canada to Japan in exchange for Japanese produced goods and services is part of Canadian imports.

6. If households in Canada increase their expenditure on final goods and services, saving decreases and as a result investment decreases.

7. Leakages include taxes, saving and exports, and injections include government purchases, investment, and imports.

8. The government of Leisure Land has a budget deficit and households save less than firm's invest. Leisure Land's stock of net financial assets in decreasing and the rest of the world's stock of net financial assets is increasing.

9. Canada has a deficit with the rest of the world. As a result, Canada lends to the rest of the world.

10. If consumer expenditure plus government purchases plus investment exceeds GDP, then either investment exceeds saving or the government has a budget deficit.

11. GDP differs from GNP in that GNP values aggregate economic activity at market prices and GDP values aggregate economic activity at factor cost.

12. Domestic income is a net measure aggregate economic activity in a year and it is measured at factor cost.

13. Real GDP is total expenditure on final goods and services, whereas nominal GDP is the inflation component of real GDP.

14. Personal disposable income is the flow of money that households receive from supplying factors of production and that households can choose to spend on final goods and services or save.

15. When Earl withdraws $100 from his deposit at the Prairies Bank, the bank's balance sheet remains balanced because both its liabilities and assets decrease by $100.

16. The Azuma Bank makes a loan to Cathy to buy a boat and to Fred to buy some bonds. The Azuma Bank has increased its stock of financial assets, Cathy has increased her stock of real assets, and Fred has made no change to his stock of financial assets.

17. Judy's wealth is equal to her stock of real assets. The loan she has taken to pay for this year at school has no effect on her wealth.

18. The underground economy is the part of the economy in which the medium of exchange used is not money.

19. Economic growth is the rate of change of either national income or nominal GDP.

20. An index number calculated as the ratio of nominal GDP to real GDP multiplied by 100 is known as the GDP inflator.

Multiple Choice

1. The total additions to the capital stock in a given period of time are
   (a) inventory investment.
   (b) fixed investment.
   (c) net investment.
   (d) gross investment.
   (e) unintended investment.

2. Which of the following are stocks?
   (a) expenditure on final goods and services but not intermediate transactions.
   (b) the output of final goods and services but not those added to inventory.
   (c) investment including the addition to inventories.
   (d) the money that people have to spend.
   (e) both (a) and (c).

3. Which of the following shows the equality of leakages and injections?
   (a) $S + T + IM = I + G - EX$.
   (b) $S - T - IM = I - G + EX$.
   (c) $S + T + IM = I + G + EX$.
   (d) $S + I + IM = T + G + EX$.
   (e) $S + I + G = T + IM - EX$.

4. In a country that has a budget deficit
   (a) leakages exceed injections.
   (b) injections exceed leakages.
   (c) exports exceed imports.
   (d) imports exceed exports.
   (e) none of the above.

5. When national income statisticians use the expenditure approach to measure GDP they do the following calculation:
   (a) $C - I - G + EX + IM$.
   (b) $C + I + G + EX - IM$.
   (c) $C + I + G + T + EX + IM$.
   (d) $C + I + G - T + EX - IM$.
   (e) $C + I + G + T + EX - IM$.

6. The three commonly used measures of the money supply in Canada today are
   (a) M1, M3 and M5.
   (b) M2, M4, and M5.
   (c) M1, M2, and M3.
   (d) M2, M3, and M4.
   (e) M1, M2, and M4.

7. In Canada, twin deficits
   (a) appeared in 1960.
   (b) declined quickly in the 1980s.
   (c) did not occur before the 1970s.
   (d) became large in the 1980s.
   (e) do not exist today.

8. Which of the following is a stock?
   (a) net exports.
   (b) investment.
   (c) government purchases.
   (d) unemployment.
   (e) interest rates.

9. During the 1980s, Canadian federal government debt increased at an annual average rate of almost
   (a) 30 percent.
   (b) 20 percent.
   (c) 16 percent.
   (d) 40 percent.
   (c) 4 percent.

10. Suppose you know that the government is running a budget deficit. Then
   (a) saving must exceed investment.
   (b) net exports must be positive.
   (c) investment plus exports must exceed saving plus imports.
   (d) the country's net exports can only be positive if saving exceeds investment.
   (e) the budget deficit can be decreased only if net exports are increased.

11. Personal income is equal to
    (a) domestic income + transfer payments from government − business retained profits.
    (b) domestic income − transfer payments from government − business retained profits.
    (c) domestic income + transfer payments from government + business retained profits.
    (d) domestic income − transfer payments from government.
    (e) domestic income − business retained profits.

12. Personal disposable income is equal to personal income minus
    (a) dividend payments.
    (b) personal saving.
    (c) transfer payments.
    (d) personal income tax payments.
    (e) none of the above.

13. Mary's wealth is equal to
    (a) her total assets.
    (b) her total assets and total liabilities.
    (c) her total assets minus her total liabilities.
    (d) her financial assets.
    (e) her financial assets minus her financial liabilities.

14. Which of the following would be included in GDP in the year 1991?
    (a) The purchase in 1991 of a used 1990 car.
    (b) The purchase in 1991 of a share of Bell Canada stock.
    (c) The purchase in 1991 of an car produced in 1991.
    (d) All of the above.
    (e) Both (b) and (c) but not (a).

15. If net exports are zero and the government has a budget deficit, then
    (a) the government's net financial assets decrease.
    (b) the government's net financial assets increase.
    (c) the private sector's net financial assets increase.
    (d) both (b) and (c).
    (e) real assets of the private sector decrease.

16. In 1990, Dream World's nominal GDP was $100 billion and its real GDP was also $100 billion. In 1991, its nominal GDP was $110 billion and its real GDP was $95 billion. In 1991, Dream World's economic growth rate was
    (a) 10 percent.
    (b) 5 percent.
    (c) −5 percent.
    (d) −10 percent.
    (e) −11 percent.

17. Which of the following measures movements in the prices of goods and services typically consumed by urban Canadian families?
    (a) The Producer Price Index.
    (b) The Consumer Price Index.
    (c) The GDP deflator.
    (d) The GDP inflator.
    (e) The CPI deflator.

18. The GDP deflator is equal to
    (a) nominal GDP ÷ real GDP.
    (b) nominal GDP x real GDP.
    (c) (real GDP ÷ nominal GDP) x 100.
    (d) (nominal GDP ÷ real GDP) x 100.
    (e) nominal GDP − real GDP.

19. The price level as measured by the GDP deflator will be higher than that measured by the CPI if
    (a) the prices of the goods typically consumed by households exceed other prices.
    (b) the basket of goods typically consumed by households doesn't change.
    (c) the prices of capital goods exceed the prices of other goods.
    (d) the economy experiences rapid growth in all sectors.
    (e) none of the above.

20. On Sandy Isle, nominal GDP in 1991 was $100 billion and real GDP was $90 billion. In 1991, Sandy Isle's GDP deflator was
    (a) 90.
    (b) between 90 and 100.
    (c) 100.
    (d) between 100 and 110.
    (e) more than 110.

Short Answers Questions

1. Explain the difference between flow and stock variables. Give some examples of macroeconomic variables that highlight the difference between flows and stocks.

2. Explain the distinction between nominal GDP and real GDP.

3. Some economists have suggested that the official measure of GDP underestimates its true value. Why?

4. What are the twin deficits?

5. (a) Explain the difference between gross national product (GNP) and gross domestic product (GDP).
   (b) How are GNP and GDP valued?

   (c) What is the difference between GNP and GDP?

6. (a) What is domestic income?
   (b) What does domestic income measure?

7. (a) Using the expenditure approach to measure GDP, what equation is used by national income statisticians?
   (b) How does the expenditure approach value GDP?

8. What are business retained profits?

9. Some economists have suggested that the official estimates of GDP overestimate the true value of GDP. Why?

10. Canada experienced a debt explosion in the 1980s. The debt of which agents in the economy increased most rapidly. Was this an explosion in nominal debt or real debt.

Problem Solving

How does it go?

1. You are given the following information about the economy in Sunny Isle:

	$ billion
GDP at market prices	250
Consumer expenditure	100
Investment	75
Government budget deficit	20
Net exports	−20

(a) Calculate saving.

Saving is a leakage from the circular flow. Total leakages equal total injections. That is,

$$S + T + IM = I + G + EX$$

or,

$$S = I + (G - T) + (EX - IM)$$
$$= 75 + 20 + (-20)$$
$$= \$75 \text{ billion.}$$

(b) Calculate the taxes paid to the government.

Households allocate their income between consumer expenditure, saving, and taxes. That is,

$$Y = C + S + T$$

or,

$$250 = 100 + 75 + T$$
$$T = \$75 \text{ billion.}$$

(c) Calculate the change in the net financial assets of the government sector.

The change in the net financial assets of the government sector is equal to $T - G$, which is -20 billion.

2. You are given the following data for an economy:

	$billion
Wages	230
Interest	85
Rent	90
Profit	115
Transfer payments	35
Consumer expenditure	225
Investment	160
Government purchases	175
Imports	124
Exports	118
Total taxes paid	150

Depreciation   34

(a) What is aggregate expenditure measured in market prices?

Aggregate expenditure at market prices is equal to

$C + I + G + EX - IM$, which is

$225 + 160 + 175 + 118 - 124$ or $554 billion.

(b) What is domestic income?

Domestic income is the sum of all factor incomes. That is, wages + interest + rent + profit. That is,

$230 + 85 + 90 + 115$ or $520 billion

(c) What is the government's budget *deficit*?

Government's budget deficit is equal to $G - T$, where T is net taxes. Net taxes equal taxes paid minus transfer payments. That is, $150 - 35$, or $115 billion.

The budget deficit is equal to $175 - \$115$, which is $60 billion.

Now try these

1. On June 1, 1991, Terry owned a 1985 boat with a current market value of $4000. In the year from June 1, 1991 to June 1, 1992, the market value of the boat dropped to $3200. On June 1, 1992, Terry sold the 1985 boat and replaced it with a 1988 boat valued at $6000. Her capital stock on June 1, 1992 was the same $6000.

(a) What was the change in Terry's capital stock from June 1, 1991 to June 1, 1992?

(b) What was Terry's investment?

2. Suppose that you purchase a strawberry flavored icecream bar from your local grocery store for $1.50. The store bought the icecream bar from a wholesaler for $1.20; the wholesaler bought it from the manufacturer for $0.98; the manufacturer bought the milk for $0.06, the strawberries for $0.12, the sugar for $0.04, and electricity for $0.20, paid wages to its workers of $0.36, and made a $0.20 profit. The profit was paid to the stockholders as a dividend.

(a) What is the total flow of money in this story of the strawberry flavored ice-cream bar?

(b) What is the expenditure on final goods and services?

3. In problem 2, what is the value added by the manufacturer? The value added by the wholesaler? The value added by the grocery store?

4. In problem 2, what are the factor incomes paid.

5. Firms produce $1000 worth of goods and services and pay incomes of $1000 to households. If households purchase $900 worth of goods and services and save $100 and that firms do not purchase any new capital equipment, then the only investment is inventory investment. By what amount do the firms' inventories change?

6. This year in Leisure Land, consumer expenditure is $3657.3 billion, investment is $741 billion, government purchases are $1098.1 billion, exports are $672.8 billion, imports are $704 billion, and indirect taxes less subsidies are $469.4 billion.

(a) What is gross national product at market prices?

(b) What is gross national product at factor cost?

7. On December 31, 1991, George had $25 of currency, $150 in his savings account, $200 in savings bonds, a $1000 bank loan, $1200 on his visa account, and a car worth $1500, and a CD player and CDs worth $1000.

Calculate George's

(a) total financial assets.
(b) total financial liabilities.
(c) total real assets.
(d) total assets.
(e) total liabilities.
(f) net worth.

8. You are given the following information about an economy:

	$ billion
Wages and salaries	$4000
Interest and investment income	$200
Rents	$1000
Profits	$500
Income taxes	$300
Indirect taxes less subsidies	$50
Capital consumption	$30

(a) What is domestic income?

(b) What is gross domestic product at factor cost?

(c) What is net domestic product at market prices?

(d) What is gross domestic product at market prices?

9. You are given the following information about Dream Land:

	$ billion
GDP	5000
Net exports	250
Government purchases	1700
Consumer expenditure	2000

(a) If the budget is balanced, what is saving?
(b) Calculate investment.
(c) Calculate the change in net financial assets of households and firms.
(d) Is Dream Land borrowing or lending to the rest of the world?
(e) Calculate the change in the net financial assets of the rest of the world.

10. You are given the following data for Desert Kingdom:

	$ billion
Wages	130
Interest	35
Rent	40
Profit (all distributed)	75
Transfer payments	45
Consumer expenditure	145
Investment	80
Government purchases	75
Imports	6
Exports	18
Total taxes paid	50
Depreciation	10

Calculate:

(a) aggregate expenditure using the expenditure approach.
(b) domestic income using the factor incomes approach.
(c) the government's budget *deficit*.
(d) personal income.
(e) indirect taxes less subsidies.

✓ *Answers*

Concept Review

1) flow, stock
2) capital, investment, fixed investment, inventory investment
3) depreciation, gross investment, net investment, gross investment, depreciation
4) income, expenditure, product
5) final goods and services, final, intermediate transactions
6) consumer expenditure. saving
7) leakage, injection
8) government purchases, transfer payments, taxes
9) exports, imports, net exports, minus
10) twin deficit
11) gross national product, domestic, domestic income
12) nominal GDP, real GDP
13) personal income, personal disposable income
14) underground economy
15) balance sheet, asset, liability
16) real assets, financial assets
17) wealth, net worth
18) medium of exchange, money
19) economic growth
20) GDP deflator, CPI, PPI, price indexes, basket

True or False

1) T	5) T	9) F	13) F	17) F
2) T	6) F	10) F	14) T	18) F
3) F	7) F	11) F	15) T	19) F
4) F	8) T	12) T	16) T	20) F

Multiple Choice

1) d	5) b	9) c	13) c	17) b
2) d	6) c	10) d	14) c	18) d
3) c	7) d	11) a	15) d	19) d
4) e	8) d	12) d	16) c	20) e

Short Answer Questions

1. A flow is a variable that measures a rate per unit of time. Examples of macroeconomic flows are income and expenditure and are expressed as dollars per unit of time. A stock is a variable measured at a point in time. Examples of macroeconomic stocks are the total amount of money in the economy at a given point in time.

2. Nominal GDP is the value of goods and services produced in a year, measured in current year prices. Real GDP is the value of the goods and services produced in a year, when output is valued at the prices prevailing in a base year.

3. Because the measured GDP omits the underground economy. The underground economy is the part of the economy that is engaged in illegal activities and includes both criminal activity (e.g., drug dealing) and activities that are not themselves illegal but are concealed to avoid government regulations or the payment of taxes (e.g., under reporting tips)

4. The government's budget deficit and the Canadian deficit with the rest of the world are called the twin deficits.

5. (a) Gross national product is the total expenditure on final goods and services in a year by Canadian resident. GNP is a gross measure because it includes gross investment. GNP is a measure of the national economic activity, that is all economic activity of the residents of Canada and it does not matter in what part of the world that activity takes place.

Gross domestic product is the total expenditure in a year on goods and services produced in the geographical domain of Canada.
(b) Both GNP and GDP are valued at market prices which are the prices paid by the final user.
(c) The difference between GDP and GDP is known as net property income from (or paid) abroad.

6. (a) Domestic income is the total income, including profit, received by residents of Canada in a year.
(b) Domestic income measures net aggregate economic activity because firms deduct the depreciation of their capital stock in calculating their profit.

7. (a) National income statisticians use the following equation to obtain a measure of GDP:

$$Y = C + I + G + EX - IM.$$

(b) The expenditure approach values GDP at market prices.

8. Business retained profits are those profits not distributed to households in the form of dividends.

9. Some economists suggest that the official estimates of GDP overestimate the true value of GDP because they omit the cost of pollution and the destruction of natural resources such as forests. Furthermore, these costs could be very large if the worst-case scenarios about global warming and ozone layer depletion are correct.

10. The debt explosion of the 1980s occurred because government debt, corporate debt and household debt all increased. Federal government debt increased most rapidly. In nominal terms, it increased at an

average rate of 16 percent a year. Federal government debt also increased in real terms at an average rate of 9 percent a year. Federal government debt also increased as a percentage of GDP.

Problem Solving

1. (a) $2000
    (b) $2800

2. (a) $4.66
    (b) $1.50

3. $0.56, $0.22, $0.30

4. $1.50

5. $100

6. (a) $5465.2 billions
    (b) $4995.8 billions

7. (a) $ 375
    (b) $2200
    (c) $2500
    (d) $2875
    (e) $2200
    (f) $ 675

8. (a) $5700 billion
    (b) $5730 billion
    (c) $5750 billion
    (d) $5780 billion

9. (a) $1300 billion
    (b) $1050 billion
    (c) $250 billion
    (d) lending
    (e) −$250 billion

10. (a) $312 billion
    (b) $280 billion
    (c) $ 70 billion
    (d) $325 billion
    (e) $ 22 billion

CHAPTER 3

Explaining Business Cycles, Growth, and Inflation

Perspective and Focus

You now know (from Chapter 1) what macroeconomics is about and (from Chapter 2) how we go about observing and measuring the main flows and stocks that keep track of our macroeconomic performance. Your job in this chapter is to move forward and learn how real GDP and the price level are determined—what determines the cycles in economic activity, the tendency for real GDP to grow all the time, and the tendency for prices to rise—for there to be inflation.

Learning Objectives

After studying this chapter, you will be able to:

- Set out and explain the aggregate demand-aggregate supply model
- Explain what determines aggregate demand
- Explain what determines aggregate supply
- Explain how aggregate demand and aggregate supply interact to determine real GDP and the price level
- Use the aggregate demand-aggregate supply model to explain the 1982 recession and the 1980s expansion
- Explain the difference between the classical and Keynesian models of aggregate demand and aggregate supply
- Explain how the classical and Keynesian models interpret fluctuations in real GDP and the price level
- Describe the objectives of the research programs of new classical and new Keynesian macroeconomists

Increasing Your Productivity

There are just two things to watch in this chapter that cause real problems for students time and time again. Get them right and you are way ahead of the game.

1. The direction of shift of the *SAS* curve.
2. What happens when *LAS* changes.

Directions of Shift of the *SAS* Curve

An increase in short-run aggregate supply shifts the *SAS* curve to the right. A decrease in short-run aggregate supply shifts the *SAS* curve to the left. Don't be confused by the positions of the *SAS* curves in the vertical direction. When short-run aggregate supply has fallen, the new

SAS curve intersects the *LAS* curve at a higher price level than the original *SAS* curve. But short-run aggregate supply has fallen. The quantity of real GDP supplied at a given price level is lower on the new *SAS* curve than on the original *SAS* curve. Take a look at Figure 3.6(a) on page 73 and convince yourself of this fact.

Effects of a Change in Long-Run Aggregate Supply

When long-run aggregate supply increases both the long-run aggregate supply curve and the short-run aggregate supply curve shifts to the right. The new *SAS* curve intersects the *AD* curve at a level of real GDP below the new long-run aggregate supply level. That is, with an increase in long-run aggregate supply, long-run real GDP increases by more than actual real GDP. Figure 3.7(c) illustrates this case. Work through the opposite case—that of a decrease in long-run aggregate supply. Draw a diagram as you follow the story that we are about to tell. A decrease in long-run aggregate supply (for example resulting from a major drought) shifts the long-run aggregate supply curve to the left. The short-run aggregate supply curve shifts leftward with it. The new short-run aggregate supply curve intersects the aggregate demand curve at a level of real GDP above the long-run level. That is, the fall in actual real GDP is smaller than the fall in long-run real GDP. Does your diagram agree with this account? If it doesn't draw it again. Make your short-run aggregate supply curve shift leftward to intersect the new *LAS* curve at the same price level as the original *SAS* curve intersects the original *LAS* curve. In other words, make a diagram that looks like Figure 3.6(c) except make the *LAS* and *SAS* curves move in the opposite direction from the shifts shown in that figure.

Self Test

Concept Review

1. A macroeconomic model is a description of how _____, _____, _____, and _____ make economic decisions and how these decisions are _____ in _____.

2. Variables whose values are determined by the model are called _____ _____. Variables whose values are determined outside the model and are taken as given are called _____ _____ _____.

3. _____ _____ is a body of laws and generalizations about how the economy works based on _____ models whose _____ have not yet been rejected.

4. The quantity of real GDP demanded or the _____ _____ of _____ ___ _____ _____ is the total value of _____ _____ , _____ , _____ _____ and ____ _____.

5. The aggregate demand schedule lists the _____ ___ ____ ____ _____ at each level of the ____ _____, holding constant all other influences on the buying plans households, firms, governments, and foreigners. Aggregate demand curve is a graph of the _____ _____ __ _____.

6. The quantity of real GDP supplied or the _____ _____ of ____ ____ _____ is the total value of all _____ and _____ _____ in the economy.

7. Aggregate supply is the relationship between the _____ __ ____ ___ _____ and the _____ _____ , holding constant all other influences on firms' production plans. It is represented by either the _____ _____ _____ or the _____ _____ _____.

8. Long-run aggregate _____ is the quantity is real GDP _____ when all _____ and _____ have adjusted so that each firm is producing its profit-maximizing output and there is _____ _____.

9. The _____ _____ of _____ is the percentage of the labor force that is unemployed when the only _____ is that arising from the normal job search activity and labor market turnover.

10. The short-run aggregate supply schedule lists the _____ __ ____ ___ _____ at each ____ _____ , holding constant the _____ of the factors of production. The short-run aggregate supply curve is a graph of the _____-___ _____ ____ ___ _____.

11. _____ _____ is the term used to refer to the relationship between the quantity of real GDP supplied and the price level.

12. The situation in which the aggregate quantity of real GDP demanded equals the aggregate quantity of real GDP supplied is called a _____ _____.

13. When macroeconomic equilibrium occurs on the long-run aggregate supply curve, the economy is at ____-_____ _____.

14. When macroeconomic equilibrium occurs to the left of the long-run aggregate supply curve, the economy is at __ _____ _____.

15. When macroeconomic equilibrium occurs at a level of real GDP that is greater than long-run aggregate supply, the economy is at an _____ __ _____ _____.

16. Household income minus total taxes paid is called _____ _____.

17. _____ _____ is money expressed in terms of the goods and services that it can buy.

18. The price of foreign goods relative to the price of domestically produced goods and services is called the ____ _____ _____.

19. The ____ ____ _____ is the money wage rate divided by the price level.

20. When real GDP is less than long-run real GDP, a ____ ___ exits.

True or False

1. The variables whose values are predicted by a macroeconomic model are called endogenous variables.

2. A macroeconomic model describes in immense detail all the decisions of households, firms, governments, and foreigners.

3. The Canadian economy experienced recession in the early 1970s, no inflation in the mid-1970s, and rapid inflation in late 1970s.

4. Both Canada and the rest of the world experienced a recession in 1982 and an expansion with increasing inflation through the 1980s.

5. From 1970 to 1990, real GDP in Canada increased by a smaller percentage than did real GDP in the rest of the world.

6. The aggregate demand schedule lists the quantity of real GDP demanded at each price level, taking account of variations in all other influences on the purchasing plans of households, firms, governments, and foreigners.

7. Aggregate demand decreases if government purchases of goods and services decrease, consumption expenditure decreases because of a decrease in wages, investment decreases because firms' expect future profits to be poor.

8. A shift of the aggregate demand curve to the left is an decrease in aggregate demand.

9. Long-run aggregate supply is the quantity of real GDP supplied when all wages and prices have adjusted so that each firm is producing its profit-maximizing output and unemployment is at its natural rate.

10. The percentage of the labor force that is unemployed when the only unemployment is that arising from the normal job-search activity of new entrants to the labor force and labor market turnover is known as the natural rate of unemployment.

11. Long-run aggregate supply increases when technology advances or the labor force increases, but it decreases if wages increase.

12. An increase in short-run aggregate supply is an upward shift of the short-run aggregate supply curve.

13. Macroeconomic equilibrium is a situation in which the quantity of real GDP demanded is equal to the quantity of real GDP supplied in the long-run.

14. The price level increases and unemployment increases if either short-run aggregate supply or aggregate demand increases.

15. The real exchange rate increases when the price of foreign goods and services increase or the price of domestic goods and services decrease.

16. The real wage rate is the real cost of labor, and it increases when the price level increases.

17. The classical model assumes that the economy works like a self-regulating mechanism and, of the many possible influences on aggregate demand, only fiscal policy is effective.

18. In the Keynesian model, the short-run aggregate supply curve is vertical—the quantity of real GDP supplied does not respond to changes in the price level.

19. New classical and new Keynesian economists agree that macro models should be built on micro foundations, but they do not agree on the facts to be used to judge macro models. If they could agree on the facts to be used, then we would have less disagreement, better macro models, and more effective macro policy.

20. Classical macroeconomists explain the expansion of Canadian real GDP in the 1980s as the result of supply-side forces, whereas for Keynesian macroeconomists it was the result of demand-side forces.

Multiple Choice

1. Aggregate quantity of goods and services demanded is
   (a) the total quantity demanded of all goods and services produced domestically plus the quantity of goods and services imported.
   (b) the total quantity demanded all the goods and services produced domestically.
   (c) the total quantity demanded of all final goods and services produced domestically.
   (d) the total quantity demanded of all goods and services produced domestically minus those that remain unsold and are put into inventory.
   (e) none of the above.

2. Long-run aggregate supply is the level of real GDP that
   (a) varies with the price level so that the long-run aggregate supply curve is upward-sloping.
   (b) varies so that the long-run aggregate supply is negatively sloped.
   (c) varies at a given price level so that the long-run aggregate supply curve is horizontal.
   (d) never varies so that the long-run aggregate supply curve is vertical.
   (e) none of the above.

3. The economy in at an unemployment equilibrium if the macroeconomic equilibrium occurs at a
   (a) level of real GDP below its long-run level.
   (b) level of real GDP on the long-run aggregate supply curve.
   (c) level of real GDP above long-run aggregate supply.
   (d) level of real GDP either above or below long-run aggregate supply.
   (e) (a), (c), and (d).

4. Aggregate demand curve shifts to the left if
   (a) disposable income increases.
   (b) investment increases.
   (c) business confidence improves.
   (d) all of the above.
   (e) none of the above.

5. The aggregate demand curve slopes downward because as the price level increases, other things being equal,
   (a) the quantity of real money decreases and consumer expenditure decreases. As a result the quantity of real GDP demanded decreases.
   (b) the real exchange rate decreases and the demand for domestically produced goods and services decreases. As a result the quantity of real GDP demanded decreases.
   (c) the real money supply decreases, interest rates increase, and consumer expenditure increase. As a result the quantity of real GDP demanded decreases.
   (d) both (a) and (b).
   (e) all the above.

6. The short-run aggregate supply curve slopes upward because when
   (a) the price level changes, wage rates also change.
   (b) the price level changes, wage rates do not change.
   (c) wage rates change, the price level does not change.
   (d) wage rates change, the price level changes.
   (e) none of the above.

7. Long-run aggregate supply increases if
   (a) the labor force increases.
   (b) the natural rate of unemployment decreases.
   (c) the wage rate increases.
   (d) both (a) and (b).
   (e) all the above.

8. Short-run aggregate supply increases if
   (a) the labor force increases or the capital stock increases.
   (b) the natural rate of unemployment decreases.
   (c) technological advances increase labor productivity.
   (d) both (a) and (b).
   (e) all of the above.

9. Aggregate demand increases if
   (a) government purchases of goods and services increase.
   (b) a tax cut increases disposable income and increases consumer expenditure.
   (c) business confidence improves and investment increases.
   (d) the dollar weakens on the foreign exchange market and net exports increase.
   (e) all of the above.

10. Short-run aggregate supply increases, but long-run aggregate supply does not change if
    (a) wage rates increase.
    (b) the minimum wage rate is increased.
    (c) labor unions push for higher wages.
    (d) all the above.
    (e) none of the above.

11. Both the long-run and the short-run aggregate supply increase if
    (a) the labor force decreases.
    (b) the natural rate of unemployment increases.
    (c) the capital stock decreases.
    (d) technological advance increases labor productivity.
    (e) all of the above.

12. Use Figure 3.1. At the macroeconomic equilibrium
    √(a) real GDP is at its long-run level.
    √(b) the price level is 120.
    (c) unemployment is zero.
    (d) both (a) and (b).
    (e) all of the above.

13. Use Figure 3.1. An increase in aggregate demand of 100 units
    (a) increases real GDP by 100 units.
    (b) increases the price level by 10 units.
    (c) decreases the natural rate of unemployment.
    (d) increases real GDP by 50 units.
    (e) none of the above.

14. Use Figure 3.1. An increase in long-run aggregate supply of 200 units
    (a) increases real GDP to 900 units.
    (b) increases the price level to 130.
    (c) decreases the price level to 110.
    (d) increases the natural rate of unemployment.
    (e) both (a) and (c).

Figure 3.1 Fantasy Land has the following aggregate demand and aggregate supply curves.

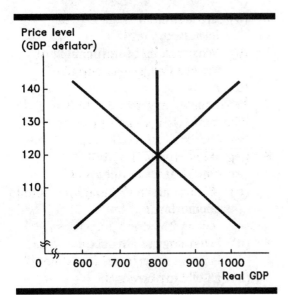

Figure 3.2 Magic Empire has the following aggregate demand and aggregate supply curves:

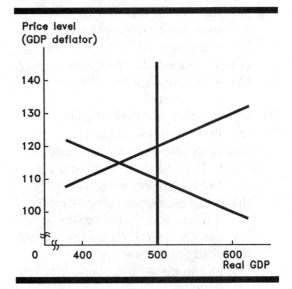

15. Use Figure 3.1. An increase in wages that shifts the short-run aggregate supply to the left by 200 units
    (a) moves the economy to an unemployment equilibrium, so wages will quickly fall to restore full employment.
    (b) increases the price level to 130.
    (c) moves the economy to an unemployment equilibrium, so aggregate demand will automatically increase to restore full employment.
    (d) increases the natural rate of unemployment.
    (e) both (b) and (d).16.

Use Figure 3.2. At the macroeconomic equilibrium
    (a) real GDP is 500 and the price level is 110.
    (b) real GDP is 500 and the price level is 120.
    (c) real GDP is 450 and the price level is 115.
    (d) unemployment is above the natural rate.
    (e) both (c) and (d).

17. Use Figure 3.2. An increase in aggregate demand of 100 units
    (a) increases real GDP by 100 units.
    (b) increases the GDP deflator by 5.
    (c) decreases the natural rate of unemployment.
    (d) increases real GDP by 50 units.
    (e) both (b) and (d).

18. Use Figure 3.2. A severe drought decreases long-run aggregate supply by 100 units and
    (a) moves the economy to a full-employment equilibrium.
    (b) moves the economy to an above full-employment equilibrium.
    (c) decreases the natural rate of unemployment.
    (d) does not change the macroeconomic equilibrium.
    (e) both (a) and (c).

19. In classical macroeconomics, an increase in aggregate demand is induced by
    (a) an increase in the money supply.
    (b) a cut in taxes.
    (c) an increase in government purchases.
    (d) an increase in investment.
    (e) all of the above.

20. In Keynesian macroeconomics,
    (a) important influences on aggregate demand are fiscal policy and those coming from the rest of the world.
    (b) a change in the money supply influences aggregate demand through its effects on investment.
    (c) changes in taxes are an important influence on aggregate demand.
    (d) changes in government purchases of goods and services are an important influence on aggregate demand.
    (e) all of the above.

Short Answers Questions

1. What is a macroeconomic model? Explain what endogenous and exogenous variables are.

2. What is the crucial difference between the aggregate demand-aggregate supply model and the micro demand-supply model?

3. Briefly summarize the Keynesian explanation of the 1980s.

4. What is meant by the quantity of real GDP demanded?

5. (a) What determines the position of the aggregate demand curve?

    (b) What factors cause aggregate demand to increase? Give some examples.

6. (a) What is meant by long-run aggregate supply?
    (b) What are the determinants of long-run aggregate supply?

7. What causes aggregate supply to increase? Give some examples.

8. (a) What is meant by full-employment equilibrium?
    (b) What is meant by unemployment equilibrium?

9. (a) What are the two main influences on firms' investment?
    (b) Briefly explain each influence.

10. If the economy is in a recession, what policies could the government adopt to restore employment to its full-employment level. Explain the effect of such policies on the price level.

Problem Solving

How does it go?

Leisure Land has the following aggregate demand and aggregate supply curves

AD curve	$Y^d = 2,000 - 10P^*$	(3.1)
SAS curve	$Y^s = -500 + 10P^*$	(3.2)
LAS curve	$Y = 600.$	(3.3)

(a) What is the macroeconomic equilibrium?

Macroeconomic equilibrium occurs at the intersection of the aggregate demand and short-run aggregate supply curves. Figure 3.3 shows the macroeconomic equilibrium.

Figure 3.3

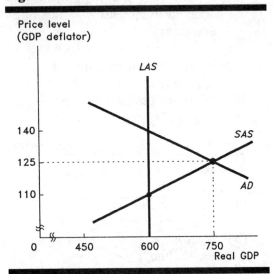

Figure 3.4

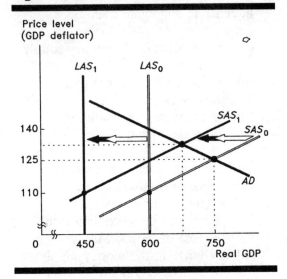

To find the equilibrium real GDP (Y^*) and price level (P^*) solve the equations to the *AD* and *SAS* curves. At the equilibrium,

AD curve $Y^* = 2,000 - 10P^*$ (3.1)
SAS curve $Y^* = -500 + 10P^*$.   (3.2)

Add Equations (3.1) and (3.2) to give
$$2Y^* = 1,500.$$
That is, $Y^* = 750$.

Substitute 750 for Y^* in Equation (3.2) to give
$$750 = -500 + 10P^*$$
$$P^* = 125.$$

Equilibrium real GDP is 750, and the equilibrium price level is 125.

(b) A severe drought decreases aggregate supply by 150 units. What is the new macroeconomic equilibrium?

A decrease in aggregate supply shifts both the long-run and short-run aggregate supply curves to the left. Figure 3.4 shows the *LAS* and the *SAS* curves shifting to the left by 150 units. The *LAS* curve shifts from LAS_0 to LAS_1, and the *SAS* curve shifts from SAS_0 to SAS_1.

Figure 3.4 shows that the new equilibrium real GDP is between 600 and 750 and that the new equilibrium price level is above 125. The new macroeconomic equilibrium lies to the right of the LAS_1 curve, so the economy is at an above full-employment equilibrium.

Before we can find the actual values of the new equilibrium we must find the equation to the SAS_1 curve. The SAS_1 curve is such that real GDP supplied at each price level is 150 units less than on SAS_0. That is, the SAS_1 curve is
$$Y^s = -500 + 10P - 150.   (3.4)$$

To find the new equilibrium, solve Equation (3.1) and (3.4) for Y^* and P^*. That is,

SAS_1 curve $Y^* = -650 + 10P$ (3.4)
AD curve $Y^* = 2,000 - 10P^*$. (3.1)

Add Equations (3.4) and (3.1) to give
$$2Y^* = 1,350.$$
That is, $Y^* = 675$.

Substitute 675 for Y^* in Equation (3.4) to give

$$675 = -650 +10P^*$$
$$10P^* = 1,325$$
$$P^* = 132.5.$$

Equilibrium real GDP is 675, and the equilibrium price level is 132.5. Notice that this macroeconomic equilibrium matches that shown in Figure 3.4.

(c) In (a) Leisure Land is at an above full-employment equilibrium. What is Leisure Land's long-run equilibrium?

At an above full-employment equilibrium there is a shortage of labor and wages will automatically begin to rise. The increase in wages shifts the short-run aggregate supply curves to the left. Wages will continue to increase until the macroeconomic equilibrium lies on the long-run aggregate supply curve. Figure 3.5 shows the SAS curves shifting to the left, and the macroeconomic equilibrium moves up the aggregate demand curve, as shown by the arrows. The short-run aggregate supply curve comes to a halt when it reaches SAS_2.

Figure 3.5 shows that the new equilibrium real GDP is 600 and the new equilibrium price level exceeds 132.5. The new macroeconomic equilibrium lies on the LAS curve, so the economy is at full-employment equilibrium.

To find the new equilibrium, solve Equation (3.1) and (3.3) for Y^* and P^*. That is,

AD curve $\qquad Y^* = 2,000 - 10P^*$ (3.1)
LAS curve $\qquad Y^* = 600.$ (3.3)

Substitute Equation (3.3) into (3.1) to give

$$600 = 2,000 - 10P^*.$$
That is, $\quad P^* = 140.$

Equilibrium real GDP is 600, and the equilibrium price level is 140. Notice that this macroeconomic equilibrium matches that shown on Figure 3.5.

Figure 3.5

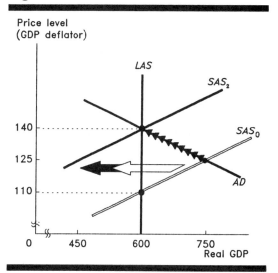

Now try these

Fact 3.1 Sunny Isle has the following aggregate demand and aggregate supply curves:

$$y^d = 4,000 - 20P$$
$$y^s = 20P$$
$$y^s = 2,000.$$

1. Use Fact 3.1. What is macroeconomic equilibrium? How would you describe the macroeconomic equilibrium?

2. Use Fact 3.1. Aggregate demand increases by 500 units.
    (a) What is the new aggregate demand curve?
    (b) How would you describe the new macroeconomic equilibrium?

3. Use Fact 3.1. Aggregate supply decreases by 500 units.
   (a) What is the new long-run aggregate supply curve?
   (b) What is the new short-run aggregate supply curve?
   (c) What is new macroeconomic equilibrium?
   (d) How would describe the macroeconomic equilibrium?

4. If long-run aggregate supply increases to $4.7 trillion, and at the same time equilibrium real GDP increases to only $4.6 trillion. How big is the GDP gap?

5. Mark has $5,000 in the bank. What happens to the quantity of real money Mark has when the price level
   (a) increases by 10 percent?
   (b) decreases by 5 percent?

6. Draw a figure to show an economy at full-employment equilibrium. Use your figure to show the effect on real GDP and the price level of a decrease in firms' confidence about future profits.

7. Draw a figure to show an economy at a full-employment equilibrium. Use your figure to show the effect on real GDP and the price level of a technological advance.

8. Draw a figure to show an economy at a full-employment equilibrium. Use your figure to show the effect on real GDP and the price level of an increase in wages.

9. Draw a figure to show an economy at a full-employment equilibrium. Use your figure to show the effect on real GDP and the price level of a simul-taneous decrease in short-run aggregate supply and increase in aggregate demand of the same magnitude.

10. Redraw your figure in problem 9 for the case in which the aggregate demand curve shifts by more than the short-run aggregate supply curve.

✓ Answers

Concept Review

1) households, firms, governments, foreigners, coordinated, markets
2) endogenous variables, exogenous variables
3) macroeconomic theory, macroeconomic, predictions
4) aggregate quantity, goods and services demanded, consumer expenditure, investment, government purchases, net exports
5) quantity of real GDP demanded, price level, aggregate demand schedule
6) aggregate quantity, real GDP supplied, goods, services produced
7) quantity of real GDP supplied, price level, aggregate supply schedule, aggregate supply curve
8) supply, supplied, wages, prices, full employment
9) natural rate, unemployment, unemployment
10) quantity of real GDP supplied, price level, prices, short-run aggregate supply schedule
11) aggregate supply
12) macroeconomic equilibrium
13) full-employment equilibrium
14) an unemployment equilibrium
15) above full-employment equilibrium
16) disposable income
17) real money
18) real exchange rate
19) real wage rate
20) GDP gap

True or False

1) T	5) T	9) T	13) F	17) F
2) F	6) F	10) T	14) F	18) F
3) F	7) F	11) F	15) T	19) F
4) F	8) T	12) F	16) F	20) T

Multiple Choice

1) c	5) d	9) e	13) d	17) e
2) e	6) b	10) e	14) e	18) a
3) a	7) d	11) d	15) b	19) a
4) e	8) e	12) d	16) c	20) e

Short Answer Questions

1. A macroeconomic model is a description of how households, firms, governments, and foreigners make economic decisions and how these decisions are coordinated in markets. Endogenous variables are those determined by the model. Exogenous variables are those taken as given by the model—they are determined outside the model.

2. The most important difference is that the aggregate demand-aggregate supply model explains how aggregate variables, such as the price level and real GDP, are determined, while the micro demand-supply model explains how the prices and quantities of individual goods and services, such as pizza and banking services, are determined.

3. The Keynesian explanation of the recession of the early 1980s is that it resulted from a sharp increase in world oil prices combined with slow growth of aggregate demand. The recovery of the 1980s resulted from strong aggregate demand growth. The most important influence on aggregate demand during the recovery was the expansionary fiscal policy—the persistent government budget deficit.

4. The quantity of real GDP demanded is the sum of consumer expenditure, investment, government purchases of goods and services, and net exports.

5. (a) The position of the aggregate demand curve is determined by all influences on the quantity of real GDP demanded other than the price level.

   (b) Aggregate demand increases if taxes are cut, interest rates fall, business confidence improves, foreign income increases, the money supply is increased, foreign prices increase, or the dollar weakens on the foreign exchange market.

6. (a) Long-run aggregate supply is the quantity of real GDP supplied when all wages and prices have adjusted so that each firm is producing its profit-maximizing output and there is full employment.

   (b) Long-run aggregate supply is determined by the size of the labor force, the size of the capital stock, the state of technology, and the natural rate of unemployment.

7. Aggregate supply increases if the labor force increases, the natural rate of unemployment decreases, the capital stock increases, or technological advance increases labor productivity.

8. (a) Full-employment equilibrium is a situation in which macroeconomic equilibrium occurs at a point on the long-run aggregate supply curve.

Unemployment is at its natural rate.

(b) An unemployment equilibrium is a situation in which macroeconomic equilibrium occurs at a level of real GDP below its long-run level—below long-run aggregate supply.

9. (a) The two main influences in firms' investment are interest rates and the state of confidence.

(b) The higher the interest rate, the more expensive it is for firms to borrow and the greater is the inducement for firms to economize on purchases of new plant and equipment. The higher the interest rate, other things being equal, the lower is investment. The major influence on firms' investment is their confidence about future business prospects. At times when firms anticipate higher future profits, investment is high. When firms anticipate lower future profits, investment is low.

10. The government can use either monetary or fiscal policy to stimulate aggregate demand and return real GDP to if full-employment level. In using such a policy the price level increases.

Problems

1. Equilibrium real GDP is 2,000, and the price level is 100. The macroeconomic equilibrium lies on the long-run aggregate supply curve, so the equilibrium is a full-employment equilibrium.

2. (a) $y^d = 4,500 - 20P$.
   (b) Equilibrium real GDP is 2,250,

and the price level is 112.5. The macroeconomic equilibrium lies to the right of the long-run aggregate supply curve, so the equilibrium is an above full-employment equilibrium.

3. (a) $y^s = 1,500$.
   (b) $y^s = 20P - 500$.
   (c) Equilibrium real GDP is 1,750, and the price level is 112.5. The macroeconomic equilibrium lies to the right of the long-run aggregate supply curve, so the equilibrium is an above full-employment equilibrium.

4. A real GDP gap arises if equilibrium real GDP is less than long-run real GDP. The GDP gap is equal to $0.1 trillion.

5. (a) Mark's real money falls by 10 percent, that is, by $500.

   (b) Mark's real money increases by 5 percent, that is, by $250.

Figure 3.6

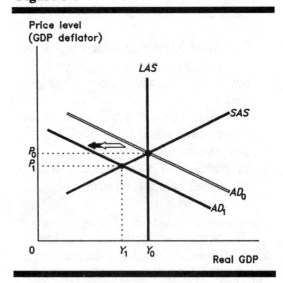

6. Figure 3.6 shows that a decrease in firms confidence about future profits decreases real GDP and lowers the price level.

7. Figure 3.7 shows that technological advance increases aggregate supply, increasing real GDP and lowering the price level.

Figure 3.7

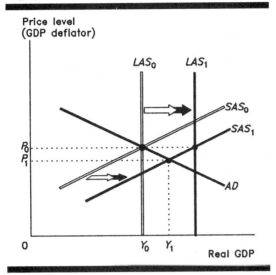

Figure 3.8

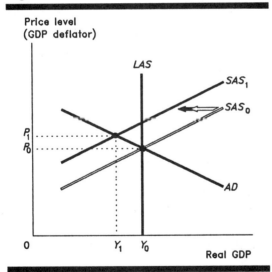

8. Figure 3.8 shows that an increase in wages decreases short-run aggregate supply. It shifts the short-run aggregate supply curve to the left, decreasing real GDP and increasing the price level.

Figure 3.9

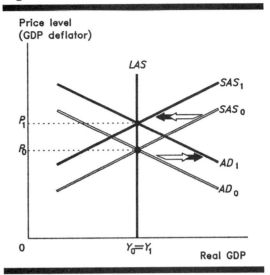

9. Figure 3.9 shows that a simultaneous increase in aggregate demand and decrease in aggregate supply of the same magnitude increase the price level and have no effect on real GDP.

10. Figure 3.10 shows that a simultaneous increase in aggregate demand and decrease in aggregate supply, where aggregate demand shifts by more increases both real GDP and the price level.

Figure 3.10

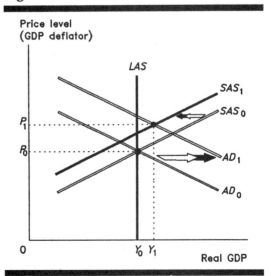

CHAPTER 4

Aggregate Expenditure and Income

Perspective and Focus

You have now studied aggregate demand and aggregate supply and know, in general terms, how real GDP and the price level are determined. This chapter is the first of four that take you behind the scenes of the aggregate demand curve. You are going to take the aggregate demand curve to pieces and study it in great detail.

To do this you are going to temporarily freeze the price level. Don't be confused about what this means. The price level is not actually fixed. You are going to study simply what happens in the economy at a particular price level. You are going to learn about the forces that influence the position of the aggregate demand curve and that make the aggregate demand curve shift to the right (for an increase in demand) and to the left (for a decrease in demand). It is easier to study the influences on the aggregate demand curve by working out what happens at a particular price level. That is why we freeze the price level in this and following three chapters.

Chapter 4 examines the immediate determinants of the components of aggregate expenditure—consumer expenditure, investment, government purchases of goods and services and net exports. The chapter begins by describing these components of aggregate expenditure and showing how they have fluctuated in recent years. It then explains what determines the various components of expenditure and finally shows you how to calculate equilibrium expenditure and the multiplier effect of a change in the components of aggregate expenditure.

Learning Objectives

After studying this chapter, you will be able to:

- Describe the components of aggregate expenditure, the relative importance of each, and the extent to which each varies
- Set out a simple model of consumption and saving
- Describe the relationship between consumption and income in the Canadian economy
- Explain how expenditure equilibrium is determined
- Explain how the economy converges to an expenditure equilibrium
- Define and derive the multiplier
- Define and derive the fiscal policy multipliers
- Explain the effects of changes in investment, government purchases, taxes, and exports on equilibrium aggregate expenditure

Increasing Your Productivity

The key to understanding what is going on in this chapter is to make a sharp distinction between actual and planned expenditure. Actual consumer expenditure plus investment plus government purchases plus net exports is always equal to real GDP *by definition*. *Planned* consumer expenditure plus investment plus government purchases plus net exports equals real GDP only *in equilibrium*. Consumption plans, government purchases plans and net export plans are always fulfilled. Investment plans *are not* always fulfilled. Firms have a desired level of investment but actual investment equals desired investment plus the unintended change in inventories. If sales are less than planned, inventories accumulate and because inventories are part of investment, *actual* investment exceeds *planned* investment. If sales exceed expectations, inventories decline and *actual* investment is below *planned* investment.

The fact that investment is not always equal to its planned level has two implications:

1. The economy is not always in a state of expenditure equilibrium.

2. When the economy is not at an expenditure equilibrium, forces work moving it toward such an equilibrium.

Since actual GDP equals the sum of consumer expenditure, investment, government purchases of goods and services, and net exports, when there is an unintended accumulation of inventories, actual investment exceeds planned investment and planned expenditure is less than real GDP. In such a situation, firms cut back production to lower inventories and real GDP falls. It keeps on falling until planned expenditure and actual expenditure are equal. Conversely, if inventories fall below the desired level, then planned expenditure exceeds actual expenditure and firms takes steps to increase production. In this case, real GDP increases and continues to do so until actual expenditure equals planned expenditure.

These ideas are the essence of this chapter. The rest of the chapter follows mechanically and is easy to understand once you have understood these fundamental ideas. The diagrammatic and algebraic presentation of the determination of equilibrium expenditure, the convergence to it, and the multiplier effect that operates when there is a change in investment or exports or government purchases can all be understood using these essential concepts.

An appendix to the chapter presents the algebra of the expenditure equilibrium and the multipliers. Study the appendix carefully and do attempt to understand how they are derived and what they mean. Translate into plain english after you have learnt how to derive them. But do not attempt to memorise all these formulas.

Self Test

Concept Review

1. The consumption function is the relationship between _____ _____ and _____ _____.

2. The amount of consumer expenditure that does not change as disposable income varies is called _____ _____ _____.

The amount of consumer expenditure that does change as disposable income varies is called _____ _____ _____.

3. The saving function is the relationship between _____ and _____ _____. When saving is negative, it is called _____.

4. The average propensity to consume is the _____ of _____ _____ to _____ _____. The marginal propensity to consume is the _____ of the _____ in _____ _____ to the _____ in _____ _____.

5. The _____ propensity to save is the ratio of _____ to _____ _____. The propensity to save is the ratio of the _____ in _____ to the _____ in _____ _____.

6. The average relationship between consumer expenditure and disposable income over several decades is called the _____ - ____ _____ _____, where as the relationship between consumer expenditure and disposable income in a particular year is called the _____ -_____ _____ _____ .

7. The sum of planned consumer expenditure, investment, government purchases of goods and services, and net exports is _____ _____ _____. Expenditure equilibrium exits when _____ __ __ _____ equals _____ _____.

8. Taxes that do not change when income varies are called _____ ____ , and taxes that do change when income varies are called _____ ____ .

9. The aggregate expenditure curve is a curve showing the relationship between _____ _____ and ____ ____ .

10. Expenditure that does not change as real GDP varies is called _____ _____ .

11. The _____ _____ is the ratio of the change in real GDP to the change in investment that caused it.

12. The government purchases multiplier is the ratio of the change in _____ _____ to the change in _____ _____ that caused it.

13. The ratio of the change in ____ ____ to the change in _____ ____ is called the autonomous tax multiplier.

14. The ratio of the change in real GDP to the change in government purchases when taxes change by the same amount as government purchases is called the _____ _____ .

15. The marginal propensity to consume out of real GDP is the fraction ot each additional dollar of ____ ___ that _____ spend on goods and services.

16. The marginal tax rate is the fraction of an _____ dollar of _____ that is paid out in _____ .

17. The _____ tax rate _____ is the ratio of the _____ in real GDP to the change in the _____ tax rate that caused it.

18. The relationship between taxes paid and income is called the __ _____ .

19. The import function is the relationship between the level of _____ and _____ _____.

20. The change in imports resulting from a one dollar increase in real GDP is called the _____ _____ to _____ .

True or False

1. Government expenditure is the largest component of aggregate expenditure, investment is the second largest component, and consumer expenditure is the third largest.

2. Exports, imports, and investment are the most volatile components of aggregate expenditure.

3. If consumer expenditure is $10,000 when disposable income is zero, then saving is equal to -$10,000.

4. A household with zero disposable income spends $5,000 a year on basic food, clothing, and shelter. Its autonomous consumer expenditure is $5,000 a year.

5. The ratio of consumer expenditure to disposable income is the average propensity to consume.

6. The ratio of a change in saving to a change in disposable income is the marginal propensity to save.

7. When real GDP increases, consumer expenditure increases as the economy moves up its consumption function. At the same time, saving decreases as the economy moves down its saving function.

8. Along a linear consumption function the marginal propensity to consume is a constant, but as real GDP increases the average propensity to consume decreases.

9. As real GDP decreases, induced expenditure and aggregate expenditure decrease, but autonomous expenditure does not change.

10. Autonomous expenditure is the fraction of aggregate expenditure that depends on real GDP.

11. As disposable income increases both the marginal propensity to consume and the marginal propensity to save increase.

12. The investment multiplier in a closed economy is $1/1 - b$.

13. The autonomous tax multiplier in a closed economy is $- by/(1 - b)$.

14. In a closed economy, the balanced budget multiplier is 2 and it tells us that if government purchases of goods and services are increased by $1 trillion and autonomous taxes are increased by $1 trillion to pay for such expenditure, then real GDP will increase by $2 trillion.

15. Aggregate expenditure is the quantity of nominal GDP demanded at a given price level.

16. At real GDP below an expenditure equilibrium, planned investment is not realized because unplanned inventories disinvestment takes place.

17. The multiplier process occurs because as real GDP increases consumer expenditure increases, which leads to an increase in investment.

18. The magnitude of the government purchases multiplier is the same a the autonomous tax multiplier.

19. The government budget deficit fluctuates over the business cycle and in such a way that allows it to work as an automatic stabilizer.

20. The multiplier in an open economy is smaller that in a closed economy.

Multiple Choice

1. Planned consumer expenditure is given by 0.050 + 0.7y trillions. If income is zero, then planned consumer expenditure is
   (a) $0.025 trillion.
   (b) $0.050 trillion.
   (c) $0.075 trillion.
   (d) $0.010 trillion.
   (e) $0.070 trillion.

2. If the marginal propensity to save is 0.25, then an increase in disposable income of $40,000, increases saving by
   (a) $ 1,000
   (b) $ 5,000.
   (c) $15,000.
   (d) $30,000.
   (e) $10,000.

3. When disposable income is $40,000 a year, consumer expenditure is $35,000. The average propensity to consume is
   (a) 40,000/35,000.
   (b) 75,000/35,000.
   (c) 40,000 x 35,000.
   (d) 35,000/40,000.
   (e) 40,000 - 35,000.

4. The slope of the saving function
   (a) is the reciprocal of the slope of the consumption function.

   (b) is the same as the slope of the consumption function.
   (c) plus the slope of the consumption function equals one.
   (d) is at least as large as the slope of the consumption function.
   (e) is larger than the slope of the consumption function.

Fact 4.1. Magic Empire's consumption function is

$$c = 10 + 0.75(y - t).$$

Magic Empire is a closed economy, government purchases are $10 billion, and autonomous taxes are $8 billion. There are no income taxes in Magic Empire. Investment is $15 billion.

5. Use Fact 4.1. Expenditure equilibrium occurs at a real GDP of
   (a) $116 billion.
   (b) $164 billion.
   (c) $148 trillion.
   (d) $38.67 trillion.
   (e) $65.33 trillion.

6. Use Fact 4.1. The government purchases multiplier is
   (a) 0.75.
   (b) 0.25
   (c) 4.
   (d) 1.33.
   (e) 3.

7. Use Fact 4.1. A $1 billion increase in government purchases, which is paid for by an increase in autonomous taxes increase real GDP by
   (a) $0 billion.
   (b) $1 billion.
   (c) $2 billion.
   (d) $3 billion.
   (e) $4 billion.

8. Use Fact 4.1. A $2 billion increase in autonomous taxes increases real GDP by
   (a) $4 billion.
   (b) $3 billion.
   (c) $2 billion.
   (d) –$3 billion.
   (e) –$6 billion.

9. In Dream World the investment multiplier is 4. A $1 trillion decrease in investment changes real GDP by
   (a) –$2 trillion.
   (b) $0.25 trillion.
   (c) $40 trillion.
   (d) –$4 trillion.
   (e) $0.4 trillion.

10. Sandy Island is a closed economy, and its marginal propensity to save is 0.4. Its autonomous tax multiplier is equal to
    (a) –1.5.
    (b) –2.976.
    (c) –0.855.
    (d) –5.970.
    (e) –9.888.

11. In a closed economy which has induced taxes, the autonomous expenditure multiplier is
    (a) $\dfrac{1}{1 - b(1 + t_1)}$
    (b) $\dfrac{1 - b}{1 + t_1}$.
    (c) $\dfrac{1 - b}{1 - t_1}$.
    (d) $\dfrac{1}{1 - b(1 - t_1)}$.
    (e) $\dfrac{1}{b - y}$.

Fact 4.2 Desert Empire is a closed economy. Its consumer expenditure is $200 billion when disposable income is zero and its marginal propensity to consume is 0.8. Investment is $500 billion. Government purchases are $100 billion and taxes are 10 percent of income.

12. Use Fact 4.2. At the expenditure equilibrium, real GDP is approximately equal to
    (a) $800 billion.
    (b) $880 billion.
    (c) $1000 billion.
    (d) $2000 billion.
    (e) $2857 billion.

13. Use Fact 4.2. At the expenditure equilibrium, the government budget deficit is
    (a) $185.7 billion.
    (b) $85.7 billion.
    (c) –$185.7 billion.
    (d) –$85.7 billion.
    (e) none of the above.

14. Use Fact 4.2. If investment increases by $10 billion, real GDP increases by
    (a) $10 billion.
    (b) more than $10 billion but less than $20 billion.
    (c) more than $20 billion but less than $30 billion.
    (d) more than $30 billion but less than $40 billion.
    (e) $50 billion.

15. Use Fact 4.2. The government can balance its budget by
    (a) increasing private investment.
    (b) increasing government purchases.
    (c) cutting the marginal tax rate.
    (d) introducing autonomous taxes.
    (e) increasing consumer expenditure.

16. The multiplier process takes place because the initial change in real GDP
    (a) produces an additional change in consumer expenditure.
    (b) produces an additional change in government purchases as taxes change.
    (c) produces an additional change in investment as saving changes.
    (d) (a) and (c).
    (e) all the above.

17. Treasure Island is an open economy. Its autonomous imports are $0.05 trillion and its marginal propensity to import is 0.1. Treasure Island's import function is
    (a) 0.10 + 0.5y trillions of dollars.
    (b) 0.05 + 0.1y trillions of dollars.
    (c) 0.05 + 0.5y trillions of dollars.
    (d) 0.15 + 0.1y trillions of dollars.
    (e) 0.01 + 1.5y trillions of dollars.

18. The import function can be written as
    (a) $im = iy - m_0 m$.
    (b) $im = im_0 + my$.
    (c) $im = im_0 - m$.
    (d) $im = a + by$.
    (e) $im = im_0 + im(y - t)$.

19. An economy has a given level of government purchases and a fixed marginal tax rate. As real GDP fluctuates, and its fluctuations are lessened because
    (a) investment automatically moves in the opposite direction to real GDP.
    (b) taxes automatically move in the opposite direction to real GDP.
    (c) the government budget deficit automatically moves in the opposite direction to real GDP.
    (d) all of the above.
    (e) none of the above.

20. On Coral Island the marginal propensity to consume is 0.75, the

marginal tax rate is 0.2, and the marginal propensity to import is 0.1. If Coral Island is a closed economy, the investment multiplier is
(a) 2.5, and if it is an open economy the investment multiplier is 4.
(b) 3.4, and if it is an open economy the investment multiplier is 1.5.
(c) 2.5, and if it is an open economy the investment multiplier is 2.
(d) 0.5, and if it is an open economy the investment multiplier is 0.9.
(e) 4.2, and if it is an open economy the investment multiplier is 2.6.

Short Answers Questions

1. What are the components of aggregate expenditure, and what is the relative importance of each of them.

2. Explain what autonomous consumer expenditure is and what induced consumer expenditure is.

3. Derive the balanced budget multiplier.

4. Distinguish between average propensity to save and marginal propensity to save.

5. (a) Define the long-run consumption function.
   (b) Define the short-run consumption function.

6. What is the investment multiplier.

7. (a) Define the marginal tax rate.
   (b) Define the marginal tax rate multiplier.
   (c) What effect does a higher marginal tax rate have on the investment multiplier?

8. Explain the term *marginal propensity to consume.*

9. Explain why consumer expenditure plus saving always equals income minus taxes.

10. (a) Distinguish between an identity and an equilibrium condition.
    (b) Provide two examples of each.

Problem Solving

How does it go?

Rose Land is a closed economy. Its consumption function is

$c = 100 + 0.75(y - t)$ billions of dollars.

Investment is $350 billion, government purchases are $200 billion, and autonomous taxes are $150 billion. There are no induced taxes.

(a) What is real GDP at the expenditure equilibrium?

Expenditure equilibrium occurs when aggregate planned expenditure equals real GDP. Aggregate planned expenditure is equal to

$e_p = c_p + i_p + g_p.$

Substitute $100 + 0.75(y - t)$ for c_p, $350 billion for i_p, and $200 billion for g_p to give

$e_p = 100 + 0.75(y - t) + 350 + 200.$

Substitute $150 billion for t to give

$e_p = 100 + 0.75(y - 150) + 350 + 200$
$\quad = 537.5 + 0.75y.$

At an expenditure equilibrium real

GDP equals aggregate planned expenditure. That is,

$y = e_p$
$\quad = 537.5 + 0.75y$
$\quad = \$2,150$ billion.

(b) What is consumer expenditure?

Consumer expenditure is determined from the consumption function $c = 100 + 0.75(y - t)$.

Substitute $2,150 billion for y and $150 billion for t to give

$c = 100 + 0.75 (2,150 - 150)$
$\quad = \$1,600$ billion.

(c) If government purchases decrease by $50 billion, what is the change in real GDP?

The change in real GDP equals

$$\Delta y = \frac{1}{1 - b} \Delta g.$$

Substitute -50 for Δg and 0.75 for b to give

$$\Delta y = \frac{1}{1 - 0.75} \times (-50)$$
$\quad = -\$200$ billion.

(d) What is the government purchases multiplier?

The government purchases multiplier is

$$\frac{1}{(1 - b)}$$

Substitute 0.75 for b. The government purchases multiplier is 4.

Now try these

1. In Star Kingdom, the consumption function in billions of dollars is

   $c = 50 + 0.6(y - t_0)$.

   Autonomous taxes are $8 billion, planned investment is $7.5 billion, and planned government purchases are $10 billion. Star Kingdom is a closed economy, and there are no induced taxes.
   (a) What is planned consumer expenditure when real GDP is zero?
   (b) What is planned consumer expenditure?
   (c) What is aggregate planned expenditure?
   (d) What is real GDP at the expenditure equilibrium?

Fact 4.3 On Green Island, the consumption function is

$c = 100 + 0.75(y - t)$ billions of dollars.

Planned investment is $500 billion, planned government purchases are $400 billion, and autonomous taxes are $400 billion. Green Island is a closed economy, and there are no induced taxes.

2. Use Fact 4.3. At the expenditure equilibrium, calculate:
   (a) real GDP.
   (b) consumer expenditure.
   (c) the government's budget deficit.

3. Use Fact 4.3. The government of Green Island cuts its purchases of goods and services by $100 billion. Calculate:
   (a) the change in real income.
   (b) the change in consumer expenditure.
   (c) the change in the government budget deficit.

(d) the government purchases multiplier.

4. Use Fact 4.3. The government of Green Island makes a balanced budget cut of $100 billion. Calculate:
   (a) the change in real income.
   (b) the change in consumer expenditure.
   (c) the balanced budget multiplier.

5. In Faraway Land, when disposable income is zero, consumer expenditure is $5,000 and when disposable income increases by $1,000, consumer expenditure increases by $600.

   (a) What is the marginal propensity to save?
   (b) When disposable income is $24,000, what is saving?
   (c) When disposable income is $24,000, what is average propensity to save?

6. In Fantasy Land all taxes are autonomous. Real GDP is $2 billion, and the autonomous expenditure multiplier is 4. If the autonomous expenditure multiplier increases to 5, what is real GDP at the new expenditure equilibrium?

7. Carla's disposable income is $40,000 per year and she saves $5,000 a year. Calculate:
   (a) Carla's average propensity to save.
   (b) Carla's average propensity to consume.

8. If an increase in aggregate income of $200 million increases consumer expenditure by $150 million, what is the marginal propensity to consume?

Fact 4.4. Green Country is an open economy. Its consumption function is

$$c = 100 + 0.75(y - t) \text{ millions of dollars.}$$

Investment is $400 million, government purchases are $300 million, autonomous taxes are $400 million, exports are $100 million, and its import function is

$$im = 50 + 0.3y \text{ million of dollars.}$$

9. Use Fact 4.4. Calculate:
   (a) equilibrium real GDP.
   (b) equilibrium consumer expenditure.
   (c) the government's budget deficit.

   The government cuts its purchases of goods and services to $200 million. Calculate:
   (d) the change in real GDP.
   (e) the change in consumer expenditure.
   (f) the change in the government's budget deficit.
   (g) the government purchases multiplier.

10. Use Fact 4.4. If taxes are not autonomous but induced and given by the tax function

    $$t = 0.15y,$$

    what now are the answers to problem 9?

✓ Answers

Concept Review

1) consumer expenditure, disposable income
2) autonomous consumer expenditure, induced consumer expenditure
3) saving, disposable income, dissaving
4) ratio, consumer expenditure, disposable income, ratio, change, consumer expenditure, change, disposable income
5) average, saving, disposable income, marginal, change, saving, change, disposable income
6) long-run consumption function, short-run consumption function
7) aggregate planned expenditure, aggregate planned expenditure, real GDP
8) autonomous taxes, induced taxes
9) aggregate planned expenditure, real GDP
10) autonomous expenditure
11) investment multiplier, real GDP
12) government purchases
13) real GDP, autonomous taxes
14) balanced budget multiplier
15) real GDP, households
16) additional, income, taxes
17) marginal, multiplier, change, marginal
18) tax function
19) imports, real GDP
20) marginal propensity, import

True or False

1) F	5) T	9) T	13) F	17) F
2) F	6) T	10) F	14) F	18) F
3) T	7) F	11) F	15) F	19) T
4) T	8) T	12) T	16) T	20) T

Multiple Choice

1) b	5) a	9) d	13) d	17) b
2) e	6) c	10) a	14) a	18) b
3) d	7) b	11) e	15) a	19) c
4) c	8) e	12) c	16) a	20) c

Short Answer Questions

1. The components of aggregate expenditure are consumer expenditure, investment, government purchases, and net exports. Consumer expenditure is the most important (the largest component), investment and government purchases are next, and net exports are the smallest component.

2. Autonomous consumer expenditure is the part of households' expenditure that does not depend on disposable income. Induced consumer expenditure is the part of households' expenditure that depends on disposable income. That is, when disposable income increases autonomous consumer expenditure does not change, but induced consumer expenditure increases.

3. A balanced budget change is a change in government purchases that is matched by a change in taxes. There is no change in the initial state of the budget. The balanced budget multiplier is the change in real GDP resulting from the balanced budget change divided by the change in government purchases. If taxes are autonomous and the economy is closed, a change in government purchases of Δg changes real GDP by

$$\frac{1}{(1-b)}\, \Delta g.$$

The change in taxes of Δt changes real GDP by

$$\frac{-b}{(1-b)}\, \Delta t.$$

Since Δg and Δt are equal, and the change in g and the change in t occur at the same time, real GDP increases by 1.

4. The average propensity to save is
$$\frac{\text{Saving}}{\text{Disposable income}}$$

The marginal propensity to save is
$$\frac{\text{Change in saving}}{\text{Change in disposable income}}$$

The marginal propensity to save tells us how much of an extra dollar of disposable income is saved, whereas the average propensity to save tells us the proportion of disposable income that is saved.

5. (a) The long-run consumption function tells us the *average* relationship between consumer expenditure and disposable income over several decades.

    (b) The short-run consumption function tells us the relationship between consumer expenditure and disposable income in a particular year.

6. A change in investment produces a change in real GDP, and the change in real GDP is bigger than the initial change in investment. The investment multiplier is the number by which the change in investment has to be multiplied to give the change in real GDP that it produced.

7. (a) The marginal tax rate is the fraction of an additional dollar that is paid out in taxes.

    (b) The marginal tax rate multiplier is the ratio of the change in real GDP to the change in the marginal tax rate that caused it.

(c) An increase in the marginal tax rate (t_1) decreases disposable income and decreases consumer expenditure. The marginal propensity to consume out of real GDP, which is equal to $b(1 - t_1)$, declines. The investment multiplier is equal to

$$\frac{1}{1 - b(1 - t_1)}.$$

So an increase in t_1, decreases $b(1 - t_1)$, which increases $1 - b(1 - t_1)$ and decreases the multiplier.

8. The marginal propensity to consume is the increase in consumer expenditure that results from a one dollar increase in disposable income.

9. Households receive income in payment for the services of the factors of production that they own. Part of their income is paid out in taxes and what is left is disposable income (income minus taxes). Households allocate their disposable income between consumer expenditure and saving. Therefore income minus taxes always equals consumer expenditure plus saving.

10. (a) An identity is a condition that always holds—it can't be violated. An equilibrium condition is a condition that hold only at an equilibrium.

(b) Identities that we've met so far in this course include the condition that aggregate expenditure $(c + i + g + ex - im)$ always equals real GDP (y) and that income (y) is always allocated among consumer expenditure (c), saving (s), and taxes (t).
Equilibrium conditions that we've met so far include the conditions at an expenditure equilibrium— aggregate planned expenditure equals real GDP and planned inventory

investment equals actual inventory investment.

Problems

1. (a) $45.2 billion
   (b) $c_p = 45.2 + 0.6y$
   (c) $e_p = 62.7 + 0.6y$
   (d) $156.75 billion

2. (a) $2,800 billion
   (b) $1900 billion
   (c) $0

3. (a) –$400 billion
   (b) –$300 billion
   (c) –$100 billion
   (d) 4

4. (a) –$100 billion
   (b) $0
   (c) 1

5. (a) 0.4
   (b) $4,600
   (c) 0.19

6. $2.5 billion

7. (a) 0.125
   (b) 0.875

8. 0.75

9. (a) $1,000 million
   (b) $550 million
   (c) –$100 million
   (d) –$181.82 million
   (e) –$136.36 million
   (f) –$100 million
   (g) 1.82

10. (a) $1,283.02 million
    (b) $917.92 million
    (c) –$107.55 million
    (d) –$150.94 million
    (e) –$96.23 million
    (f) –$77.36 million
    (g) 1.51

CHAPTER 5

Aggregate Expenditure, Interest Rates, and Money

Perspective and Focus

In Chapter 4, you learnt how to determine equilibrium expenditure, for a *given level of investment*. But investment is influenced by many economic factors, and one of the key influences on investment is the cost of capital, as measured by the interest rate. Fluctuations in interest rates, among other things, bring fluctuations in investment. In this chapter, you study the influences on investment. Because investment is influenced by the interest rate and investment influences equilibrium expenditure, there is a relationship between aggregate expenditure and the interest rate. This relationship is called the *IS* curve.

Since equilibrium expenditure depends on the interest rate, we cannot determine the actual level of aggregate expenditure until we know the interest rate. This chapter takes that next step and shows you how interest rates are determined in the markets for financial assets and money. In studying the determination of the interest rate in the market for money, you will discover that the demand for money depends on income. Because the demand for money depends on income the equilibrium interest rate also depends on income. This fact gives rise to another relationship between the interest rate and real GDP, a relationship called the *LM* curve. You will learn about the *LM* curve in this chapter.

Bringing the *IS* and *LM* curves together enables us to determine equilibrium aggregate expenditure and the interest rate simultaneously. The chapter also teaches you how to do this.

Learning Objectives

After studying this chapter, you will be able to:

- Describe the fluctuations in Canadian investment and interest rates in the 1970s and 1980s
- Explain what determines investment
- Explain the distinction between the nominal interest rate and the real interest rate
- Define and derive the investment function
- Describe the shifts in the Canadian investment function in the 1970s and 1980s
- Define and derive the *IS* curve
- Describe the fluctuations in Canadian money supply and interest rates in the 1970s and 1980s
- Explain what determines the demand for money
- Describe the shifts in the Canadian demand for money function in the 1970s and 1980s
- Define and derive the *LM* curve
- Determine the equilibrium interest rate and real GDP
- Derive the aggregate demand curve

Increasing Your Productivity

The *IS-LM* analysis lies at the heart of the theory of aggregate demand and it is important that you thoroughly master this material at this stage of your study. Do not attempt to go beyond this point without being thoroughly on top of this material.

A key thing to remember when studying *IS* and *LM* curves is that they are a different type of curve from any other that you have thus far encountered in your study of economics. You have been accustomed to curves that describe plans of consumers and producers and how those plans are influenced by prices—demand and supply curves. The *IS* and *LM* curves are *not* like demand and supply curves. The *IS* and *LM* curves are curves that trace out an *equilibrium relationship*.

Along the *IS* curve, the market for goods and services is in equilibrium in the sense that aggregate planned expenditure equals real GDP. At points to the left of the *IS* curve, aggregate planned expenditure exceeds real GDP. At points the right of the *IS* curve, aggregate planned expenditure is less than real GDP. Only when the economy is on the *IS* curve is aggregate planned expenditure is equal to real GDP.

Work at understanding the intuition behind the slope of the *IS* curve. The curve slopes downward because: The lower the interest rate, the greater the level of planned investment; and the greater the level of planned investment, the higher the level of equilibrium expenditure and equilibrium real GDP.

Like the *IS* curve, the *LM* curve is also an equilibrium relationship. Along the *LM* curve the quantity of money demanded equals the quantity of money supplied. If the economy was to the left of the *LM* curve, the quantity of money demanded would be less than the quantity of money supplied. If the economy was the right of the *LM* curve, the quantity of money demanded would exceed the quantity of money supplied. Only on the *LM* curve is the money market in equilibrium.

Where the *IS* and *LM* curves intersect, there is *simultaneous equilibrium* in the markets for goods and money.

You have already learnt, in Chapter 4, that when aggregate planned expenditure is less than actual expenditure, actual expenditure falls until actual expenditure and planned are equal. Thus whenever the economy is to the right of the *IS* curve, forces operate to bring the economy back onto the *IS* curve. These forces are changes in production—real GDP. Inventories are piling up above their planned level, so firms cutback their production and real GDP decreases. Conversely, when the economy is to the left of the *IS* curve forces operate in the opposite direction. Inventories are below their planned level, so firms increase production and real GDP increases.

Similarly, if the economy if off the *LM* curve, forces operate to bring it back onto that curve. These forces are changes in interest rates. If the economy is to the right of the *LM* curve, interest rates rise and if the economy is to the left of the *LM* curve, interest rates fall.

The combined effect of all these forces keep the economy moving toward the intersection point of the *IS* and *LM* curves.

With the tools of the *IS—LM* model, you are able to derive the aggregate demand curve explicitly. To do this, you vary the price level and enquire how the level of aggregate demand changes as the price level changes, *everything else held constant*. A change in the price level changes the real money supply and shifts the *LM* curve. The lower the price level, the larger is the quantity of real money supplied and the farther to the right is the *LM* curve, and at the intersection point with the *IS* curve the higher is equilibrium real GDP and the lower is the interest rate. The points traced by the falling price level and the rising equilibrium real GDP form the aggregate demand curve. As the economy moves along an aggregate demand curve the interest rate changes. Specifically, as the price level decreases and real GDP increases along the aggregate demand curve, the interest rate falls.

Although the algebra of the *IS-LM* model is presented as an appendix in this chapter, it will definitely require careful study. Do not attempt to memorise the formulas for equilibrium income, interest rate, and the aggregate demand curve. But do attempt to understand how they are derived and what they mean. Translate each of them into plain english after you have learnt how to derive it.

Work harder at this chapter than any other you have ever worked on and do all the exercises as many times as is necessary to feel completely on top of this material. A thorough knowledge of this chapter will pay handsome dividends in subsequent parts of the course.

Self Test

Concept Review

1. The real interest rate is equal to
   _____ minus
   _____.

2. The nominal interest rate is equal to
   the _____ plus the
   inflation rate.

3. The quantity of money deflated by
   the price level (that is the quantity of
   money expressed in units of goods
   and services) is the quantity of
   _____.

4. The rate of return on a piece of
   capital equipment is equal to
   _____ received
   from using that piece of equipment
   _____ of the
   price of the equipment.

5. The quantity of money
   _____ is equal to the
   amount of money that people plan to
   _____ on a particular day
   under particular circumstances.

6. The ratio of the amount of money
   that people plan to hold to real
   income is called the
   _____.

7. The relationship between the interest
   rate and real GDP such that the
   money market is in equilibrium is
   called the _____.

8. The *IS* curve is the relationship
   between the interest rate and real
   GDP such that the
   _____ is
   in equilibrium.

9. The investment function is the
   relationship between the
   _____ and
   _____.

10. _____ is the planned rate of purchases of new capital.

11. The demand for real money is the relationship between the quantity of real money demanded and _____ , given _____ .

12. The _____ is the relationship between the quantity of _____ money , real income and the interest rate.

True or False

1. At points below the *LM* curve, the demand for money is less than the supply of money.

2. The relationship between aggregate planned expenditure in a given period of time and the price level is known as the aggregate demand curve.

3. The *IS* curve shifts if government purchases, taxes, or any other component of autonomous expenditure changes.

4. The quantity of money demanded is the amount of money that people plan to hold on a given day in given circumstances.

5. The demand curve for real money shows the quantity of real money demanded at a given real income assuming that the interest rate remains constant.

6. If a bond pays $10 a year in perpetuity and its current market price is $100, then the interest rate is 10 percent—$10 divided by $100 expressed as a percent.

7. A change in the real money supply does not shift the *LM* curve.

8. A change in the demand for money arising from any source other than a change in real GDP or a change in the interest rate shifts the *LM* curve.

9. Along the *IS* curve, planned leakages equal planned injections.

10. The real interest rate is equal to the nominal interest rate plus the inflation rate.

11. The nominal interest rate is the interest rate actually paid and received.

12. If the economy is at a point above the *LM* curve, the real GDP adjusts to restore money market equilibrium.

13. If the economy is off the *IS* curve than investment adjusts to restore equilibrium.

14. As an economy moves up its *LM* curve the demand for money is constant.

15. As an economy moves down its *IS* curve, the interest rate decreases and so investment increases. As investment decreases, aggregate expenditure decreases and the *IS* curve shifts to the left.

16. An increases in the money supply shifts the *LM* curve to the right, decreasing the interest rate and increasing the quantity of money demanded.

17. As real income increases, the demand for money increases and consumer expenditure increases. The *LM* curve shifts to the left and the *IS* curve shifts to the right. Interest rate increases.

18. An increases in interest rates decreases investment but does not shift the *IS* curve.

19. As an economy moves up its *IS* curve, leakages and injections both decrease by the same amount.

20. As an economy moves up along its *LM* curve the demand for money decreases because the interest rate increases.

Multiple Choice

1. The rate of return on capital is equal to
   (a) the inflation rate.
   (b) 1 divided by the inflation rate.
   (c) the unemployment rate.
   (d) minus the inflation rate.
   (e) minus the unemployment rate.

2. The relationship between investment and the interest rate, holding all other influences on investment constant, is known as the
   (a) interest rate function.
   (b) capital function.
   (c) investment function.
   (d) *IS* function.
   (e) aggregate expenditure function.

3. Which of the following equations describes the investment function?
   (a) $i = i_0 - hr$ $i_0, h > 0$.
   (b) $i = i_0 + hr$ $i_0, h > 0$.
   (c) $i = hr - i_0$ $i_0, h > 0$.
   (d) $i = hr + i_0$ $i_0, h > 0$.
   (e) $i = hr + i_0$ $i_0, h > 0$.

4. The relationship between real GDP and the interest rate such that aggregate planned expenditure-planned consumer expenditure plus investment plus government purchases—is equal to real GDP is known as the

   (a) investment function.
   (b) *IS* curve.
   (c) *LM* curve.
   (d) short-run aggregate supply curve.
   (e) demand for money function.

5. Along an *IS* curve,
   (a) aggregate planned expenditure is less than real GDP.
   (b) aggregate planned expenditure is greater than real GDP.
   (c) aggregate planned expenditure equals real GDP.
   (d) may be greater or less than real GDP.
   (e) the rate of return on capital always equals the inflation rate.

6. Because the *IS* curve slopes downward,
   (a) an increase in the interest rate brings about an increase in real GDP in order to keep the economy at an expenditure equilibrium.
   (b) constant interest rate brings about an increase in real GDP in order to keep the economy at an expenditure equilibrium.
   (c) decrease in the interest rate brings about a decrease in real GDP in order to keep the economy at an expenditure equilibrium.
   (d) decrease in the interest rate brings about an increase in real GDP in order to keep the economy at an expenditure equilibrium.
   (e) increase in the interest rate causes real GDP to remain constant in order to keep the economy at an expenditure equilibrium.

7. Since *b* is a fraction, 1 − *b* is also a fraction, and 1/(1 − *b*) is a number
   (a) larger than one.
   (b) equal to one.
   (c) less than one.
   (d) which is negative.
   (e) equal to zero.

8. An increase in government purchases shifts the *IS* curve by 1/(1 − *b*)
   (a) times the change in government purchases.
   (b) divided by the change in government purchases.
   (c) plus the change in government purchases.
   (d) minus the change in government purchases.
   (e) none of the above.

9. The measure of money that includes currency, demand deposits, other checkable deposits, and savings deposits is
   (a) M1.
   (b) M2.
   (c) M3.
   (d) M7.
   (e) L.

10. The quantity of money demanded depends on
    (a) price level.
    (b) real income.
    (c) interest rate.
    (d) both (a) and (b).
    (e) all the above.

11. The interest rate is the opportunity of holding money, therefore
    (a) the higher the rate of interest, the smaller is the quantity of money people are planning to hold.
    (b) the lower the rate of interest, the smaller is the quantity of money people are planning to hold.
    (c) the higher the rate of interest, the greater is the quantity of money people are planning to hold.
    (d) the lower the rate of interest, the greater is the quantity of money people are planning to hold.
    (e) none of the above.

12. The combinations of real GDP and the interest rate at which the quantity of money demanded equals the quantity supplied traces out the
    (a) *IS* curve.
    (b) *LM* curve.
    (c) long-run aggregate supply curve.
    (d) short-run aggregate supply curve.
    (e) none of the above.

13. If the economy is at a point to the right of the *IS* curve, investment
    (a) plus government purchases exceeds saving plus taxes.
    (b) plus government purchases equals saving plus taxes.
    (c) minus government purchases exceeds saving plus taxes.
    (d) plus government purchases is less than saving plus taxes.
    (e) minus government purchases is less than saving plus taxes.

14. A movement downward along *IS* curve results when
    (a) the interest rate increases.
    (b) business taxes decrease.
    (c) real income increases.
    (d) expected future profits increase.
    (e) government purchases increase.

15. In the closed economy *IS-LM* model, equilibrium occurs when
    (a) the quantity of money supplied equals injections and the quantity of money demanded equals leakages.
    (b) the quantity of money supplied equals the quantity of money demanded and investment equals saving.
    (c) the quantity of money supplied equals the quantity of money demanded and investment plus government purchases equals taxes plus saving.
    (d) investment equals saving and government purchases equal taxes.
    (e) none the above.

16. Which of the following statements about the *IS* curve in a closed economy is *false*?
    (a) The *IS* curve is steeper than the investment demand curve.
    (b) The *IS* curve describes an equilibrium of flows.
    (c) Along the *IS* curve, the increase in investment resulting from a decline in the interest rate equals the increase in saving resulting from the increase in income.
    (d) The more sensitive investment is to changes in interest rate, the flatter is the *IS* curve.
    (e) Both (a) and (c).

17. If the quantity of money demanded exceeds the quantity of money supplied,
    (a) a decrease in the interest rate can restore equilibrium in the money market.
    (b) the economy is to the right of the *LM* curve.
    (c) an increase in the price level can not restore equilibrium in the money market.

    (d) an increase in government spending will not restore equilibrium in the money market.
    (e) both (a) and (b).

18. Coral Island is a closed economy and its marginal propensity to consume is 0.75. An increase in taxes of $100
    (a) moves the economy up its *LM* curve.
    (b) moves the economy down its *IS* curve.
    (c) shifts the *IS* curve to the right by 100.
    (d) shifts the *IS* curve to the left by 400.
    (e) none of the above.

19. A decrease in government purchases
    (a) shifts the *LM* curve to the right.
    (b) shifts the *IS* curve to the left.
    (c) shifts the *IS* curve to the right.
    (d) leaves the *IS* curve unchanged.
    (e) both (a) and (c).

20. An increase in government purchases matched by an increase in taxes
    (a) shifts the *LM* curve to the right.
    (b) shifts the *IS* curve to the left.
    (c) shifts the *IS* curve to the right.
    (d) leaves the *IS* curve unchanged.
    (e) both (a) and (c).

Short Answers Questions

1. How does the nominal interest rate differ from the real interest rate?.

2. What does the quantity of money demanded depend on?.

3. What happens to the *IS* curve when

    (a) taxes decline?
    (b) government purchases increase?
    (c) interest rates increase?

4. (a) What are the two main determinants of investment?
   (b) What is meant by investment demand?.

5. (a) What is the rate of return on a piece of capital equipment equal to.
   (b) What determines whether a particular investment is worthwhile.

6. What happens to the *LM* curve when
   (a) both the price level and the money supply increase by the same percentage?
   (b) the price level decreases?

7. What determines investment?.

8. Explain the change in aggregate expenditure as an economy moves down its *IS* curve.

9. Explain why an increase in government purchases shifts the *IS* curve to the right.

10. Use the *IS-LM* model to explain why the aggregate demand curve slopes downward.

Problem Solving

How does it go?

Rose Land is a closed economy. Its consumption function is

$c = 100 + 0.75(y - t)$ billions of dollars.

Its investment function is

$i = 1000 - 25r$ billions of dollars.

Government purchases are $200 billion, and autonomous taxes are $150 billion. There are no induced taxes.

(a) What is the equation to Rose Land's *IS* curve?

Along the *IS* curve, aggregate planned expenditure equals real GDP. The equation to the *IS* curve is

$$y = c + i + g$$
$$= 100 + 0.75(y - 150) + 1000 - 25r + 200$$
$$= 1,187.5 + 0.75y - 25r$$
$$= 4,750 - 100r.$$

(b) Calculate the slope of the *IS* curve.

The *IS* curve is

$$y = 4,750 - 150r. \tag{5.1}$$

The slope of the *IS* curve is $\Delta r/\Delta y$ as the economy moves along its *IS* curve. From Equation (5.1), as r increases to $r + \Delta r$, y decreases to $y - \Delta y$, such that

$$y - \Delta y = 4,750 - 150(r + \Delta r) \tag{5.2}$$

Subtracting Equation (5.1) from Equation (5.2) gives

$$-\Delta y = 150\Delta r.$$

The slope of the *IS* curve is

$$\Delta r/\Delta y = -1/150.$$

(c) Rose Land's demand for money is

$$M^d = (100 + 0.2y - 5r)P.$$

If Rose Land's supply of money is 1,000 and its price level is 1, what is the equation to Rose Land's *LM* curve?

Along the *LM* curve, the quantity of money demanded equals the quantity supplied. That is,

$$1,000 = (100 + 0.2y - 5r). \quad (5.3)$$

Re-arranging Equation (5.3) gives

$$y = 4,500 + 25r. \quad (5.4)$$

(d)   What is the slope of Rose Land's *LM* curve?

The slope of the *IS* curve is $\Delta r/\Delta y$ as the economy moves along its *LM* curve. From Equation (5.4), as *r* increases to $r + \Delta r$, *y* increases to $y + \Delta y$, such that

$$y + \Delta y = 4,500 + 25(r + \Delta r) \quad (5.5)$$

Subtracting Equation (5.4) from Equation (5.5) gives

$$\Delta y = 25\Delta r.$$

The slope of the *LM* curve is

$$\Delta r/\Delta y = 1/25.$$

(e)   Calculate Rose Land's equilibrium interest rate and real GDP in Rose Land.

Rose Land's *IS* and *LM* curves are

$$y = 4,750 - 100r \quad (5.1)$$
$$y = 4,500 + 25r. \quad (5.4)$$

To solving these equation for *r*, subtract Equation (5.4) from Equation (5.1), which gives

$$0 = 250 - 125r.$$
or, $r = 2.$

To find the value of *y*, substitute 2 for *r* in either Equation (5.1) or Equation (5.4), which gives

$$y = 4,550.$$

(f)   Find the equation to Rose Land's aggregate demand curve.

Rose Land's *IS* and *LM* curves are

$$y = 4,750 - 100r \quad (5.1)$$
$$y = 4,500 + 25r. \quad (5.4)$$

The aggregate demand curve traces out the quantity of real GDP demanded as the price level varies. The quantity of real GDP demanded is equilibrium real GDP as determined by the intersection of the *IS* curve and the *LM* curve.

To find how real GDP is related to the price level, we need to go back to the *LM* curve and find the equation to it that includes the price level. Above we substituted the particular value (1) for the price level. Now we must go back and replace the price level with *P*.

The equation to the *LM* curve is found as follows:

$$1,000 = (100 + 0.2y - 5r)P. \quad (5.5)$$

Re-arranging Equation (5.5) gives

$$y = 5,000/P - 500 + 25r. \quad (5.6)$$

You can see that as the price level changes the *LM* curve shifts and the intersection of the *LM* and *IS* curves traces out the level of real GDP.

To find the equation to the *AD* curve, use the *IS* and *LM* curves, eliminate the interest rate *r* and get the relationship between the price level and real GDP. That is, from the *IS* curve, Equation (5.1), the interest rate is equal to

$$r = 47.5 - 0.01y.$$

Substitute for *r* in the *LM* curve, Equation (5.6), which gives

$$y = 4,000/P + 550.$$

Equation (5.7) is Rose Land's aggregate demand curve.

Now try these

1. In Star Kingdom, the consumption function in billions of dollars is

   $$c = 50 + 0.6(y - t_0).$$

   Autonomous taxes are $8 billion and planned government purchases are $10 billion. Star Kingdom is a closed economy, and there are no induced taxes. It investment function is

   $$i = 750 - 15r.$$

   (a) What is the equation to Star Kingdom's *IS* curve?
   (b) What is the slope of the *IS* curve?
   (c) What is aggregate expenditure when the interest rate is 4 percent a year?
   (d) What is real GDP when the interest rate is 2 percent a year?

2. On Green Island, the consumption function in billions of dollars is

   $$c = 100 + 0.75(y - t).$$

The investment function in billions of dollars is

$$i = 1000 - 75r.$$

Government purchases are $400 billion and autonomous taxes are $400 billion. Green Island is a closed economy, and there are no induced taxes.

(a) What is the equation to Green Island's *IS* curve?
(b) The government of Green Island cuts its purchases of goods and services by $100 billion. Calculate the shift of the *IS* curve.
(c) The government of Green Island makes a balanced budget cut of $100 billion. Calculate the shift of the *IS* curve.

3. Shark Island is a closed economy and its *IS* and *LM* curves are as follows:

   IS curve: $y = 600 - 30r$
   LM curve: $y = 520 + 48r$.

   (a) Calculate Shark Island's equilibrium interest rate.
   (b) Calculate Shark Island's equilibrium real GDP.
   (c) Calculate the slope of Shark Island's *IS* curve.
   (d) Calculate the slope of Shark Island's *LM* curve.

4. You are given the following data about the economy of Fish Point:

   IS curve: $y = 1400 - 25r$
   Demand for money:
   $$M^d/P = 200 + 0.4y - 10r$$
   Supply of money: $M = 1000$.

   The price level at Fish Point is 2.

   (a) What is the equilibrium quantity of real money demanded?

(b) Calculate the equilibrium real GDP and the interest rate.

(c) Calculate the slope of the *IS* curve.

(d) Calculate the equation to the aggregate demand curve.

5. You have the following data about Coral Island, a closed economy:

$$c = 100 + 0.75(y - t)$$
$$i = 50 - 25r$$
$$g = 200$$
$$t = 200.$$

(a) What is the equation to Coral Island's *IS* curve?

(b) Calculate the slope of Coral Island's *IS* curve.

(c) Calculate the shift of the *IS* curve if government purchases increase by 100.

(d) Calculate the shift of the *IS* curve if taxes increase by 100.

(e) Calculate the shift of the *IS* curve if government purchases and taxes each increase by 100.

6. Silly Isle's *LM* curve is

$$y = 3500 + 25r.$$

(a) Calculate the slope of Silly Isle's *LM* curve.

(b) Silly Isle's real money supply increases by 100. Calculate the change in the slope of its *LM* curve.

(c) Silly Isle's interest rate increases by 1 percentage point. Calculate the change in the quantity of money demanded.

7. Heron Island is a closed economy and its *IS* and *LM* curves are as follows:

IS curve: $y = 1300 - 30r$
LM curve: $y = 520 + 48r$.

(a) Calculate Heron Island's equilibrium interest rate.

(b) Calculate Heron Island's equilibrium real GDP.

8. Shark Island's investment demand function is given by:

$$i = 750 - 250r.$$

Calculate the slope of Shark Island's investment function.

9. On Heron Island, the marginal propensity to consume is 0.75. Autonomous consumption is 100. Investment is less than or equal to 500 and decreases by 25 if the interest rate increases 1 percentage point. Government purchases are 300, the government's budget is balanced, and all taxes are autonomous.

(a) What is the equation to Heron Island's *IS* curve?

(b) Calculate the slope of Heron Island's *IS* curve.

(c) Compare the slopes of Heron Island's *IS* curve and investment function.

10. You are given the following data about the economy of Sail Island:

IS curve: $y = 2400 - 50r$
Demand for money:
$$M^d/P = 200 + 0.5y - 10r$$
Supply of money: $M = 2000$.

The price level at Sail Island is 2.

(a) What is the equilibrium quantity of real money demanded?

(b) Calculate the equilibrium real GDP and the interest rate.

(c) Calculate the slope of the *IS* curve.

(d) Calculate the equation to the aggregate demand curve.

✓ Answers

Concept Review

1) nominal interest rate, inflation rate
2) real interest rate
3) real money
4) net income, expressed as a percentage
5) demanded, hold
6) propensity to hold money
7) *LM* curve
8) goods market
9) interest rate, investment
10) investment demand
11) interest rate, real income
12) demand for money function

True or False

1) F	5) F	9) T	13) F	17) F
2) T	6) T	10) F	14) T	18) F
3) T	7) F	11) T	15) F	19) T
4) T	8) T	12) F	16) T	20) F

Multiple Choice

1) d	5) c	9) b	13) d	17) b
2) c	6) d	10) e	14) c	18) a
3) a	7) a	11) a	15) c	19) c
4) b	8) a	12) b	16) a	20) c

Short Answer Questions

1. The nominal interest rate is also called the market interest rate and includes an inflation component. This is the interest rate actually paid in dollar terms. The real interest rate is the nominal interest rate minus the inflation rate. This is the interest rate that is really paid and received after taking inflation into account.

2. The quantity of money demanded depends on the price level, real income, and the interest rate.

3. (a) The *IS* curve shifts to the right.

   (b) The *IS* curve shifts to the right.

   (c) The *IS* curve does not shift.

4. (a) The two main determinants of investment are the interest rate and the rate of return on capital.

   (b) Investment demand is the planned rate of purchase of new capital that is the planned rate of investment.

5. (a) The rate of return on a piece of capital equipment is equal to the net income received from using the equipment expressed as a percentage of the equipment's price.

   (b) To determine whether a particular investment is worthwhile, we compare its rate of return with the interest rate.

   Investment projects are undertaken if the rate of return is greater than or equal to the interest rate.

6. (a) The *LM* curve remains constant.

   (b) The *LM* curve shifts to the right.

7. Investment is determined by the rate of return on capital and the interest rate.

8. Along the *IS* curve aggregate expenditure equals real GDP. As an economy moves down its *IS* curve real GDP increases, so aggregate expenditure also increases.

9. Along the *IS* curve leakages equal injections. An increase in government purchases increases injections, so leakages must increase for goods market equilibrium. Leakages are saving and taxes and these increase as real GDP increases.

10. A decrease in the price level shifts the *LM* curve to the right. The new intersection point of the *IS* and *LM* curves occurs at a greater real GDP. That is, a decrease in the price level increases the level of aggregate expenditure and increases the level of aggregate demand. The aggregate demand curve slopes downward.

7. (a) 10
   (b) 1,000

8. 0.04

9. (a) $y = 2,700 - 100r$
   (b) −0.01
   (c) slope of the investment function is −0.04. The *IS* curve is flatter than the investment function

10. (a) 1,000
    (b) $r = 11.43, y = 1,828.57$
    (c) −0.02
    (d) $y = 2,857.14/P + 400$
    (e) −$96.23 million
    (f) −$77.36 million
    (g) 1.51

Problems

1. (a) $y = 2,3013 - 37.5r$

   (b) −0.0267
   (c) $1,863 billion
   (d) $1,938 billion

2. (a) $y = 4,800 - 300r$
   (b) 400 to the left
   (c) 100 to the left

3. (a) 1.026
   (b) 569.23
   (c) −0.033
   (d) 0.021

4. (a) 500
   (b) $r = 13, y\ 1,075$
   (c) −0.04
   (d) $y = 1,250/P + 450$

5. (a) $y = 800 - 100r$
   (b) −0.01
   (c) 400 to the right
   (d) 300 to the left
   (e) 100 to the right

6. (a) 0.04
   (b) no change
   (c) no change

CHAPTER 6

Monetary and Fiscal Policy Influences on Aggregate Demand

Perspective and Focus

This chapter puts the *IS-LM* model of aggregate demand to work and studies the effects of changes in monetary policy and fiscal policy on the equilibrium interest rate and level of real GDP at a given price level. In other words it studies how the aggregate demand curves shifts when the money supply changes (monetary policy) and when government purchases or taxes (fiscal policy) change.

If you find you are having difficulties with this chapter, your problems could arise from the fact that you did not take our advice seriously enough concerning the need to study the previous chapter extremely thoroughly. You may find it necessary, from time to time, to go back to Chapter 5 and review and refresh your memory and understanding of certain key things.

Although this chapter deals with monetary and fiscal policy, do not be mislead into regarding the results you will be finding as telling you the full and final effects of policy. They tell you how policy shifts the aggregate demand curve. To work out the ultimate effects of policy we have to see how the shifted aggregate demand curve interacts the aggregate supply curve. That is, we have to place the effects of policy on the aggregate demand curve in the context of the *AD-AS* analysis of Chapter 3.

Learning Objectives

After studying this chapter, you will be able to:

- Describe the fluctuations in money supply growth, government purchases, and taxes in Canada recent years
- Explain how a change in the money supply influences interest rates, real GDP, and the price level
- Describe how monetary policy has been used to slow down the Canadian economy
- Explain how changes in government purchases influence interest rates, real GDP, and the price level
- Explain how changes in taxes influence interest rates, real GDP, and price level

Increasing Your Productivity

One of the neatest things about the *IS-LM* model is the way in which it helps us to understand the impacts of monetary and fiscal policy. The key thing to notice is that fiscal policy effects the *IS* curve but not the *LM* curve while monetary policy effects the *LM* curve but not the

IS curve. These facts enable us to analyze the effects of monetary and fiscal policy and to obtain clear predictions about the effects of various policy actions.

Work hard first of all to understand why a change in the money supply shifts the *LM* curve. An increase in the money supply shifts the *LM* curve to the right and a decrease shifts the *LM* curve to the left. Work at understanding at why this occurs. Similarly work hard to understand why a decrease in taxes shifts the *IS* curve to the right, while an increase in government purchases of goods and services shifts the *IS* curve to the right. Similarly, an increase in taxes shifts the *IS* curve to the left and a decrease in government purchases shifts the *IS* curve to the left.

Once you have understood these shifts in the *IS* and *LM* curves you are ready to analysis how monetary and fiscal policy influences interests rates and real GDP at a given price level—how they shift the aggregate demand curve.

In studying these influences of monetary and fiscal policy, *always draw the diagram*. Don't try to work things out in your head. It is not that they are impossible to work out in your head, but it is just that much easier to work them out with a diagram. A diagram lets you check with your eyes as well as your reasoning that you are getting the right answers.

Once you have learnt how to shift the aggregate demand curve as a result of changes in monetary and fiscal policy you are ready to integrate the aggregate demand analysis back into the *AD-AS* analysis. There is nothing fundamentally new here, just a richer understanding of the forces that make the aggregate demand curve shift.

This chapter contains an appendix on the algebra of fiscal and monetary policy multipliers. It is worth spending some time trying to understand the material in this appendix. *It is not* worth spending one second trying to *memorize* the formulas. The way to study this material is to begin the appendix of Chapter 5 and then build on that set of results by changing the equilibrium. To change an equilibrium we change some exogenous variables—in this case the money supply, government purchases of goods and services, or taxes. We then work out the new equilibrium and find out the multiplier effects on the endogenous variables—*in this case* real GDP and the interest rate. Work through these formulas and check that you can understand how they are derived. Once you understand their derivation, work to understand the intuition behind the multipliers and connect them back to the shifts in the *IS* and *LM* curves. Then go onto convince yourself that you understand the story about what is happening in a real economy when these forces are at work. Also check that you can interpret these equations in terms of the forces at work. Once you have done all this you will be able to derive these equations whenever you need them and understand and interpret the results that you obtain from them.

Self Test

Concept Review

1. During the _____s (since World War II), the world operated a gold exchange standard.

2. On the gold exchange standard, Canada kept its monetary policy

    _____
    _____
    _____.

3. The world monetary order that had prevailed since World War II collapsed in _____.

4. When the world operated on a gold exchange standard, exchange rates were _____.

5. Monetary targetting began in the _____.

6. A policy of announcing a target growth rate for the money supply is called

   _____.

7. During the 1970s, monetary targets were _____.

8. In the late 1970s, the Bank of Canada targetted the

   _____.

9. During the early 1980s, the growth rate of the money supply

   _____.

   The real money supply

   _____.

10. During the mid to late 1980s, the Bank of Canada kept its eye on several _____ such as _____, _____ , and

    _____.

11. The most obvious and dramatic feature of recent fiscal policy is the

    _____.

12. The budget deficit is the excess of _____ over

    _____.

13. Since 1980, government spending increased _____ than did tax revenue.

14. An increase in _____ that leads to a decrease in _____ is called crowding out.

15. Crowding out is complete if when

    _____ increases _____ decreases by _____ ; and crowding out is partial when the decrease in_____ is _____ the increases in

    _____.

True or False

1. When the Bank of Canada targetted the money supply, it chose as its target M2.

2. The most obvious and dramatic feature of Canadian fiscal policy is the large deficit that emerged between government spending and the tax revenue during the 1980s.

3. The flatter the *IS* curve, the less the rightward shift in the aggregate demand curve for any given increase in the money supply.

4. The steeper the *LM* curve, the larger is the effect of a change in the money supply on aggregate demand.

5. A flatter *LM* curve makes monetary policy less potent because the demand for money is more sensitive to interest rates.

6. Since 1970, the real money supply in the Canada has declined in three periods—1971-1976, 1980-1982, and 1985-1988.

7. An increase in government purchases of goods and services will shift the *IS* curve to the left.

8. The combination of the rightward shift of the *IS* curve and the leftward shift of the *LM* curve increases the interest rate.

9. Crowding out is the name for the effect of an increase in investment on government purchases.

10. In the *IS-LM* model, an increase in autonomous taxes changes real GDP in a similar manner as an increase in government purchases does, but the magnitude of the change in real GDP resulting from a 1 unit increase in autonomous taxes is greater.

11. Fiscal policy is any policy that changes aggregate demand.

12. Fiscal policy is any government policy that shifts the *IS* curve.

13. Fiscal policy is not very effective if the *IS* curve is fairly steep.

14. Fiscal policy is more effective, the more sensitive investment is to the interest rate.

15. Monetary policy crowds out fiscal policy if investment is very sensitive to interest rate changes.

16. Expansionary monetary policy lowers interest rates, increases investment, and increases aggregate demand.

17. An increase in government purchases increases the aggregate demand for goods and services and shifts the *IS* curve to the right. The interest rate increases. As a result, investment decreases and aggregate demand for goods and services decreases. The *IS* curve shifts to the left.

18. A decrease in the money supply shifts the *LM* curve to the left. Interest rates increase. As a result, investment decreases, and aggregate expenditure decreases.

19. An increase in the money supply increases aggregate demand only because it results in an increase in government purchases.

20. If investment is not very sensitive to changes in the interest rates, then an increase in government purchases does not result in crowding out.

Multiple Choice

1. During the 1960s, Canada kept its monetary policy in close harmony with those of other countries in a system of fixed exchange rates by using
   (a) special drawing rights.
   (b) silver exchange standard.
   (c) gold exchange standard.
   (d) fiat exchange standard.
   (e) none of the above.

2. During the 1970s, money supply growth rates fluctuated dramatically, climbing to double digits. This was a period of formal commitment to
   (a) fiscal targetting.
   (b) gold targetting.
   (c) silver targetting.
   (d) fiat targetting.
   (e) monetary targetting.

3. In the late 1970s, the Bank of Canada targetted
   (a) interest rates.
   (b) the money supply growth rate.
   (c) the monetary base.
   (d) all of the above.
   (e) none of the above.

4. The flatter the *IS* curve, then the larger is the
   (a) leftward shift in the aggregate demand curve for any increase in the money supply.
   (b) rightward shift in the aggregate demand curve for any decrease in the money supply.
   (c) rightward shift in the aggregate demand curve for any given increase in the money supply.
   (d) leftward shift in the aggregate demand curve for an absence of change in the money supply.
   (e) movement up along the aggregate demand curve for any given increase in the money supply.

5. Monetary policy is less potent, the
   (a) steeper *IS* curve.
   (b) steeper *LM* curve.
   (c) flatter *IS* curve.
   (d) flatter *LM* curve.
   (e) both (c) and (d).

6. Which of the following are *incorrect* with respect to an increase in governmental purchases of goods and services?
   (a) The *IS* curve shifts to the left.
   (b) The aggregate demand curve shifts to the right.
   (c) Equilibrium real GDP increases.
   (d) The equilibrium price level increases.
   (e) The higher price level shifts the *LM* curve to the left.

7. The slope of the *IS* curve depends on the sensitivity of
   (a) the money demand to the interest rate.
   (b) saving to the interest rate.
   (c) government purchases of goods and services to the interest rate.
   (d) investment to the interest rate.
   (e) the money supply to the interest rate.

8. The effect of an increase in government purchases on investment is known as
   (a) expulsion.
   (b) arbitrage.
   (c) crowding out.
   (d) overshadowing.
   (e) restructuring.

9. A complete crowding out occurs at less than full employment provided that the *LM* curve
   (a) and *IS* curve are vertical.
   (b) and *IS* curve are horizontal.
   (c) is horizontal or the *IS* curve is vertical.
   (d) is vertical or the *IS* curve is horizontal.
   (e) and *IS* curve are negatively sloped.

10. The economy is approaching full employment. If government purchases have increased and the investment function has shifted to the right, there will be
    (a) downward pressure on interest rates, which will to, some degree, choke off additional investment.
    (b) upward pressure on interest rates, which will not have any effect on additional investment.
    (c) downward pressure on interest rates, which will not have any effect on additional investment.
    (d) upward pressure on interest rates, which will, to some degree, choke off additional investment.
    (e) no pressure on interest rates, but additional investment will be chocked off to some degree.

11. On Green Island, the demand for real balances is independent of interest rates. As a result
    (a) monetary policy will be effective in changing output.
    (b) monetary policy will not be very effective in changing output.
    (c) both fiscal and monetary policy will be very effective in changing output.
    (d) only fiscal policy will be effective in changing output.
    (e) none of the above.

12. The government of Lizard Island is considering the following expansionary policies: Policy 1 removes an investment tax and Policy 2 increases the money supply. Which of the following statements best describes the outcome of these policies?
    (a) Each policy increases aggregate demand, interest rates, and investment.
    (b) Each policy increases aggregate demand and investment but interest rate increases under Policy 1 and decrease under Policy 2.
    (c) Each policy increases aggregate demand and investment but decreases interest rates.
    (d) Each policy increases aggregate demand but interest rat e increases and investment decreases under Policy 1 and interest rates decrease and investment increases under Policy 2.
    (e) None of the above.

Fact 6.1 You are given the following data about Sandy Island, a closed economy,:

$$c = 100 + 0.8(y - t)$$
$$i = 500 - 50r$$
$$g = 200$$

$$t = 250$$
$$M^d/P = 0.5y + 200 - 10r$$
$$M = 1000$$
$$P = 1.$$

13. Use Fact 6.1. The equation to the *IS* curve is
    (a) $y = 1600 - 60r$.
    (b) $y = 3000 - 250r$.
    (c) $y = 1600 + 100r$.
    (d) $y = 1800 - 100r$.
    (e) $y = 4250 - 250r$.

14. Use Fact 6.1. The equation to the *LM* curve is
    (a) $y = 1600 + 20r$.
    (b) $y = 1425 + 10r$.
    (c) $y = 2800 - 100r$.
    (d) $y = 600 + 30r$.
    (e) $y = 1600 - 60r$.

15. Use Fact 6.1. Sandy Island's equilibrium real GDP and interest rate are
    (a) 877, 9.2 percent respectively.
    (b) 1459, 3.41 percent respectively.
    (c) 1800, 10 percent respectively.
    (d) 1704, 5.19 percent respectively.
    (e) 1450, 2.5 percent respectively.

16. Use Fact 6.1. The government of Sandy Island increases its purchases of goods and services by 100. As a result,
    (a) the *IS* curve shifts right by 100 and the *LM* curve remains constant.
    (b) the *IS* curve shifts right by 500 and the *LM* curve remains constant.
    (c) the *IS* curve shifts right by 100 and the *LM* curve shifts right by 100.
    (d) the *IS* curve shifts right by 500 and the *LM* curve shifts right by 400.
    (e) the *IS* curve shifts right by 800 and the *LM* curve shifts right by 100.

17. Use Fact 6.1. The government of Sandy Island increases its purchases of goods and services by 100. As a result, investment
    (a) increases by 100.
    (b) increases by more than 100.
    (c) decreases by 100.
    (d) decreases by less than 100.
    (e) none of the above.

18. Use Fact 6.1. If the government of Sandy Island increases its purchases of goods and services
    (a) by 100, complete crowding out results.
    (b) by more than 100, complete crowding out results.
    (c) by 100, partial crowding out results.
    (d) by less than 100, partial crowding out results.
    (e) none of the above.

19. Use Fact 6.1. An increase in the money supply of 100,
    (a) increases the equilibrium interest rate to 6 percent.
    (b) increases the equilibrium interest rate to more than 6 percent.
    (c) increases real GDP by less than 200.
    (d) both (a) and (c)
    (e) none of the above.

20. Use Fact 6.1. An increase in the money supply by 100,
    (a) increases the investment by 100.
    (b) decreases the investment by 100.
    (c) increases investment by less than 100.
    (d) decreases investment by less than 100.
    (e) none of the above.

Short Answers Questions

1. How does the slope of the *IS* curve and the slope of the *LM* curve affect the potency of a change in the money supply?.

2. The slope of the *IS* curve and *LM* curve have what effect on equilibrium real GDP when there is a change in government purchases?.

3. Why is monetary policy less potent with a flatter *LM* curve?.

4. What monetary arrangement did Canada use during the 1960s?.

5. What is crowding out? Explain why crowding out arises.

6. Explain the effect of an increase in taxes on investment.

7. Under what conditions is the *LM* curve very steep.

8. What is the effect on the slope of the *IS* curve if investment become more sensitive to interest rate changes.

Problem Solving

How does it go?

You are given the following information about Stony Island.

$$c = 100 + 0.75(y - t)$$
$$i = 900 - 20r$$
$$g = 100$$
$$t = 100$$
$$M^d/P = 0.2y + 150 - 75r$$
$$M = 500$$
$$P = 1.$$

(a) Calculate equilibrium real GDP and the interest rate.

ρ=4.55

Equilibrium real GDP and the interest rate are determined at the intersection of the *IS* and *LM* curves. By using the method set out in Chapter 5, the *IS* and *LM* curves are as follows:

36863l− 2350 +295 ✓

IS curve: $y = 4100 - 80r$
LM curve: $y = 1750 + 375r$.

Equilibrium real GDP equals 3,68-6.81 and the equilibrium interest rate equals 5.165 percent a year.

(b) Calculate the equilibrium level of investment.

The investment function tells us the level of investment:

$i = 500 - 20 \times 5.165$
  $= 396.70$.

(c) If the money supply increases by 100, how far does the *LM* curve shift?

The increase in the money supply shifts the *LM* curve to the right.

The equation to the new *LM* curve is derived by equating the quantities of real money demanded and supplied:

$600 = 0.2y + 150 - 75r$

which is

$y = 2250 + 375r$.

The *LM* curve has shifted to the right by 2250 − 1750, which is 500.

(d) Calculate the change in aggregate demand resulting from an increase in the money supply of 100.

When the money supply increases by 100, the *LM* curve shifts to the right and becomes

$y = 2250 + 375r$.

The increase in aggregate demand is equal to the increase in equilibrium real GDP. Solve the equations to the *IS* and *LM* curves for real GDP—the new level of aggregate demand.

Equilibrium real GDP is equal to 3,774.73. Therefore the increase in aggregate demand is equal to 89.92.

(e) Calculate the change in investment that results from an increase in the money supply of 100.

When the money supply increases by 100, the *LM* curve shifts to the right, real GDP increases to 3,774.73. By substituting for *y* in the *IS* curve, you can calculate the new equilibrium interest rate. It is 4.066.

With an interest rate of 4.006, investment, from the investment function, increase to

$i = 900 - 20 \times 4.066$
  $= 818.68$.

The increase in the money supply decreases the interest rate and increases investment by 818.68 − 794.38, which is 24.30.

(f) Calculate the shift of the *IS* curve that results from an increase in government purchases of 100.

The increase in government purchases shifts the *IS* curve to the right by $1/(1 - b)$ times the increase in government purchases. That is, the *IS* curve shifts by

$1/(1 - 0.75) \times 100$, which is 400.

(g) Calculate the change in investment resulting from an increase in government purchases of 100.

The new *IS* curve is

$$y = 4500 - 80r.$$

The new interest rate, at the intersection of the new *IS* curve and the *LM* curve is found by solving the equations to the new *IS* curve and the *LM* curve. It is 6.044.

Investment, from the investment demand function, is

$$i = 900 - 20 \times 6.044$$
$$= 779.21.$$

(h) Has the increase in government purchases crowded out investment?

The increase in government purchases increases the interest rate form 4.066 to 6.044. As a result, investment decreases from 818.68 to 779.12, a decrease of 39.56. The decrease in investment is less than the increase in government purchases so there is partial crowding out.

Now try these

1. You are given the following data about Lizard Island:

$$c = 100 + 0.7(y - t)$$
$$i = 900 - 25r$$
$$g = 100$$
$$t = 100$$
$$M^d/P = 0.2y + 100 - 50r$$
$$M = 500$$
$$P = 1.$$

Calculate the equilibrium value of

(a) real GDP.

(b) the interest rate.

2. You are given the following data about Green Island:

$$c = 200 + 0.6(y - t)$$
$$i = 500 - 100r$$
$$g = 300$$
$$t = 400$$
$$M^d/P = 0.2y + 500 - 50r$$
$$M = 700$$
$$P = 1$$

(a) Calculate the equilibrium real GDP.
(b) Calculate the equilibrium value of consumption.
(c) Calculate the equilibrium value of investment.
(d) Calculate the equilibrium interest rate.
(e) Calculate the effect on equilibrium real GDP of a unit increase in the money supply.
(f) Calculate the effect on equilibrium real GDP of a unit increase in taxes.
(g) Calculate the effect on equilibrium real GDP of a unit increase in government spending.

3. You are given the following data concerning the economy of Easter Island:

$$c = 150 + 0.75(y - t)$$
$$i = 900 - 40r$$
$$g = 100$$
$$t = 100$$
$$M^d/P = 0.2y + 100 - 5r$$
$$M = 500.$$
$$P = 1.$$

(a) Calculate Easter Island's equilibrium real GDP.
(b) Calculate Easter Island's equilibrium real interest rate.
(c) Calculate Easter Island's equilibrium consumption.

(d) Calculate Easter Island's equilibrium investment.

4. In Problem 3, the government of Easter increases taxes by 50.

   (a) Calculate the change in Easter Island's real GDP.
   (b) Calculate the change in Easter Island's real interest rate.

5. In Problem 3, the government of Easter increases government purchases by 50.

   (a) Calculate the change in Easter Island's real GDP.
   (b) Calculate the change in Easter Island's real interest rate.

6. In Problem 3, the government of Easter increases government purchases by 50 and also increases taxes by 50.

   (a) Calculate the change in Easter Island's real GDP.
   (b) Calculate the change in Easter Island's real interest rate.

7. You are given the following data about the economy of Windy Isle:

   IS curve: $y = 2000 - 25r$
   Demand for
     money: $M^d/P = 200 + 0.4y - 10r$
   Supply of
     money: $M = 800.$

   Price level is 2 and the marginal propensity to consume is 0.85.

   The government of Windy Isle increases its purchases by 150.

   (a) Calculate the change in Windy Isle's real GDP.
   (b) Calculate Windy Isle's new interest rate.

(c) Calculate the change in Windy Isle's investment.
(d) Is there crowding out? Explain.

✓ Answers

Concept Review

1) 1960s
2) in close harmony with the policies of other countries
3) 1971
4) fixed
5) 1970s
6) monetary targetting
7) rarely achieved
8) growth rate of M1
9) decreased to zero, decreased
10) intermediate targets, money supply growth rate, interest rate, exchange rate
11) large budget deficit
12) government spending, taxes
13) faster
14) government purchases, investment
15) government purchases, investment, the same amount, investment, less than, government purchases

True or False

1) F	5) T	9) F	13) F	17) F
2) T	6) T	10) F	14) F	18) T
3) F	7) F	11) F	15) F	19) F
4) T	8) T	12) T	16) T	20) T

Multiple Choice

1) c	5) e	9) d	13) b	17) d
2) e	6) a	10) d	14) a	18) c
3) b	7) d	11) a	15) d	19) c
4) c	8) c	12) d	16) b	20) c

Short Answer Questions

1. The flatter the *IS* curve, the larger is the effect of a change in the money supply on equilibrium real GDP.

   The steeper the *LM* curve, the larger is the effect of a change in the money supply on equilibrium real GDP.

2. The steeper the *IS* curve, the larger is the effect of a change in government purchases on real GDP.

   The flatter the *LM* curve, the larger is the effect of a change in government purchases on real GDP.

3. The flatter the *LM* curve, the more sensitive to interest rates is the demand for money. When the money supply increases, interest rates fall, but how far they fall depends on the demand for money function.

   If the demand for money is highly responsive to changes in the interest rate, then a large increase in the money supply brings only a small fall in interest rates.

   The smaller the fall in the interest rate, the smaller is the increase in investment and, therefore, the smaller the increase in aggregate demand.

4. During the 1960s, the world operated on a gold exchange standard, a monetary arrangement in which Canada kept its monetary policy in close harmony with the policies of other countries in a system of fixed exchange rates.

The value of the U.S. dollar was fixed in terms of gold. Thirty-five dollars bought one fine ounce of gold. The Canadian dollar was fixed against the U.S. dollar

5. Crowding out results when an increase in government purchases decreases private investment. Crowding out arise because an increase in government purchases shifts the *IS* curve to the right and increases the interest rate. As a result, private investment decreases.

6. An increase in taxes shifts the *IS* curve to the left. The interest rate decreases, and as a result investment increases.

7. The slope of the *LM* curve is equal to k/l. The *LM* curve is very steep when k/l is very small and this arises if l is very large—money and bonds are very close substitutes.

8. If investment becomes more sensitive to interest rate changes, then the parameter h increases. The slope of the *IS* curve is equal to $(1 - b)/h$. As h increases, the slope of the *IS* curve gets smaller. The *IS* curve becomes flatter.

Problems

1. (a) 3075
   (b) 4.3 percent

2. (a) 1450
   (b) 830
   (c) 320
   (d) 1.8 percent
   (e) increases by 2.5 units
   (f) decreases by 1.5 units
   (g) increases by 2.5 units

3. (a) 2,310.81
   (b) 12.43 percent
   (c) 1,808.11
   (d) 402.70

4. (a) −20.27 units
   (b) −0.81 percentage points

5. (a) 27.03
   (b) 1.08 percentage points

6. (a) 6.76 units
   (b) 0.27 percentage points

7. (a) 2250
   (b) 30 percent
   (c) −75
   (d) There is partial crowding out
         because investment falls by 75
         which is less than the increase in
         government purchases of 150

CHAPTER 7

World Influences on Aggregate Demand

Perspective and Focus

Up to now we have been studying a "closed" economy. The only "closed economy" the world economy. This economy is an important one and it is very worthwhile studying how an open economy operates. But national economies are the ones which focus most of our interest and attention, especially when it comes to discussing and evaluating the effects of macroeconomic policy.

This chapter takes the step of expanding the model of aggregate demand to include features of the open economy—of the linkages between the Canadian economy and the rest of the world.

Learning Objectives

After studying this chapter, you will be able to:

- Describe the trends in Canadian international trade, deficit, and indebtedness
- Describe the balance of payments accounts
- Explain how net exports are determined
- Explain the behavior of net exports in the 1980s
- Explain how foreign exchange markets work and how the foreign currency value of the Canadian dollar is determined
- Describe the behavior of interest rates around the world in the 1980s
- Explain why interest vary from one country to another and why they are really equal
- Explain the open economy *IS-LM* model
- Explain how fiscal policy operates with a fixed exchange rate
- Explain how fiscal and monetary policy operate with a flexible exchange rate

Increasing Your Productivity

The key part of this chapter on which you will spent most of your time is the open economy *IS-LM* model. However, it is important that you spend enough time before getting to the open economy *IS-LM* model to ensure that you understand thoroughly the concepts of the real exchange rate, the determination of the net exports, and the concept of interest rate parity. Work hard to thoroughly master these topics.

The open economy *IS-LM* model has three relationships between the interest and real GDP—the *IS* curve, the *LM* curve, and the interest rate parity condition *IRP*. But only two of these relationships operate to determine real GDP and the interest rate. The two in question depend on the exchange rate regime.

With a fixed exchange rate, equilibrium is determined at the intersection of the *IS* and *IRP* curves, the money supply adjusting to shift the *LM* curve to satisfy the equilibrium. With a flexible exchange rate, equilibrium is determined at the intersection of the *IS* and *LM* curves, the interest rate and expected exchange rate change adjusting to shift the *IRP* curve to satisfy the equilibrium.

It is the fundamental difference in the determination of equilibrium under fixed and flexible exchange rates that lies at the heart of the differences in the monetary policy and the fiscal policy multipliers under the two exchange rate regimes. You will discover that monetary policy has no effect under fixed exchange rates. The reason is that the monetary authority has tied its hands by fixing the exchange rate and cannot control the quantity of money supplied. Like a monopoly producer of any kind of good or service, the monetary authority can only pick one—the exchange rate or the quantity of money supplied. Having chosen the exchange rate, the monetary authority must let the market determine the quantity of money that will be held at that exchange rate. If there is any change in the money supply, it immediately sets off a balance of payments movement that offsets the initial change.

Conversely, under a flexible exchange rate regime the monetary authority can determine the money supply and its actions do indeed influence domestic interest rates and the exchange rate, as well the expected future exchange rate.

Under fixed exchange rates, fiscal policy is highly potent. It's potency arises from the fact that the interest rate is determined on world markets and there is no crowding out (or much less crowding out, in general) than under a flexible exchange rate regime.

Like its two predecessors, this chapter has a algebraic appendix. This appendix on the algebra of the open economy *IS-LM* model is a little more intensive in notation than the two previous ones. It is not vital that you study this appendix and we suggest that unless you genuinely enjoy and easily gain insights from an algebraic approach that you do not devote a large amount of time to this material.

Self Test

Concept Review

1. The account that records the receipts from nonresidents and payments to residents arising from transactions involving debt is called the

    _____.

2. Capital exports are investments by _____ of the _____ in _____.

3. Capital _____ increase the capital account surplus.

4. The balance of payments is equal to the sum of the _____ account balance and the _____ account balance.

5. A decrease in the number of yen that one dollar buys is _____ of the yen and a _____ of the dollar.

6. _____ are U.S. dollar deposited in foreign banks outside the United States.

7. The official settlements balance plus the _____ always equals zero.

8. An exchange rate that is market determined is called a _____ exchange rate.

9. An exchange rate that is declared and maintained by the central bank is called a _____ exchange rate.

10. An index that is the weighted average of the values of a unit of currency is called _____ exchange rate.

11. The exchange rate between two currencies for immediate delivery is the _____ exchange rate, whereas the exchange rate between currencies for delivery in one year is called the _____ exchange rate.

12. The net export curve shows the relationship between _____ and _____, holding _____ constant.

13. The equality of the value of money in all countries is called _____.

14. The equality of rates of return on assets denominated in different currencies is _____.

15. The equality of rates of return when the investor takes the risk is called _____.

16. The equality of rates of return when the investor does not take the risk _____.

17. A _____ exchange rate the number of units of foreign money that one dollar buys, whereas the _____ exchange rate is the number of units of foreign goods that one dollar buys.

18. Unilateral transfers are transactions that are pert of the _____ account of the balance of payments.

19. Net foreign investment income is entered in the _____ account of the balance of payments.

20. The account the records international transactions in gold and foreign currency is the _____ account of the balance of payments.

True or False

1. Net foreign investment income is the earnings of Canadian residents on assets held in the rest of the world minus the earnings of foreigners on assets held in Canada.

2. Gifts from Americans to people in the rest of the world minus gifts to Americans from people in other countries are known as bilateral transfers.

3. The real exchange rate is the price of domestic goods and services relative to the price of foreign goods and services.

4. A managed floating exchange rate is an exchange rate whose value is determined by market forces.

5. Purchasing power parity explains day-to-day fluctuations in the exchange rate.

6. Since the early 1970s, the Canadian economy has operated with a flexible exchange rate.

7. The exchange rate between two currencies for immediate delivery is called the forward exchange rate.

8. In an economy with a fixed exchange rate, fiscal policy has no influence on aggregate demand.

9. A country's capital account balance is its capital imports minus its capital exports.

10. The net export function is the relationship between net exports and the variables that influence it—real GDP, income in the rest of the world, and the real exchange rate.

11. An increase in real income in the rest of the world shifts the *IS* curve to the right.

12. As an economy moves up its *LM* curve, the balance of payments becomes smaller.

13. As domestic interest rates increase the *LM* curve shifts because the demand for money decreases.

14. A depreciation of the domestic currency does not shift the *IS* curve.

15. In a flexible exchange rate regime, a balance of payments deficit occurs at all points below the *IS* curve.

16. In a fixed exchange rate regime, an increase in foreign real income increases interest rates and increases the capital account.

17. In a fixed exchange rate regime, an increase in foreign real income increases exports and increases the domestic money supply.

18. An increase in real income in the rest of the world when the exchange rate is flexible has no effect on the balance of payments but appreciates the domestic currency.

19. A rise in foreign interest rates decreases the money supply and decreases domestic real income if the exchange rate is fixed.

20. A rise in foreign interest rates depreciates the domestic currency and increases the balance of payments surplus if the exchange rate is flexible.

Multiple Choice

1. Since 1984, foreign investments in Canada have
   (a) been equal to Canadian investments in other countries.
   (b) outstripped Canadian investments in the rest of the world.
   (c) been less than Canadian investments in the rest of the world.
   (d) come to a virtual standstill whereas Canadian investments in other countries are blooming.
   (e) been almost nil but they have been more than Canadian investments in other countries.

2. The capital account
   (a) records new investments by Canadian residents in some specified countries.
   (b) records new investments by Canadian residents in the rest of the world and foreign investments in Canada.
   (c) shows capital imports as investments by Canadian residents in the rest of the world.
   (d) balance is obtained by subtracting capital imports from capital exports.
   (e) records gifts from Canadians to people in the rest of the world.

3. Fiscal policy,
   (a) decreases interest rates and, to some degree, crowds out investment.
   (b) increases interest rates and, to some degree, increases investment.
   (c) increases interest rates and, to some degree, crowds out investment.
   (d) decreases interest rates and, to some degree, decreases investment.
   (e) none of the above.

4. The government budget deficit and the Canadian deficit with the rest of the world are known as the
   (a) bilateral deficit.
   (b) twin deficits.
   (c) unilateral deficit.
   (d) structural deficit.
   (e) multilateral deficit.

5. The equality of rates of return when no risk is taken and when the investor covers the transaction by taking out a forward contract is known as
   (a) spot interest parity.
   (b) forward interest parity.
   (c) uncovered interest parity.
   (d) covered interest parity.
   (e) real interest parity.

6. With a fixed exchange rate, the
   (a) *IS* curve is flatter than in a closed economy.
   (b) *LM* curve is flatter than in a closed economy; but because the money supply is endogenous, so is the position of the *LM* curve.
   (c) *IS* curve is vertical in both a closed and an open economy.
   (d) *LM* curve is steeper than in the closed economy; but because the money supply is exogenous, so is the position of the *LM* curve.
   (e) *IS* curve is steeper than in a closed economy.

7. The equality of rates of return when the investor takes a risk and does not cover the transaction by taking out a forward contract is referred to as
   (a) entrepreneurial parity.
   (b) managed floating interest parity.
   (c) nominal exchange parity.
   (d) uncovered interest parity.
   (e) official settlements parity.

8. The relationship between net exports and real GDP, holding the real exchange rate constant, is known as the
   (a) fixed exchange rate curve.
   (b) current account curve.
   (c) capital exports curve.
   (d) real dollar curve.
   (e) net export curve.

9. An index number calculated as a weighted average of the value of the Canadian dollar in terms of all other currencies, where the weight on each currency is a proportion of Canadian international trade undertaken in that currency is known as
    (a) dollar exchange rate.
    (b) appreciation exchange rate.
    (c) depreciation exchange rate.
    (d) current exchange rate.
    (e) effective exchange rate.

10. The position of the open economy *IS* curve depends on
    (a) government purchases of goods and services.
    (b) taxes.
    (c) real income of the remainder of the world.
    (d) interest rates in the rest of the world.
    (e) all of the above.

11. The Bretton Woods system
    (a) pegged the national currencies to the U.S. dollar.
    (b) established a system of flexible exchange rates.
    (c) required nations with deficits to revalue their currencies.
    (d) pegged the world's currency to silver.
    (e) required nation's with serious inflation to revalue their currencies.

12. The Bretton Woods system collapsed
    (a) at the end of World War II.
    (b) during the Korean War.
    (c) during the Great Depression.
    (d) in the early 1970s.
    (e) in the early 1980s.

13. If the German demand for Japanese cars increases, then
    (a) the supply of German marks increases.
    (b) the supply of Japanese yen increases.
    (c) a smaller quantity of German marks will be bought and sold.
    (d) the Japanese yen will appreciate relative to the German mark.
    (e) the demand for German marks will decrease.

14. In an open economy, an increase in the real income in the rest of the world shifts
    (a) the *IS* curve.
    (b) the *LM* curve.
    (c) the *IRP* curve.
    (d) both (a) and (c).
    (e) none of the above.

15. An increase in the money supply in a flexible exchange rate economy moves down its *IS* curve and
    (a) increases its capital account.
    (b) appreciates its currency.
    (c) depreciates its currency.
    (d) both (a) and (c).
    (e) none of the above.

16. As a flexible-exchange rate economy moves down its *IS* curve,
    (a) its currency appreciates.
    (b) its net exports remain constant.
    (c) its net exports decrease.
    (d) its currency depreciates.
    (e) both (a) and (d).

17. In an open economy, as real income in the rest of the world decreases
    (a) the domestic economy's *LM* curve shifts.
    (b) the domestic economy's *IS* curve shifts to the right.
    (c) the domestic economy's *IS* curve shifts to the left.
    (d) both (a) and (b).
    (e) both (a) and (c).

18. If the Canadian interest rate is lower than the U.S. interest rate
    (a) Canadian currency is expected to appreciate.
    (b) Canadian currency is expected to depreciate.
    (c) rational economic agents will always invest in Canada.
    (d) rational economic agents will always borrow funds in the United States.
    (e) inflation in Canada must be higher than inflation in the United States.

19. A fax machine costs $1,295.00 and the current exchange between the dollar and the Japanese yen is 180 yen per dollar. The price of the fax machine in yen is
    (a) 7.194 yen.
    (b) 180 yen.
    (c) 1,295 yen.
    (d) 233,100 yen.
    (e) none of the above.

20. As an economy moves up its *LM* curve
    (a) its current account balance becomes larger.
    (b) its capital account becomes smaller.
    (c) its current account balance becomes smaller.
    (d) its balance of payments becomes smaller.
    (e) both (c) and (d).

3. Briefly explain what a flexible exchange rate regime and a managed floating exchange rate regime are.

4. (a) What is the interest rate parity theory based on?
   (b) What does the interest rate parity theory predict?
   (c) When does interest rate parity prevail?

5. (a) What are the balance of payments accounts?
   (b) What do they record?

6. How are net imports determined?

7. Briefly summarize Canadian fiscal and monetary policy during the 1980s.

8. What is meant by a forward contract?

9. What is meant by purchasing power parity.

10. Explain why a central bank does not have control of the money supply if the exchange rate is fixed.

Short Answers Questions

1. Briefly explain the difference between an open-economy model and a closed-economy model.

2. What are the main influences on exports and imports?

Problem Solving

How does it go?

1. Last year, Rose Island had the following international transactions:

   Exports of goods and services $6,000
   Imports of goods and services $5,000
   Dividends paid by Rose Island-
      ers to the rest of the
      world $2,000
   Dividends received by Rose
      Islanders from the
      rest of the world $1,000
   Rose Islanders' gifts to
      residents of the rest
      of the world $700
   Gifts to Rose Islanders from
      the rest of the world $500
   Rose Islanders' purchases of
      debt issued by the rest
      of the world $4,000
   Purchases of Rose Island debt
      by residents of the rest of
      of the world $3,000
   Reduction in Rose Island foreign
      exchange reserves $2,000

   (a) Calculate the current account balance.

   The current account balance is equal to (exports + dividends received from the rest of the world + gifts received from the rest of the world) minus (imports + dividends paid to the rest of the world + gifts from the rest of the world). That is, ($6,000 + $1,000 + $500) – ($5,000 + $2,0000 + $700), which equals –$700.

   (b) Calculate the capital account balance.

   The capital account balance equals purchases of Daisy Island

   debt minus debt purchased by Daisy Islander. That is, $3,000 – $4,000, which equals –$1,000.

   (c) Calculate the official settlements balance.

   The official settlements balance is equal to minus the change in the foreign exchange reserves. That is, $2,0000.

2. The price of a television set in Japan is 100,000 yen. The spot exchange rate is 350 yen per dollar. Calculate the price of the television set in Canada.

   The price of the television set in Canada is equal to the price in yen converted to dollars at the spot exchange rate. That is, 100,000/350 dollars, which is $285.71.

Now try these

1. A Honda sells for 1,200,000 yen in Japan and for 10,000 dollars in Canada. The exchange rate is 120 yen per dollar.

   (a) What is the Canadian real exchange rate.
   (b) In which country is the Honda cheaper?

2. Seal Island had the following international transactions in 1991:

Exports of goods and services	$3,000
Imports of goods and services	$4,000
Dividends and interest paid by Seal Islanders to the rest of the world	$500
Dividends and interest received by Seal Islanders from the rest of the world	$1,000
Seal Islanders' gifts to residents of the rest of the world	$250
Gifts to Seal Islanders from the rest of the world	$500
Seal Islanders' purchases of debt issued by the rest of the world	$1,500
Purchases of Seal Island debt by residents of the rest of the world	$2,000

Calculate Seal Island's
(a) current account balance.
(b) capital account balance.
(c) balance of payments.
(d) official settlements balance.

3. You are considering buying a bond. The interest rate on dollar denominated bonds is 10 percent per year and on pound denominated bonds is 20 percent per year. Today's spot exchange rate is £1.20 per dollar and the expected exchange rate in one year is £1.32 per dollar. Which bond will you buy? Explain your answer.

4. Big Wave Island as a fixed exchange rate. Its *IS* curve and demand for money are

IS curve: $y = 10550 - 15r + (200/P)$

Demand for
money: $M^d/P = 0.2y + 200 - 10r$.

The price level in Big Wave Island is 4 and the interest rate in the rest of the world is 2 percent a year.

(a) Calculate equilibrium real income and interest rate in Big Wave Island.

(b) Calculate the equilibrium money supply in Big Wave Island.

(c) The government of Big Wave Island decreases its purchases of goods and services and as a result the *IS* curve shifts to the left by 100. Calculate the immediate change in the interest rate.

(d) In (c), calculate its real income in the long run.

(e) In (d), calculate the change in its money supply in the long run.

5. Big Wave Island as a fixed exchange rate. Its *IS* curve and demand for money are

IS curve: $y = 10550 - 15r + (200/P)$

Demand for
money: $M^d/P = 0.2y + 200 - 10r$.

The price level in Big Wave Island is 4 and the interest rate in the rest of the world is 2 percent a year.

(a) The government of Big Wave Island increases the money supply and as a result the *LM* curve shifts to the right by 50. Calculate the immediate change in the interest rate.

(b) In (a), calculate its real income in the long run.
(c) In (b), calculate its interest rate in the long run.

✓ Answers

Concept Review

1) capital account
2) domestic economy, rest of the world
3) imports
4) current, capital
5) an appreciation, a depreciation
6) Eurodollars
7) balance of payments
8) flexible
9) fixed
10) effective
11) spot, forward
12) net exports, real GDP, real exchange rate
13) purchasing power parity
14) interest rate parity
15) uncovered interest parity
16) covered interest parity
17) nominal, real
18) current
19) current
20) official settlements

True or False

1) T	5) F	9) T	13) F	17) T
2) F	6) T	10) T	14) T	18) T
3) T	7) F	11) T	15) T	19) T
4) F	8) T	12) F	16) F	20) F

Multiple Choice

1) b	5) d	9) e	13) a	17) c
2) b	6) e	10) e	14) a	18) a
3) c	7) d	11) a	15) c	19) d
4) b	8) e	12) d	16) d	20) c

Short Answer Questions

1. An open-economy model takes linkages between the domestic economy and the rest of the world into account whereas a closed-economy model excludes international considerations.

2. The main influences on exports are the real exchange rate and income of the rest of the world.

   The main influences on imports are the real exchange rate and Canadian real GDP.

3. A flexible exchange rate is one whose value is determined by market forces. The central bank does not declare a target value for the exchange rate and has no direct interest in the value of the exchange rate. The central bank does not intervene and manipulate the relative price of its currency in the foreign exchange market.

   A managed-floating exchange rate is one that is manipulated but is not necessarily held constant by the central bank. As a rule, the central bank announces that it is floating but does not tell the market what course the exchange rate should follow.

4. (a) Interest rate parity theory is based on the idea that investors try to do the best they can and seek the highest rate of return available.

   (b) The interest rate parity theory predicts that rates of return on assets denominated in different currencies are equal once the expected rate of currency depreciation or appreciation is taken into account.

Furthermore, the theory also predicts that the exchange rate will adjust from hour to hour and day to day to ensure that interest rate parity prevails.

(c) Interest parity prevails when investors make the same rate of return regardless of the currency in which they borrow and lend.

5. (a) The balance of payment accounts are the current account, the capital account, and the official settlements account.

(b) The current account records the values of net exports, net income from foreign investment, and unilateral transfers.

The capital account records the difference between Canadian investments in the rest of the world and foreign investments in Canada.

The settlements account records the net receipts and payments of gold and foreign currency resulting form the transactions in the current and capital accounts.

6. Net exports are determined by the real exchange rate, income in the rest of the world, and Canadian real GDP.

7. During the early 1980s, government purchases increased and taxes decreased as a percentage of GDP. This was an expansionary fiscal policy. Its effects were similar to those predicted by the *IS-LM* model with flexible exchange rates. Real GDP and interest rates increased, as did the real exchange rate. Net exports decreased sharply.

In the second half of the 1980s, fiscal policy was not expansionary. Government purchases decreased as a percentage of real GDP by more than taxes. The leftward shift of the *IS* curve brought lower interest rates, slower real GDP growth, and a lower real exchange rate. Furthermore, net exports increased.

8. A forward contract is a contract that is negotiated today to purchase or sell an agreed quantity at an agreed future date and at an agreed price.

9. Purchasing power parity is the condition that exits when the value of money in one country is equal to the value of money in another country. Purchasing power parity holds in the long-run.

10. In a fixed exchange regime the money supply is endogenous. Central bank monetary policy is conducted to maintain the chosen value of the exchange rate. The money supply is determined by the actions of private individuals in choosing the currency in which to hold their wealth.

Problems

1. (a) 1
   (b) The prices are the same

2. (a) −$250
   (b) $500
   (c) +250
   (d) −250

3. (a) If you buy the dollar denominated bond, you lend $100 and a year later you receive $110. Your rate of return is 10 percent per year.

If you buy the pound denominated bond, you have to buy pounds first. You get £120 for your $100 and lend it at an interest rate of 20 percent a year. You receive £144 at the end of the year. Converting £144 into dollars, you expect to get $110 and this is exactly the same as if you had bought the dollar denominated bond.

4. (a) $y = 10,570$, $r = 2$ percent a year
    (b) $9,176
    (c) falls by 1.54 percentage points to 0.46 percent a year
    (d) 10,470
    (e) decreases by $880 to $8,296

5. (a) decreases by 0.77 percentage points to 1.23 percent a year
    (b) 10,570
    (c) 2 percent a year

CHAPTER 8

The Labor Market and Aggregate Supply

Perspective and Focus

You have now completed your study of the details of aggregate demand. It is time to move on to probing details of aggregate supply. This chapter and the next two do just that.

Chapter 8 takes you to the heart of the major disagreement in macroeconomics today—a disagreement about how flexible wages are and how quickly the automatic stabilization mechanism of flexible wages operates to keep the economy at or near full employment.

Learning Objectives

After studying this chapter, you will be able to:

- Describe the behavior of cycles in real GDP, unemployment and real wages
- Explain how labor productivity influences the demand for labor
- Compare the changes in labor productivity and the demand for labor in Canada and Japan
- Explain how labor supply decisions are made
- Derive the long-run aggregate supply curve
- Derive the short-run aggregate supply curve
- Explain the main competing theories of wage determination
- Explain the behavior of wages over the business cycle.

Increasing Your Productivity

The key to understanding the theory of aggregate supply is to recognize that the long-run aggregate supply curve is the place toward which the economy is tending to move, while the short-run aggregate supply curve is the place where it is. At any given point in time, there is a given level of wages that determines the position of the short-run aggregate supply curve. If the price level equals that at which the short-run aggregate supply curve intersects the long-run aggregate supply curve, then the economy is at a full-employment equilibrium. When the price level is above that at which the short-run aggregate supply curve intersects the long-run aggregate supply curve, then the economy is at an above full-employment equilibrium. When the price level is below that at which the short-run aggregate supply curve intersects the long-run aggregate supply curve, then the economy is at an unemployment equilibrium.

The second key thing to remember in this chapter is that the positions of the production function, the demand for labor curve, the supply of labor curve and the aggregate supply curves, are constantly changing. Most of the time productivity increases, shifting the production function upward. As a result, the demand for labor and aggregate supply increase. Also, most of the time, the population increases, shifting the supply of labor curve to the right and increasing both short-run and long-run aggregate supply.

Occasionally forces operate in the opposite direction bringing a decrease in aggregate supply.

Self Test

Concept Review

1. Households allocate their time between _____ and _____ .

2. Nonmarket activities include _____ and _____ .

3. Market activities include _____ and _____ .

4. The labor supply curve is the relationship between _____ and _____ .

5. The demand for labor is the relationship between _____ and _____ .

6. There is a tendency for _____ to be procyclical and for _____ to be countercyclical.

7. The price of labor measured in constant purchasing power is the _____ .

8. An increase in the capital stock produces a movement along the short-run _____ , whereas technological progress produces a _____ _____ of it.

9. The theory that money wage rates adjust slowly in response to excess demand or supply of labor is called _____ .

10. The theory that money wage rates adjust continuously and quickly in response to excess demand or supply of labor is called the _____ .

True or False

1. A variable is procyclical when its fluctuations match fluctuations in real GDP.

2. Massive disruption to the world supply of oil during the 1970s produced a shift in the short-run production function and the demand for labor curve.

3. The real interest rate does not affect the supply of labor because it does not affect intertemporal substitution.

4. A close relationship does not exist between fluctuations in real GDP and unemployment over the course of the business cycle.

5. The long-run aggregate supply curve shows the relationship between the quantity of real GDP supplied and the price level when wages and other factor prices are flexible and have adjusted to achieve full employment and when firms are producing their profit maximizing output.

6. The two theories of wage determination are known as labor market clearing and gradual adjustment.

7. The short-run aggregate supply curve shows the relationship between the quantify of real GDP supplied and the price level when wages are variable.

8. The Canadian short-run production function shifted upward by about 80 percent between 1975 and 1990.

9. It is possible for a single shock in either aggregate supply or aggregate demand to generate a business cycle.

10. In order to measure the marginal product of labor, one must measure the slope of the long-run aggregate supply curve.

11. The opportunity cost is the goods and services foregone by giving up the wage that an hour of work earns.

12. The slope of the short-run production function measure the money wage rate.

13. The marginal product of labor is the increase in the real wage rate after the last worker has been employed.

14. Firms hire maximize profit by hiring the quantity of labor that makes the marginal product of labor equal to the wage rate.

15. The quantity of labor supplied changes if the real wage changes.

16. If a change in the price level changes the money wage rate by the same percentage then the real wage constant and the long-run aggregate supply curve is vertical.

17. The business cycle refers to fluctuations in the general price level.

18. The effect of a change in the real wage rate on the timing of work depends on whether the change in the wage rate is anticipated.

19. The gradual adjustment theory of wages implied that the short-run aggregate supply curve moves only slowly.

20. The labor market clearing theory of wages implies that unemployment fluctuates around its natural rate.

Multiple Choice

1. The price of labor measured in constant purchasing power is given by
   (a) W/P.
   (b) $W \times P$.
   (c) $W + P$.
   (d) $W - P$.
   (e) P/W.

2. In order to maximize profits, firms hire labor up to the point at which
   (a) $1/W = 1/MP \times P$.
   (b) $W = MP \times 1/P$.
   (c) $W/P = 1/P$.
   (d) $W/P = MP$.
   (e) $W/MP = P$.

3. Which of the following shift the production function and the demand for labor curve over time?
   (a) Changes in inflation.
   (b) Changes in unemployment.
   (c) Capital accumulation.
   (d) Technological change.
   (e) Both (c) and (d).

4. Capital accumulation and technological change shift the short-run production function upward over time. Simultaneously, the short-run production function
   (a) becomes flatter—that is, at any level of employment the marginal product of labor is less.
   (b) gets steeper—that is, at any level of employment the marginal product of labor is higher.
   (c) remains constant—that is, at any level of employment the marginal product of labor remains the same.
   (d) becomes quite variable—that is, at any level of employment the marginal product of labor can be either higher or lower.
   (e) becomes negative throughout—that is, at any level of employment the marginal product of labor is negative.

5. Market activity includes:
   (a) work.
   (b) job search.
   (c) work in the home.
   (d) leisure.
   (e) both (a) and (b).

6. A change in the real wage has the following effect(s) on the quantity of labor supply supplied:
   (a) an activities effect.
   (b) a leisure effect.
   (c) an income effect.
   (d) a substitution effect.
   (e) both (c) and (d).

7. Which of the following induces a change in the quantity of labor supplied and a movement along the labor supply curve?
   (a) A change in the real wage rate.
   (b) A change in the population.
   (c) A change in the real interest rate.
   (d) All of the above.
   (e) None of the above.

8. The relationship between the quantity of real GDP supplied and the price level, when wages and other factor prices are flexible and have adjusted to achieve full employment and when firms are producing their profit-maximizing output is given by the
   (a) short-run aggregate supply curve.
   (b) long-run aggregate supply curve.
   (c) short-run production function.
   (d) long-run production function.
   (e) Okun's Law.

9. An increase in capital stock or technological advance increases the level of real GDP that can be produced from a given level of employment. As a result, the short-run production function
   (a) shifts upward and the marginal product of labor increases, so the demand for labor curve shifts to the right.
   (b) shifts downward and the marginal product of labor decreases, so the demand for labor curve shifts to the right.
   (c) shifts upward, so that the marginal product of labor remains constant and the demand for labor curve shifts to the right.
   (d) remains constant, so that the marginal product of labor increases and the demand for labor curve shifts to the right.
   (e) shifts downward and the marginal product of labor remains constant, so the demand for labor curve remains unchanged.

10. An increase in the working age population or in the real interest rate
    (a) increases the quantity of labor supplied at each real wage rate and shifts the labor supply curve to the right.
    (b) decreases the quantity of labor supplied at each real wage rate and shifts the labor supply curve to the left.
    (c) increases the quantity of labor supplied at each real wage rate and leaves the labor supply curve unchanged.
    (d) decreases the quantity of labor supplied at each real wage rate and leaves the labor supply curve unchanged.
    (e) increases the quantity of labor supplied at each real wage rate and shifts the labor supply curve to either the right or the left.

11. An increase in the money wage rate
    (a) decreases long-run aggregate supply.
    (b) decreases short-run aggregate supply.
    (c) increases short-run aggregate supply.
    (d) increases long-run aggregate supply.
    (e) leaves short-run aggregate supply constant.

12. In order to maximize profit, firms hire the quantity of labor such that the real wage rate is equal to the
    (a) marginal product of labor divided by the price of the output.
    (b) marginal product of labor times the price of the output.
    (c) average product of labor times the price of the output.
    (d) average product of labor divided by the price of the output.
    (e) the marginal product labor.

13. The quantity of labor supplied decreases if the
    (a) labor force increases.
    (b) real wage rate decreases.
    (c) money wage decreases.
    (d) technology advances.
    (e) both (b) and (d).

14. Labor market equilibrium determines the
    (a) the marginal product of labor.
    (b) real wage rate.
    (c) level of employment.
    (d) both (a) and (b).
    (e) (a), (b), and (c).

15. The long-run aggregate supply curve shifts to the right over time if
    (a) firms begin to work overtime.
    (b) the farm sector goes into boom.
    (c) firms accumulate capital.
    (d) the real wage rate incrcases.
    (e) (a), (b), and (c).

16. The relationship between real GDP and the level of employment, holding the capital stock and the state of technology constant is illustrated by the
    (a) short-run aggregate supply curve.
    (b) supply of labor curve.
    (c) short-run production function.
    (d) long-run aggregate supply curve.
    (e) aggregate demand curve.

17. The gradual adjustment theory of wages implied that
    (a) the short-run aggregate supply curve moves only slowly.
    (b) unemployment fluctuates around its natural rate.
    (c) the short-run aggregate supply curve shifts slowly.
    (d) both (a) and (b).
    (e) both (a) and (c).

18. The labor market clearing theory of wages implied that
    (a) the short-run aggregate supply curve moves only slowly.
    (b) unemployment fluctuates around its natural rate.
    (c) the short-run aggregate supply curve shifts every time the price level changes.
    (d) both (a) and (b).
    (e) both (b) and (c).

19. All the following statements are true *except*
    (a) Along the short-run aggregate production function, the marginal product of labor decreases as more labor is employed.
    (b) The quantity of labor demanded is such that the marginal product of labor equals the money wage rate.
    (c) The quantity of labor demanded is such that the marginal product of labor multiplied by the output price equals the money wage rate.
    (d) As larger the quantity of labor employed, the smaller is the marginal product of labor.
    (e) Marginal product of labor decreases as the amount of labor hired decreases.

20. Technological advances that increase the marginal product of labor
    (a) increase the real wage rate.
    (b) decrease employment.
    (c) shift the long-run aggregate supply curve to the right.
    (d) increase the real wage rate and shifts he long-run aggregate supply curve to the left.
    (e) both (a) and (c).

Short Answers Questions

1. Explain why the long-run aggregate supply curve is vertical.

2. Briefly summarize the main implication of the labor market-clearing theory of wages.

3. Explain how the demand for labor is determined.

4. Briefly explain what two effects the real wage rate has on the quantity of labor supplied.

5. Explain the two theories of wage determination.

6. Explain why technological progress shifts the demand for labor curve.

7. Explain why the official unemployment rate underestimates the actual unemployment rate.

8. What is a *countercyclical variable*?

9. Explain why firms will hire more hours of labor only at a lower wage rate.

10. Explain the effect of a decrease in aggregate demand on employment when wages are sticky.

Problem Solving

How does it go?

Elk Island's short-run production function, demand for labor, and supply of labor are as follows:

$$y = 100n - 0.1n^2, \qquad (8.1)$$
$$n^d = 500 - 5(W/P) \qquad (8.2)$$
$$n^s = 110 + 2.5(W/P). \qquad (8.3)$$

(a) Calculate Elk Island's equilibrium employment level.

Equilibrium employment is determined by the intersection of the demand for labor and the supply of labor. That is, solve Equations (8.2) and (8.3) for n. To do this, multiple Equation (8.3) by 2 and then add it to Equation (8.2). Equilibrium employment is 240.

(b) Calculate Elk Island's equilibrium real wage rate.

To find the equilibrium real wage rate substitute 240 for n in either the demand for labor os the supply of labor—Equations (8.2) and (8.3). The equilibrium real wage is 52.

(c) Calculate Elk Island's equilibrium real GDP.

To find the equilibrium level of real GDP substitute 240 for n in the production function—Equation (8.1). Equilibrium real GDP is 18,240.

(d) Calculate the equation to Elk Island's long-run aggregate supply curve.

Long-run aggregate supply shows what happens to real GDP as the price level varies. As the price level varies employment remains at 240 and real GDP remains at 18,240. Therefore the equation to the long-run aggregate supply curve is

$$y = 18{,}240.$$

Now try these

1. In Magic Empire the money wage rate is $10 an hour and the price level is 80; in Frontierland, the money wage rate is $10 an hour and the price level is 125; and in Desert Kingdom the moncy wage rate is $10 an hour and the price level is 100.

In which country is the real wage biggest? And in which country is it least?

2. Sandy Island's production function, demand for labor, and supply of labor are given by

$$y = 100 - 0.2n^2$$
$$n^d = 250 - 2.5(W/P)$$
$$n^s = 100 + 2.5(W/P)$$

Calculate the equilibrium level of
(a) employment.
(b) real wage.
(c) real GDP.

3. On Seal Isle the short-run production function, demand for labor curve, and supply of labor curve are as follows:

$$y = 56n - 0.04n^2$$
$$n^d = 700 - 12.5(W/P)$$
$$n^s = 175 + 5(W/P)$$

(a) Calculate Seal Isle's equilibrium employment and money wage rate when the price level is 1.
(b) Calculate Seal Isle's employment when the price level increases form 1 to 1.25.
(c) Calculate the quantity of real GDP supplied on Seal Isle when the labor market is in equilibrium at a price level of 1.
(d) Calculate the quantity of real GDP supplied on Seal Isle when the money wage is sticky and the price level increases form 1 to 1.25.

4. Tomorrow's real wage rate is 5 percent higher than today's and the interest rate is 10 percent a year. Calculate the opportunity cost of more nonwork activities today and less tomorrow, when total nonwork activities are held constant.

5. In Problem 4, today's real wage rate increases by 6 percent and the increase is permanent. Calculate the opportunity cost of more nonwork activities today and less tomorrow, when total nonwork activities are held constant.

6. Pleasure Land has the following short-run production function, demand for labor, and supply of labor:

$$y = 72n - n^2$$
$$n^d = 36 - 0.5(W/P)$$
$$n^s = 8 + 1.5(W/P).$$

   (a) Calculate the real wage rate and the level of employment.

   Suppose that homemakers in Pleasure Land decide to work outside the home and that the supply of labor become:

$$n^s = 16 + 1.5(W/P).$$

   Calculate the effect of the change in the willingness to work outside the home on
   (a) the real wage.
   (b) equilibrium employment.
   (c) real GDP.

✓ Answers

Concept Review

1) market, nonmarket
2) work performed at home, leisure
3) work and job search
4) quantity of labor supplied, real wage rate
5) quantity of labor demanded, real wage rate
6) real wages, unemployment
7) real wage rate
8) production function, shift, upward
9) gradual adjustment theory of wages
10) labor market clearing theory of wages

True or False

1) T	5) T	9) F	13) F	17) F
2) T	6) T	10) F	14) F	18) F
3) F	7) F	11) T	15) T	19) T
4) F	8) F	12) F	16) T	20) F

Multiple Choice

1) a	5) e	9) a	13) b	17) e
2) d	6) e	10) a	14) e	18) b
3) e	7) a	11) b	15) c	19) b
4) b	8) b	12) e	16) c	20) e

Short Answer Questions

1. The long-run aggregate supply curve is vertical because any change in the price level changes the money wage rate by the same percentage so as to preserve the equilibrium real wage rate. There is only one equilibrium employment level and this determines a unique level of real GDP.

2. The main implication of the labor market clearing theory of wages is that the short-run aggregate supply curve moves only slowly.

   When real GDP is above its long-run aggregate supply level, the short-run aggregate supply curve moves slowly upward.
   On the other hand, when real GDP is below the long-run equilibrium level, the short-run aggregate supply curve moves slowly downward.

3. The demand for labor is determined by the marginal product of labor.

4. The two effects are the income effect and the substitution effect. The substitution effect encourages more work, the higher the real wage rate. The income effect is not so straightforward. At low income levels, an increase in the real wage rate will likely induce an increase in the quantity of labor supplied. But at a high enough income level, a higher real wage rate will likely induce a decrease in the quantity of labor supplied.

5. The labor market clearing theory of wages is that the money wage rates adjusts continuously to keep the real wage rate at the level that makes the quantity of labor demanded equal to the quantity of labor supplied.

   The gradual adjustment theory of wages is that the money wage rate responds to excess demand and supply of labor, gradually adjusting toward its market clearing level.

6. Technological progress shifts the short-run production function upwards and increases the marginal product of labor. The demand for labor is determined by the marginal product of labor. As the marginal product of labor increases, the demand for labor increases. As a result, the demand for labor curve shifts to the right.

7. The official unemployment rate understates the actual unemployment rate because it does not include discouraged workers. If discouraged workers were included the number of unemployed people would be larger and so too would the labor force. The unemployment rate would also be larger.

8. A countercyclical variable is one that moves in the opposite direction to real GDP. For example, unemployment is a countercyclical variable. When real GDP increases, employment increases and unemployment decreases.

9. The demand for labor curve slopes downward because the demand for labor is determined by the marginal product of labor. As more labor is hired marginal product decreases, therefore the firm would be willing to hire more labor only at a lower real wage rate.

10. A decrease in aggregate demand lowers the price level. With wage rates sticky, the real wage rate increases, and employment decreases.

Problems

1. Biggest in Magic Empire, smallest in Frontierland

2. (a) 200
   (b) 20
   (c) 8,000

3. (a) 325, $30
   (b) 400
   (c) 13,975
   (d) 16,000

4. 1.048

5. 1.048

6. (a) $W/P = 14, n = 29$
   (b) W/P falls to 14, n increases to 31, and y increases to 1,271

CHAPTER 9

Unemployment

Perspective and Focus

In Chapter 8, you studied the labor market and the determination of the real wage rate and the level of *employment*. Implicitly, there is a level of *unemployment* lying behind the labor market but in Chapter 8, we did not bring the level of unemployment to the forefront.

Chapter 9 focusses on one of the central macroeconomic issues of the day, high and persistent unemployment. This chapter expands the theory of demand and supply in the labor market and the key feature of the chapter that you need to pay attention to is the distinction between the supply of labor and the labor force.

Learning Objectives

After studying this chapter, you will be able to:

- Describe the patterns of unemployment in Canada and Europe during the 1980s
- Describe Okun's Law
- Explain exactly what unemployment is and how it is measured
- Describe how employment, unemployment, and average work hours fluctuate over the business cycle
- Explain why average work hours fluctuate much less than employment and unemployment
- Explain the meaning of the natural rate of employment and the reasons it fluctuates
- Describe the variations in the natural rate of unemployment during the 1970s and 1980s
- Explain why unemployment fluctuates and sometimes rises above its natural rate
- Explain the unemployment during the recession of the early 1980s

Increasing Your Productivity

One of the key diagrams in this chapter to focus on is Figure 9.7(a). Be sure that you understand how that diagram works. Once you have got it you are ready to race through the analysis in the rest of the chapter. But until you understand how Figure 9.7(a) works you will be wasting your time to move forward. Be sure that you know what the distances *DB* and *AC* mean.

You learnt in Chapter 8 that economists disagree about how the labor market works. But bear in mind when studying this chapter is that although economists do not agree on how quickly wages adjust to achieve equilibrium, they do agree about the facts. Nobody denies that there is, on occasion, a high and persistently high unemployment rate. Economists disagree about how to interpret that phenomenon. Those who emphasize wage stickiness believe that to some degree the phenomenon results from the fact that wages are indeed sticky and that they do not always clear the labor market. Economists who emphasize wage flexibility believe that such a phenomenon rises from other real underlying forces that change the natural rate of unemployment.

Although there is a lot going on in Figures 9.11(a) and 9.11(b), these two figures are two alternative ways of looking at the same phenomenon. They reinforce the point that we have just made about what economists agree and disagree on. Economists agree that the amount of unemployment in 1982 is the amount indicated by the double headed arrow labeled "82" in both parts of the figure. What economists disagree about is exactly how much of that unemployment was "natural" and how much resulted from wages being at a non-market clearing level.

In reviewing this material and understanding it, try to think critically about the two alternative theories and ask yourself the question: what would we have to observe in a real world labor market to reject one or other of these two theories? Nobody has yet found a satisfactory (truly satisfactory) answer to this question but that might not prevent you from putting your mind to it. Students have often found answers to problems that professors have been struggling with for years. In fact, almost all major scientific advance is made by young people whose minds are less rigid than those who have been steeped in the subject for some years.

Self Test

Concept Review

1. People who are willing to work but have quit looking for work because they have given up job search are called _____.

2. The percentage of the labor force that is _____ and _____ _____ is called the natural rate of unemployment.

3. The _____ comprises the people who are employed and unemployed.

4. A person who is looking for work and is available for work but has no job is counted as being _____.

5. The number of people who are in the wrong location or who have the wrong skills is _____ _____.

6. Unemployment in excess of the natural rate of unemployment is called _____ unemployment.

7. The ratio of unemployment benefits to the wage rate is the _____.

8. The unemployment rate is the percentage of _____ that is unemployed.

9. The labor force is equal to the number of people _____ and _____.

10. _____ workers are not counted as part of the labor force.

True or False

1. During the 1980s, unemployment was not considered to be a serious problem in the United States.

2. Unemployment in the United States and Canada fluctuates in a similar manner. Nevertheless, Canadian unemployment became significantly higher than U.S. unemployment during the 1980s.

3. The unemployment rate in Japan barely fluctuated in the 1980s. It began the decade at 2 percent, rose to a gentle peak of 2.8 percent in 1987, and then fell to end the decade at 2.2 percent.

4. The unemployment rate is the number of people unemployed expressed as a percentage of the labor force, where the labor force is the number of people employed plus the number of people unemployed.

5. Discouraged workers are people who do not have jobs, are willing to work, and are available for work but have stopped searching for work because of their discouraging experience.

6. Frictional unemployment is the number of people who are in the wrong location and have the wrong skills for the available jobs.

7. The cyclical unemployment rate is the actual unemployment rate minus its natural rate.

8. The scale of unemployment benefits multiplied by the wage rate a worker can earn is known as the replacement ratio.

9. The minimum wage, first introduced in the United States in the Fair Labor Standards Act of 1938, influences the rate at which unemployed workers can find jobs by increasing the total number of jobs available.

10. The natural rate of unemployment is such that the unemployment rate is variable.

11. Labor market equilibrium is determined where the actual rate of unemployment is equal to the natural rate of unemployment.

12. The actual unemployment rate minus its natural rate is the frictional unemployment rate.

13. The actual unemployment rate minus its natural rate is the structural unemployment rate.

14. Actual unemployment minus the frictional and structural unemployment is cyclical unemployment rate.

15. The official unemployment rate is obtained from information provided by the government about the number of people receiving unemployment insurance benefits.

16. Over the business cycle, the unemployment rate fluctuates, mainly because the average work week remains constant and the number of people employed fluctuates.

17. Households prefer stable work hours because it enables them to use their time efficiently and reduces uncertainty about future income.

18. On Shell Island, the rate of job loss is 2 percent and the rate of finding a job is also 2 percent. Therefore, Shell Island's natural rate of unemployment is 2 percent.

19. On Turtle Island more people are employed than are unemployed, and the rate at which jobs are being lost is less than the rate at which job are being found. Turtle Island's natural rate of unemployment is decreasing.

20. An increase in unemployment benefits decreases the value placed on job search by each person in the labor force because the opportunity cost of searching for a job has decreased.

Multiple Choice

1. The types of unemployment include:
   (a) frictional unemployment.
   (b) structural unemployment.
   (c) cyclical unemployment.
   (d) discouraged unemployment.
   (e) (a), (b), and (c).

2. The number of people counted as unemployed increases as a result of
   (a) new entrants.
   (b) job losers.
   (c) job finders.
   (d) discouraged workers.
   (e) both (a) and (b).

3. Which of the following equations represents the change in unemployment (ΔU)?
   (a) $U = lE + fU.$
   (b) $U = lE/fU.$
   (c) $U = lE \times fU.$
   (d) $U = lE - fU.$
   (e) $U = fU - lE.$

4. The unemployment rate is represented by which of the following equations?
   (a) $U/L = 1 + f/L.$
   (b) $L/U = 1 + f/L.$
   (c) $U/L = 1/1 + f.$
   (d) $U/L = l \times (1 + f).$
   (e) $U/L = 1/(1 - f).$

5. Which of the following factors influence the outcome of job search and determine the rate at which unemployed workers find jobs? The
   (a) scale of unemployment benefits.
   (b) minimum wage.
   (c) degree of structural mismatch between the skills of the unemployed and of the jobs available.
   (d) Social security benefits.
   (e) (a), (b), and (c).

6. Between 1970 and 1981, the Canadian economy contracted severely because of
   (a) an adverse supply shock (a hugh increase in the oil price).
   (b) restrictive monetary policy.
   (c) expansionary monetary policy.
   (d) favorable supply shock (a decline in the oil price).
   (e) both (a) and (b).

7. Lucy Samson of Laval University perceives that most of the fluctuations in the
   (a) actual unemployment rate are fluctuations in the structural unemployment rate.
   (b) actual unemployment rate are fluctuations in the cyclical unemployment rate.
   (c) natural unemployment rate are fluctuations in the cyclical unemployment rate.
   (d) natural unemployment rate are fluctuations in the structural unemployment rate.
   (e) actual unemployment rate are fluctuations in the natural unemployment rate.

8. The job-finding rate depends on the following factors *except*
   (a) the unemployment rate.
   (b) the degree of mismatch.
   (c) unemployment benefits.
   (d) minimum wage rate.
   (e) both (b) and (c).

9. Type of unemployment that exists at a full-employment equilibrium is
   (a) frictional.
   (b) cyclical.
   (c) structural.
   (d) both (a) and (c).
   (e) all of the above.

10. Which of the following publishes standardized unemployment rates for the major countries? The
    (a) International Bank for Reconstruction and Development.
    (b) International Monetary Fund.
    (c) Organization for Economic Cooperation and Development.
    (d) Bank of Canada.
    (e) Statistics Canada.

11. When a discouraged worker starts to look for work again and becomes unemployed
    (a) the official unemployment rate increases.
    (b) the official unemployment rate decreases.
    (c) the official unemployment rate does not change.
    (d) the official unemployment rate gives an exact measure of the unemployment rate.
    (e) not enough information to know.

12. A decrease in aggregate supply when money wage rates are sticky
    (a) increases employment and decreases unemployment.
    (b) decrease employment and increases unemployment.
    (c) increase both employment and unemployment.
    (d) decrease both employment and unemployment.
    (e) has no effect on employment and unemployment.

13. A decrease in the demand for labor when money wage rates are flexible result in
    (a) a decrease in employment and unemployment.
    (b) an increase in the real wage rate and employment and a decrease in unemployment.
    (c) an increase in the real wage rate and a decrease in employment.
    (d) no change in real wage rates.
    (e) no change in employment and unemployment.

14. The value placed on job search
    (a) by the marginal person in the labor force is constant as the labor force grows.
    (b) by the marginal person employed is more than the value placed on job search by the marginal person in the labor force.
    (c) by the marginal person employed increases as the labor force grows.
    (d) by the marginal person in the labor force decreases as the labor force grows.
    (e) none of the above.

15. Unemployment decreases if
    (a) the flow of new entrants and job losers is less than the flow of retirees and job finders.
    (b) more people become discouraged about the prospect of finding a job.
    (c) the rate of job loss decreases and the rate at which jobs are found increases.
    (d) the rate of job loss and the rate at which jobs are found decrease but the rate at which jobs are found decreases by less.
    (e) both (b) and (c).

16. All the following people are in the labor force *except*
    (a) A person who is not looking for a job, but has a new job starting in one week from now.
    (b) A person who is not looking for a job, but already has a job.
    (c) A person who does not have a job, but has been looking for a job for the past six months.
    (d) A person who has a job.
    (e) A person who wants a job but has given up looking because the wage is too low.

17. The natural rate of unemployment is equal to the rate at which people
    (a) lose jobs plus the rate at which people find jobs.
    (b) find jobs minus the rate at which people lose jobs.
    (c) find and lose jobs divided by the rate at which people find jobs.
    (d) lose jobs divided by the rate at which people lose and find jobs.
    (e) none of the above.

18. The horizontal distance between the labor force curve and the labor supply curve measures
    (a) unemployment of discouraged workers.
    (b) cyclical unemployment.
    (c) natural unemployment.
    (d) structural unemployment.
    (e) actual unemployment.

19. The vertical distance between the labor force curve and the labor supply curve measures
    (a) real wage rate.
    (b) the value placed on job search.
    (c) unemployment benefits.
    (d) cost of job search plus unemployment benefits.
    (e) actual unemployment.

20. The labor force curve describes how the
    (a) number of persons willing to work remains constant as the real wage rate varies.
    (b) number of persons willing varies as the real wage rate varies.
    (c) number of people willing to search for a job varies as the real wage rate varies.
    (d) the number of people willing to search for a job varies as the real wage rate remains constant.
    (e) none of the above.

Short Answers Questions

1. In general, why are stable hours preferred by
   (a) households?
   (b) firms?

2. Explain Okun's Law.

3. Explain the difference between frictional and structural unemployment.

4. Why does unemployment fluctuate and sometimes rise above its natural rate?

5. What factors influence the rate of job loss?

6. What is meant by "startup costs?"

7. What is the replacement ratio?

8. How does Statistics Canada define people as being unemployed?

9. (a) How is the job finding rate determined?
   (b) What is the cost of job search?
   (c) What is the benefit of job search?
   (d) What are the three factors that influence the outcome of job search and determine the rate at which unemployed workers find jobs?

10. What is the disagreement about how fluctuations in the actual unemployment rate decompose into fluctuations in the natural rate of unemployment and fluctuations in cyclical unemployment?

11. Explain the
    (a) natural rate of unemployment.
    (b) cyclical unemployment rate.

12. How does the business cycle influence the rate of job loss?

13. (a) How is unemployment measured in Canada?
    (b) What persons are not included in measured unemployment?

Problem Solving

How does it go?

You have the following information about Turtle Island:

Demand for labor: $n^d = 90 - 1.5(W/P)$
Supply of labor: $n^s = 0.75(W/P)$
Supply of job search: $j^s = 0.25(W/P)$.

(a) Calculate the equilibrium real wage rate.

   The equilibrium real wage rate is the (W/P) determined by the intersection of the demand for labor and supply of labor curves.

$$n^d = 90 - 1.5(W/P) \qquad (9.1)$$
$$n^s = 0.75(W/P) \qquad (9.2)$$

Solving Equations (9.1) and (9.2) gives

$$(W/P) = 40.$$

(b) Calculate the equilibrium level of employment.

   The number of people employed at the equilibrium real wage rate of 40 can be found by substituting 40 for (W/P) in either Equation (9.1) or (9.2). The equilibrium level of employment is 30.

(c) Calculate the equilibrium labor force.

   The number of people in the labor force is equal to the number employed plus the number who are job searching. That is, at any real wage rate the labor force is equal to the quantity of labor supplied (willing to take a job without further search) plus the quantity of job searchers.

   The equation to the labor force curve is

$$lf = n^s + j^s$$
$$lf = 0.75(W/P) + 0.25(W/P)$$
$$lf = (W/P).$$

   At the equilibrium real wage rate of 40, the labor force is 40.

(d) Calculate the equilibrium level of unemployment.

The equilibrium level of unemployment is the labor force minus the level of employment, which is equal to the level of job search. Therefore

$$\text{unemployment} = 0.25(W/P)$$
$$= 10.$$

(e) Calculate the value placed on job search by the last person employed.

The last person employed is the 30th person. This person is willing to join the labor force and search for a job at a real wage rate given by the labor force curve. It is the real wage rate that makes the labor force equal to 30. That is,

$$lf = (W/P)$$
$$30 = (W/P).$$

This person is willing to take a job at a real wage rate of 40. Therefore the value placed on job search by the last person employed is equal to 40 – 30, which is 10.

(f) Calculate the value placed on job search by the last person to join the labor force.

The last person in the labor force is the 40th person. This person is willing to join the labor force and search for a job at a real wage rate of 40.

This person is willing to take a job at a real wage rate equal to that which makes the quantity of labor supplied equal to 40. That is,

$$n^s = 0.75(W/P)$$
$$40 = 0.75(W/P)$$
$$(W/P) = 53.33.$$

This person is willing to take a job at a real wage rate of 53.33. Therefore the value placed on job search by the last person employed is equal to 53.33 – 40, which is 13.33.

Now try these

1. You are given the following information concerning the demand for labor, supply of labor, and supply of job search:

$$n^d = 10 - 0.5(W/P)$$
$$n^s = 0.5(W/P)$$
$$j^s = 0.1(W/P).$$

At the equilibrium, calculate
(a) the real wage rate.
(b) employment.
(c) labor force.
(d) unemployment.
(e) the value placed on job search by the last person employed.
(f) the value placed on job search by the last person to join the labor force.

2. In Problem 1, the government introduces a minimum wage and the real wage rate increases to 12.

Calculate
(a) the labor force.
(b) the quantity of labor supplied.
(c) the level of employment.

3. An economy has 100 competitive firms and each firm has the following short-run production function:78

n	1	2	3	4	5	6	7
y	50	95	135	170	200	225	245

The aggregate supply of labor is

(W/P)	8	10	12	15	18	20	25
n	200	300	400	500	600	700	800

At the equilibrium, calculate
(a) the real wage.
(b) employment.
(c) real GDP.

✓ Answers

Concept Review

1) discouraged workers
2) frictional, structural, unemployment
3) labor force
4) structural unemployment
5) cyclical
6) replacement ratio
8) labor force
9) employed, unemployed
10) discouraged

True or False

1) F	5) T	9) F	13) F	17) T
2) T	6) F	10) F	14) T	18) T
3) T	7) T	11) F	15) F	19) F
4) T	8) F	12) F	16) T	20) F

Multiple Choice

1) e	5) e	9) d	13) c	17) d
2) e	6) e	10) c	14) e	18) c
3) d	7) e	11) a	15) e	19) b
4) c	8) a	12) b	16) e	20) e

Short Answer Questions

1. (a) Stable hours are preferred by households because it enables them to use time efficiently, reduce income uncertainty, and minimize startup cost.

    (b) With stable hours, firms are able to obtain optimal work effort, and team production is more efficiently organized.

2. Okun's Law states that the higher the level of real GDP as a percentage of capacity real GDP, the lower is the unemployment rate.

3. Frictional unemployment is the number of people who are searching for a job. These people are new entrants into the labor force and those who have reentered the labor force or voluntarily quit their jobs to search for a better one.

    Structural unemployment is the number of persons who are in the wrong location and have the wrong skills for the available jobs.

4. Unemployment can fluctuate either because of a change in the natural unemployment rate or because of a change in cyclical unemployment. An increase in the rate of job loss or a decrease in the rate of job finding shifts the labor supply curve to the left thereby increasing the natural unemployment rate.

    Furthermore, a decrease in aggregate demand that decreases the price level increases the real wage. If money wages adjust only gradually, the real wage exceeds the market-clearing real wage. The quantity of labor demanded is less than the quantity of labor supplied and unemployment increases above the natural rate.

5. The rate of job loss is influenced by technological change, changes in international competitiveness, regional effects, and the phase of the business cycle.

6. Startup costs are the costs associated with beginning an activity. The startup costs of work include the costs of both time and transportation to and from work. These costs have to be borne whether a person works for one hour or ten hours a day.

7. The scale of unemployment benefit divided by the wage rate a worker can earn is called the replacement ratio.

8. Statistics Canada defines unemployed people as those who did not work during the survey week, made specific efforts to find a job within the four previous weeks and were available for work during the survey week.

   Also counted as unemployed are the people who did not work at all during the survey week, were available for work and were waiting either to be called back to a job from which they had been laid off or to report to a new job within 4 weeks.

9. (a) The job-finding rate is determined by the decision made by each unemployed worker's deciding to stop looking for a better job and accept the best job currently available.

   Unemployment and job search can be viewed as an investment an unemployed person makes. This investment has a cost and an expected return.

   (b) The cost of job search is the loss of wages while unemployed minus any unemployment benefit received.

   (c) The benefit from job search is the expected higher wage that might be obtained from looking longer and larger for a better job than what is currently available.

   (d) The three main factors that influence the outcome of job search and determine the rate at which unemployed workers find jobs are the scale of unemployment benefits, the minimum wage, and the degree of structural mismatch between the unemployed and jobs available.

10. Some economists believe that the natural rate of unemployment is almost constant so that all the fluctuations in unemployment are fluctuations in cyclical unemployment.

    Other economists believe that the natural rate of unemployment itself has a large cyclical component.

11. (a) The natural rate of unemployment is the percentage of the labor force that is frictionally and structurally unemployed.

    (b) The cyclical unemployment rate is the actual unemployment rate minus the natural rate.

12. As the economy moves from recession through recovery to boom, the demand for labor of all types increases and as the economy moves from boom to recession, the demand for labor across all types of jobs and skills decreases.

13. (a) In Canada, unemployment is measured by the Labour Force Survey, which surveys 56,000 households each month.

    (b) Discouraged workers are not included in measured unemployment.

Problems

1. (a) 10
   (b) 5
   (c) 6
   (d) 1
   (e) 1.67
   (f) 2

2. (a) 7.2
   (b) 6
   (c) 4

3. (a) 20
   (b) 700
   (c) 24,500

CHAPTER 10

Capital, Technology, and Economic Growth

Perspective and Focus

Chapters 8 and 9 focus on the short run. Actually, in macroeconomics the terms *short run* and *long run* have ambiguous meanings. In microeconomics, the term *short run* always means a period in which some factors of production are fixed in quantity. In the case that we have studied so far, the stock of capital is fixed and so is the state of technology. The only factor of production whose quantity varies is the labor employed. This is the *microeconomic* short-run. But macroeconomics makes another kind of distinction between short-run long-run which is really part of the microeconomic short-run. The *macroeconomic short-run* is a period in which not only are the capital stock and technology fixed but so are factor prices. The *macroeconomic long-run* is a *microeconomic* short-run in which wages and other factor prices are flexible so that full employment prevails.

Until this chapter, we have studied the *macroeconomic* short-run and long-run and the *microeconomic* short-run. It is now time to study the *microeconomic* long-run—the period in which the quantities of all factors of production can be varied. This chapter explains how economies grow. It shows how investment and saving lead to the accumulation of capital and how technological change along with capital accumulation produce ongoing increases in output per person.

Learning Objectives

After studying this chapter, you will be able to:

- Describe the main features of expansion of Canadian output since 1869.
- Describe the sources of economic growth.
- Explain the neoclassical model of economic growth.
- Explain how the saving rate influences the rate of economic growth.
- Explain how technological change influences economic growth.
- Describe the importance of the contribution of technological change to Canadian economic growth.
- Describe the Canadian productivity slowdown of the 1970s and explain its origins.

Increasing Your Productivity

The key to understanding the theory of neoclassical economic growth is to understand Figures 10.4, 10.5, and 10.6. Focus you attention on these figures and be sure you understand exactly what is going on in them. Once you have got it you will be able to do the rest of the chapter with ease. The key to Figure 10.4 is that it explains a steady-state relationship. It does not describe someone's behavior. Figure 10.4 tells you the rate at which the economy must save *and invest* if the level of capital per person is to remain constant. The text and algebra on pages 288 and 289 explain how the steady-state investment line is derived.

Figure 10.5 explains behavior. It tells us the amount of saving *and investment* that will take place at each level of capital per person.

Figure 10.6 brings Figure 10.4 and Figure 10.5 together. It tells us that if capital per person is below its steady-state level ($60,000 in Figure 10.6), actual saving and investment exceeds that required to keep the capital per person constant. Capital per person increases. If capital per person exceeds its steady-state level, then the amount of saving and investment falls short of that required to keep the capital per person constant. In this case, capital per person decreases. In either case, whether the capital per person is initially below or above its steady-state level, the process of adjustment forces the economy's capital per person back to its steady-state level.

With your understand of Figures 10.4, 10.5, and 10.6 and the analysis that surrounds them you are ready to study the effects of changes in the population growth rate, the saving rate, and the rate of technological change. These are the key exogenous influences on steady-state output per person and the rate of economic growth.

Self Test

Concept Review

1. As more capital is employed by a given quantity of labor, the marginal product of capital _____.

2. As more of one factor of production is employed, given a fixed quantity of other factors, the economy experiences _____.

3. When the value of the relevant variables are constant over time, the economy is in a _____.

4. The _____ shows the relationship between real GDP per person and capital per person.

5. The _____ is the situation when consumption per person in the economy is maximized.

6. The _____ product of capital is the _____ in _____ resulting from _____.

7. An externality is a _____ or _____ experienced by one person that _____ the _____.

8. The neoclassical growth model determines _____, _____, _____, and the _____.

9. The Solow _____ is an estimate of the contribution of technological change to the change in _____.

10. Increasing returns arise when an increase in a factor of production, holding the quantities of all other factors constant, increases the _____.

True or False

1. The increase of real GDP per person resulting from a one-unit increase in capital per person is known as the marginal technical change of capital.

2. When capital per person is constant, the economy is said to be in a variable state—a situation in which the relevant variables are constant over time.

3. The situation in which consumption per person is maximized in the steady state is called the golden rule.

4. When technological change occurs, the per capita production function shifts downward.

5. Diminishing returns are the increases in the marginal product of a factor of production as more of the factor is employed, other inputs held constant.

6. The Solow residual underestimates the contribution of technological change to economic growth because it does not recognize the fact that the pace of capital accumulation is faster with technological change than without it.

7. In the 1980s, the slowest growth rates occurred in the farming and construction sectors, while the fastest growth occurred in the computer and electronics industries.

8. The neoclassical growth model determines real GDP per person, consumption and saving per person, capital per person, and the economic growth rate.

9. Canada and other major industrial countries spend close to 10 percent of GDP on research and development every year.

10. The presence of externalities and increasing returns to knowledge make it impossible for a large and wealthy economy to grow indefinitely at a faster pace than a small and poor economy.

11. Capital per person increases if investment per person exceeds the population growth rate.

12. A technological advance moves the economy down along its per capita production function.

13. Economywide knowledge is an externality—one firm invests resources in advancing its own knowledge, it is at the same time expanding the production possibilities of all the other firms in the economy.

14. Romer's model of the economy does not include the economywide technological knowledge in the economy.

15. The slope of the steady-state investment line is equal to saving per person.

16. The Solow residual tends to overestimate the importance of technological change because it combines many separate influences that are hard to measure, such as the accumulation of human capital and the composition of the labor force.

17. The steady-state rate of growth of output increases if the population growth rate increases.

18. The government can increase the steady-state growth rate by persuading everyone to save more.

19. An increase in the growth rate of population rotates the steady-state investment line upward.

20. In the steady-state, the capital-labor ratio is increases at a constant rate.

Multiple Choice

1. Which of the following determines real GDP per person, consumption and saving per person, capital per person, and the economic growth rate? The
   (a) Keynesian growth model.
   (b) Malthus growth model.
   (c) monetarist growth model.
   (d) neoclassical growth model.
   (e) Denison growth model.

2. Romer's model of the economy has a large number of competitive firms. Each firm is small relative to the size of the economy and uses four factors of production to produce its output. These factors include
   (a) labor.
   (b) capital.
   (c) its own technological knowledge.
   (d) economywide (aggregate) technological knowledge.
   (e) all of the above.

3. The Solow residual attempts to isolate the effects of technological change, but it is difficult to separately identify it from which of the other following influences?
   (a) Technological advantage.
   (b) The accumulation of human capital.
   (c) Variations in the capacity utilization rate.
   (d) Changes in the composition of output.
   (e) All of the above.

4. Which of the following accounted for the Canadian productivity slowdown of the 1970s?
   (a) Energy price shocks.
   (b) Composition of output.
   (c) Inflation.
   (d) Composition of the work force.
   (e) All of the above.

5. Capital accumulation alone cannot bring sustained growth in real GDP per person because the marginal product of capital
   (a) increases.
   (b) remains constant.
   (c) diminishes.
   (d) is normally negative.
   (e) none of the above.

6. An estimate of the contribution of technological change to a change in output is known as the
   (a) Denison surplus.
   (b) Ricardian equivalent.
   (c) Solow surplus.
   (d) Solow residual.
   (e) Fisher equality.

7. Which of the following occurs when the marginal product of a factor of production increases as the quantity of the factor employed increases, other inputs held constant?
   (a) Diminishing returns.
   (b) Variable returns.
   (c) Increasing returns.
   (d) Constant returns.
   (e) Negative returns.

8. A situation in which capital per person and real GDP per person are constant is known as the
   (a) golden state.
   (b) normal state.
   (c) neoclassical state.
   (d) steady state.
   (e) Solow state.

9. Which of the following equations tells us that the capital stock per person will be constant if investment per person equals the growth rate of the population multiplied by capital per person?
   (a) $k/n = k/n/(n/k)$.
   (b) $k/n = k/k/(k/n)$.
   (c) $k/n = n/n/(k/n)$.
   (d) $k/n = n/n$.
   (e) $n/k = k/n$.

10. According to the neoclassical model, consumption per person is maximized when the
    (a) marginal product of labor equals the population growth rate.
    (b) marginal product of capital equals the population growth rate.
    (c) so-called normal rule is achieved.
    (d) so-called Solow rule is achieved.
    (e) so-called golden state is achieved.

11. Capital per person increases if investment per person
    (a) is less than the population growth rate.
    (b) exceeds the population growth rate.
    (c) exceeds saving per person.
    (d) is less than saving per person.
    (e) is more than consumption per person.

12. A technological advance
    (a) moves the economy up along its steady-state investment line.
    (b) shifts the per capita consumption function upward.
    (c) shifts the per capita saving function downward.
    (d) shifts the per capita production function downward.
    (e) moves the economy down along its per capita production function.

13. The slower is technological change,
    (a) the larger is the economywide stock of knowledge because it gives time for the knowledge of one firm to be transferred to all firms.
    (b) the larger is the firm-specific stock of knowledge.
    (c) the larger is the economy's capital stock.
    (d) both (a) and (b).
    (c) none the above.

14. The per capita production function shifts up over time as a result of
    (a) saving.
    (b) labor productivity increasing as the population grows.
    (c) the labor employed increasing.
    (d) technological advances.
    (e) capital per person employed increasing.

15. The steady-state rate of growth of output increases if
    (a) investment per person increases.
    (b) saving per person increases.
    (c) the population growth rate increases.
    (d) both (b) and (c).
    (e) all of the above.

16. At the golden rule:
    (a) investment per person equals saving per person.
    (b) consumption per person equals output per person.
    (c) investment per person equals the population growth rate.
    (d) the marginal product of capital equals the population growth rate.
    (e) both (a) and (d).

Fact 10.1 On Heron Island, the per capita production function is:

$$y/n = (k/n) - 0.15(k/n)^2.$$

The population growth rate is 0.03.
The marginal propensity to save is 0.2.

17. Use Fact 10.1. The steady-state growth rate is
    (a) between 11 and 15 percent a year.
    (b) between 8 and 10 percent a year.
    (c) between 2 and 7 percent a year.
    (d) less than 2 percent a year.
    (e) none of the above.

18. Use Fact 10.1. The steady-state saving per person is
    (a) greater than 0 and less than or equal to 0.02.
    (b) greater than 0.02 and less than or equal 0.03.
    (c) greater than 0.03 and less than or equal to 0.05.
    (d) greater than 0.05 and less than or equal to 1.
    (e) greater than 1.

19. Use Fact 10.1. The steady-state investment per person is
    (a) greater than 0 and less than or equal to 0.01.
    (b) greater than 0.01 and less than or equal 0.03.
    (c) greater than 0.03 and less than or equal to 0.08.
    (d) greater than 0.08 and less than or equal to 1.
    (e) greater than 1.

20. Use Fact 10.1. The golden rule capital per person is
    (a) greater than 0 and less than or equal to 0.5.
    (b) greater than 0.5 and less than or equal 0.9.
    (c) greater than 0.9 and less than or equal to 1.5
    (d) greater than 1.5 and less than or equal to 2.
    (e) greater than 2.

21. Use Fact 10.1. The golden rule consumption per person is
    (a) greater than 0 and less than or equal to 1.
    (b) greater than 1 and less than or equal 1.5.
    (c) greater than 1.5 and less than or equal to 1.7.
    (d) greater than 1.7 and less than or equal to 2.
    (e) greater than 2.

22. Use Fact 10.1. The golden rule saving per person is
    (a) greater than 0 and less than or equal to 0.5.
    (b) greater than 0.5 and less than or equal 0.6.
    (c) greater than 0.6 and less than or equal to 0.9.
    (d) greater than 0.9 and less than or equal to 1.2.
    (e) greater than 1.2.

23. Use Fact 10.1. The golden rule output growth rate
    (a) between 11 and 15 percent a year.
    (b) between 8 and 10 percent a year.
    (c) between 5 and 7 percent a year.
    (d) less than 5 percent a year.
    (e) none of the above.

24. Use Fact 10.1. The golden rule marginal product of capital is
    (a) between 0.11 and 0.15.
    (b) between 0.08 and 0.10.
    (c) between 0.05 and 0.07.
    (d) less than 0.05.
    (e) none of the above.

Short Answers Questions

1. Briefly explain the per capita production function.

2. What is determined by the neoclassical growth model?

3. Productivity growth in Canada slowed in the 1980s by more than 1 percent per year when compared with its level of the 1960s and 1970s. List four of the more important factors that have been identified as contributing to this productivity slowdown.

4. Define the steady state.

5. What is meant by the golden rule?

6. What are the two main sources of economic growth?

7. Which country has the highest saving rate in the world and where does Canada fit in?

8. When does capital per person increase?

9. Technological change increases income per person for two reasons. What are they?

10. Explain why an increase in the saving rate does not increase the steady-state growth rate.

Problem Solving

How does it go?

Wetland has the following per capita production function

$$(y/n) = (k/n) - 0.2(k/n)^2.$$

Wetland's marginal propensity to save is 0.2 and its population growth rate is 0.03.

(a) Calculate Wetland's steady-state investment line.

The steady-state investment line shows the relationship between capital per person (k/n) and investment per person $(\Delta k/n)$, such that the stock of capital per person is constant.

The population is growing at 3 percent a year, so the equation to the steady-state investment line is

$$(\Delta k/n) = 0.03(k/n).$$

(b) Calculate Wetland's per capita saving function.

Since the marginal propensity to save is 0.2, the per capita saving function is

$$\begin{aligned}
(s/n) &= 0.2(y/n) \\
&= 0.2[(k/n) - 0.2(k/n)^2] \\
&= 0.2(k/n) - 0.04(k/n)^2
\end{aligned}$$

(c) Calculate Wetland's steady-state capital per person.

The steady-state capital per person is the capital stock per person that generates the amount of saving and in turn investment to maintain the capital stock per person constant. The saving line tells us saving per person and the steady-state investment line tells us the relationship between investment per person and the capital stock per person. These two lines together determine the steady-state capital per person.

$$(\Delta k/n) = 0.03(k/n). \tag{10.2}$$

Since saving equals investment,

$$(s/n) = (\Delta k/n). \tag{10.3}$$

Substituting Equations (10.1) and (10.2) into Equation (10.3) and solving for (k/n) gives steady-state capital per person:

$$(k/n) = 4.25.$$

(d) Calculate Wetland's real GDP per person.

Steady-state real GDP per person is found by substituting for the capital per person in the per capita production function. Steady-state capital per person is 4.25. Therefore real GDP per person is

$$(y/n) = (k/n) - 0.02(k/n)^2 \quad (10.1)$$
$$= 4.25 - 0.02(4.25)^2$$
$$= 3.89.$$

(d) Calculate Wetland's consumption per person.

The marginal propensity to consume is 0.8, so steady-state consumption per person is 0.8(y/n), which is 3.11.

Now try these

1. The per capita production function of an economy is shown as

$$(y/n) = (k/n) - 0.25(k/n)^2.$$

The marginal propensity to consume is 0.9 and the population growth rate is 4 percent per year.

(a) What is the steady-state investment line?
(b) What is the per capita saving function?
(c) What is the steady-state per capita capital?
(d) What is the steady-state per capita output?
(e) What is the steady-state per consumption?

2. In problem 1, the population growth decreases to 2 percent per year.

(a) What is the steady-state investment line?

(b) What is the per capita saving function?
(c) What is the steady-state per capita capital?
(d) What is the steady-state per capita output?
(e) What is the steady-state per consumption?

3. An economy is in a steady state. Its population growth rate is 5 percent and the capital stock per person is $50,000. Calculate investment per person.

4. Sunny Isle's per capita production function is

$$(y/n) = (k/n) - 0.1(k/n)^2.$$

Sunny Isle's marginal propensity to consume is 0.75 and its population growth rate is 8 percent a year.

(a) Calculate Sunny Isle's steady-state capital per person.
(a) Calculate Sunny Isle's steady-state output per person.
(b) Calculate Sunny Isle's steady-state consumption per person.
(c) Calculate Sunny Isle's steady-state saving per person.

5. An economy's per capita production function is

$$(y/n) = (k/n) - 0.7(k/n)^2.$$

Its marginal propensity to consume is 0.6 and its population growth rate is 10 percent a year.

(a) Calculate the slope of the steady-state investment line.
(b) Calculate the steady-state output per person.
(c) Calculate the steady-state saving per person.
(d) Calculate the golden rule level of consumption per person.

(e) Calculate the golden rule invest-
     ment per person.
(f) Technological change increases
     output per person by 10 percent.
     What is the new steady-state
     capital per person?

✓ Answers

Concept Review

1) decreases
2) diminishing returns
3) steady state
4) per capita production function
5) golden rule
6) marginal, real GDP per person, one
    unit increase in capital per person
7) cost, benefit, results from, action of
    another person
8) real GDP per person, consumption
    per person, saving per person,
    economic growth
9) residual, real GDP
10) marginal product of the factor

True or False

1) F	5) F	9) F	13) T	17) F
2) F	6) T	10) F	14) F	18) F
3) T	7) T	11) T	15) F	19) T
4) F	8) T	12) F	16) T	20) F

Multiple Choice

1) d	5) c	9) c	13) e	17) c	21 b
2) e	6) d	10) b	14) d	18) a	22 a
3) e	7) c	11) d	15) c	19) b	23 e
4) e	8) d	12) b	16) e	20) e	24 d

Short Answer Questions

1. The per capita production function is
    the relationship between output per
    person and capital per person.
    Output per person is equal to income
    per person and these two equivalent
    concepts are measured as real GDP
    per person.

2. The neoclassical growth model
    determines real GDP per person,
    consumption and saving per person,
    capital per person and the economic
    growth rate.

3. Energy price shocks, inflation, work
    force composition and composition of
    output.

4. The steady state is defined as a
    situation in which capital per person
    and real GDP per person are
    constant.

5. The golden rule is the situation in
    which consumption per person is
    maximized in the steady state.

6. The two main sources of economic
    growth are capital accumulation and
    technological change.

7. Japan has the highest saving rate at
    35 percent of GDP and Canada fits
    into the intermediate saving rate of
    between 22 and 26 percent of GDP.

8. Capital per person increases if
    investment per person exceeds the
    population growth rate.

9. First, with the new technology we are
    able to produce more output from
    given inputs. Furthermore, with
    more real income, we save more and,
    therefore, accumulate more capital.

10. An increase in the saving rate
    increases steady-state capital per
    person and increases steady-state
    output per person. It does not
    increase the steady-state rate of
    growth as output grows at a rate
    equal to the population growth rate
    and it has not changed.

Problems

1. (a) $(\Delta k/n) = 0.04(k/n)$
   (b) $(s/n) = 0.1(k/n) - 0.025(k/n)^2$
   (c) 2.4
   (d) 0.96
   (e) 0.864

2. (a) $(\Delta k/n) = 0.02(k/n)$
   (b) $(s/n) = 0.1(k/n) - 0.025(k/n)^2$
   (c) 3.2
   (d) 0.64
   (e) 0.576

3. $2,500

4. (a) 6.8
   (b) 2.18
   (c) 1.63
   (d) 0.54

5. (a) 0.1
   (b) 0.27
   (c) 0.11
   (d) 0.21
   (e) 0.14
   (f) 0.10

CHAPTER 11

Inflation, Interest Rates, and Exchange Rates

Perspective and Focus

At this point of your study of macroeconomics you have completed the basic theoretical framework. You now understand the theory of aggregate demand and aggregate supply and much of what lies behind those concepts and relationships. This chapter and the next two begin to apply what you have learnt—to study macroeconomic issues and problems using the tools of macroeconomic theory.

This chapter focuses on inflation at full employment. It studies the determination of the rate of change of the price level, the interest rate, and the exchange rate. It doesn't worry about the simultaneous fluctuation in aggregate activity that may accompany the inflation. You can think of this chapter as explaining the trend in inflation but not the cycles and fluctuations in its rate.

Learning Objectives

After studying this chapter, you will be able to:

- Describe the diversity of inflation, interest rates, and money growth around the world in the 1980s
- Explain the effects of an anticipated increase in the growth rate of the money supply on inflation and real GDP
- Illustrate the effects of anticipated inflation with Israel's experience in the 1980s
- Explain the effects of inflation on interest rates
- Illustrate the effects on inflation on interest rates with Switzerland's and Brazil's experiences in the 1980s
- Explain how inflation is determined in an open economy with a fixed exchange rate
- Illustrate inflation in a fixed exchange rate economy with the experiences of the major companies in the 1960s and the countries of the European Monetary System (EMS) in the 1980s
- Explain how inflation is determined in an open economy with a flexible exchange rate
- Illustrate inflation in a flexible exchange rate economy with the world inflationary experience in the 1980s

Increasing Your Productivity

A key thing to keep at the front of your mind when studying this chapter is the fundamental difference between a fixed exchange rate and a flexible exchange rate economy when it comes to understanding the forces that determine inflation and interest rates.

With a fixed exchange rate, a country has no choice but to accept the inflation and interest rates that the rest of the world throw at it. With a flexible exchange rate, a country has complete freedom to set its own course independently of what is happening in the rest of the world.

With this lesson and basic understanding in mind you will have no difficulty in working through the analysis of this chapter. But there is just one other thing that you need to pay attention you—the chapter studies *inflation*, not the determination of the *price level*.

The *AD-AS* model has the price level on the vertical axis and so the process of inflation can only be captured in such a model with the *AD* curve and *AS* curve constantly shifting and intersecting at higher and higher price levels. It is inconvenient, as well as a waste of ink and paper, to draw the *AD* curve forever shifting upward. Therefore in the figures in the text, we shift them just once. This gives the impression that we are talking about only an increase in the price level. You must always remember that this is just a convenience. The process is ongoing. The curves never stop moving in a real-world situation.

Self Test

Concept Review

1. Aggregate expenditure is equal to the quantity of money multiplied by _____.

2. Unanticipated inflation is equal to _____ minus _____.

3. Anticipated inflation plus anticipated inflation is equal to _____ inflation.

4. A forecast made on the basis of all available information is called a _____.

5. The expected inflation rate is the _____ for some future period.

6. The agreement among the five major industrial countries to coordinate their monetary policies is the _____.

7. The proposition that an increase in the growth rate of the money supply brings an _____ increase in _____ is called the quantity theory of money.

8. The European Monetary _____ is an agreement between members of the European Community to _____.

9. Arbitrage results in profit opportunities being _____.

10. The quantity theory of money is based on _____. The quantity theory of money holds if _____ is constant and real GDP is _____ of _____.

True or False

1. Inflation, the process of rising prices, is measured as the percentage rate of change in the price level.

2. The actual inflation rate plays an important role in determining the rate of wage increase and wage increases influence the expected inflation rate.

3. By definition, the growth rate of the money supply plus the growth rate of the velocity of circulation equal the inflation rate plus the growth rate of real GDP.

4. The Plaza Agreement was an agreement to bring national monetary policies into closer coordination with each other, thereby lowering the degree of exchange rate volatility.

5. With unanticipated inflation, the actual inflation rate is equal to the expected inflation rate.

6. The equilibrium real wage rate is the real wage rate when the unemployment rate equals the natural rate of unemployment.

7. The higher the expected inflation rate, the higher is the equilibrium quantity of real money balances.

8. A country with a fixed exchange rate is able to control its money supply growth rate.

9. The fundamental relationship that influences inflation in a fixed exchange rate economy is purchasing power parity.

10. The United Kingdom is a member of the European Monetary System.

11. An equal percentage increase in the money supply and the price level shifts the *LM* curve to the right.

12. A rational expectation is a forecast made about the future value of an economic variable that is correct.

13. The equation of exchange states that the quantity of money multiplied by the velocity of circulation equals aggregate expenditure.

14. The European Monetary System is system of managed exchange rates.

15. Suppose that a slice of cheesecake can be purchased for £2.50 in

England and for 480 yen in Japan. Purchasing parity to hold if the exchange rate is 192 yen per pound.

16. The inflation rate in an open economy is determined by the domestic money supply growth if the exchange rate is fixed.

17. If the price level on Sandy Island is increasing at 10 percent a year and the price level in the rest of the world is increasing at 8 percent a year, then the value of the Sandy Island dollar against all other currencies is appreciating by 2 percent a year.

18. Christmas Island has a fixed exchange rate. Therefore it cannot choose its money supply growth rate and inflation rate independent of the rest of the world.

19. A country that has a flexible exchange rate can use its stock of foreign reserves to influence the value of the exchange rate.

20. The overshooting proposition holds because an increase in the money supply growth rate shifts the *LM* curve to the right, increases aggregate demand and increases the inflation rate. The inflation rate increases quickly and returns the *LM* curve to its original position.

Multiple Choice

1. Inflation is a process of rising prices and the inflation rate is measured as the percentage change in a price index such as the
   (a) Consumer Price Index.
   (b) GDP deflator.
   (c) Producer Price Index.
   (d) Real Price Index.
   (e) both (a) and (b).

2. The point of intersection of the *IS* and *LM* curves determines the equilibrium
   (a) interest rate and equilibrium level of real GDP at various price levels.
   (b) price level and equilibrium level of real GDP at various interest rates.
   (c) interest rate and equilibrium price level at various equilibrium levels of real GDP.
   (d) interest rate and equilibrium level of real GDP at a given price level.
   (e) interest rate for various levels of real GDP and price levels.

3. The money wage rate is the real wage rate
   (a) multiplied by the price level.
   (b) divided by the price level.
   (c) minus the price level.
   (d) plus the price level.
   (e) factored by the price level.

4. A forecast of the future value of an economic variable made using all the available information is called
   (a) an adaptive expectation.
   (b) a random expectation.
   (c) an irrational expectation.
   (d) a rational expectation.
   (e) a steady-state expectation.

5. A process in which prices increase at a pace that has been incorrectly forecasted to some degree is known as
   (a) anticipated inflation.
   (b) unanticipated inflation.
   (c) hyperinflation.
   (d) autocorrelated inflation.
   (e) erroneous inflation.

6. The equation stating that the quantity of money multiplied by the velocity of circulation equals total expenditure is called the
   (a) Liquidity Equation.
   (b) Speculative Equation.
   (c) Transactions Equation.
   (d) Equation of Exchange.
   (e) Oxford Equation.

7. Planned investment depends not only on the
   (a) interest rate but also on the unanticipated inflation rate.
   (b) unemployment rate but also on the unanticipated inflation rate.
   (c) exchange rate but also on the anticipated inflation rate.
   (d) interest rate but also on the anticipated inflation rate.
   (e) saving rate but also on the unanticipated inflation rate.

8. If the money supply growth rate exceeds the inflation rate, the
   (a) *IS* curve is shifting to the left.
   (b) *IS* curve is shifting to the right.
   (c) *LM* curve is shifting to the left.
   (d) *LM* curve is shifting to the right.
   (e) *LM* curve is not shifting to the right or the left.

9. If goods are cheaper in one country then in another, it will pay people to purchase goods in the country where they are cheap and sell goods in the country where they are more expensive. Such a process known as
   (a) arbitrage.
   (b) circulation.
   (c) trade targeting.
   (d) quota circumvention.
   (e) none of the above.

10. A system of fixed exchange rates between some members of the European Community is known as (the)
    (a) International Monetary System.
    (b) Plaza Monetary System.
    (c) Rational Agreement.
    (d) European Monetary System.
    (e) Benelux Agreement.

11. If the price level increases by the same percentage rate as the increase in the money supply, then the *LM* curve
    (a) shifts to the right.
    (b) shifts to the left.
    (c) becomes vertical.
    (d) becomes horizontal.
    (e) does not shift.

12. Seal Isle's inflation rate is 10 percent a year, while inflation in the rest of the world is 12 percent a year. Seal Isle's currency is
    (a) appreciating by 2 percent a year.
    (b) depreciating by more than 2 percent a year.
    (c) depreciating by 2 percent a year.
    (d) appreciating by more than 2 percent a year.
    (e none of the above.

13. A country with a flexible exchange rate
    (a) cannot choose its money supply and inflation rate independent of the rest of the world.

    (b) cannot choose its inflation rate but it can choose its money supply growth rate independent of the rest of the world.
    (c) keeps the value of the exchange rate constant and so insulates the domestic economy from inflation in the rest of the world.
    (d) can choose its money supply and inflation independent of the rest of the world.
    (e) can choose its inflation rate independent of the rest of the world but not its money supply growth rate.

14. In a country with a fixed exchange rate
    (a) domestic inflation is equal to inflation in the rest of the world.
    (b) the central bank can use its stock of foreign reserves to influence the value of the exchange rate.
    (c) the value of the exchange rate is determined by both domestic and rest-of-world monetary policies.
    (d) the value of the exchange rate is determined by domestic monetary policy but not rest-of-world monetary policy.
    (e) both (a) and (b).

15. Windy Island's inflation rate is 12 percent a year and its long-run real GDP growth rate is 5 percent a year. A change in Windy Island's money supply growth rate to 9 percent a year changes its inflation rate in the long-run to
    (a) less than or equal to 13 percent a year.
    (b) more than 13 percent a year and less than or equal to 14 percent a year.
    (c) more than 14 percent a year and less than 15 percent a year.
    (d) 15 percent a year.
    (e) more 15 percent a year.

16. Cactus Country increases its money supply growth rate by 10 percent and everyone anticipates the increase. As a result,
    (a) its inflation rate gradually increases by 10 percent.
    (b) real wages in Cactus Country increase by 10 percent.
    (c) its *LM* curve does not shift.
    (d) its *IS* curve shifts to the left.
    (e) none of the above.

17. When the money supply growth rate decreases, the inflation rate responds more quickly, the faster
    (a) the real money supply increases.
    (b) expectations change.
    (c) money wages change.
    (d) both (b) and (c).
    (e) none of the above.

18. An anticipated increase in the money supply growth rate from 4 percent a year to 10 percent a year, increases the inflation in the long run by
    (a) 4 percentage points.
    (b) more than 6 percentage points.
    (c) between 1 and 4 percentage points.
    (d) 6 percentage points.
    (e) none of the above.

19. The assumptions that turn the equation of exchange into the quantity theory of money include a constant
    (a) price level.
    (b) velocity of circulation.
    (c) real GDP growth independent of the quantity of money.
    (d) both (b) and (c).
    (e) all the above.

20. The position of the *IS* curve depends on the
    (a) saving rate.
    (b) interest rate.
    (c) exchange rate and on the antici-pated inflation rate.
    (d) unemployment rate and the

unanticipated inflation rate.
    (e) anticipated inflation rate.

Short Answers Questions

1. Briefly explain the European Monetary System.

2. Briefly summarize how inflation is determined
    (a) in a fixed exchange rate regime.
    (b) in a flexible exchange rate regime.

3. What is the difference between anticipated inflation and unanticipated inflation?

4. (a) What is a rational expectation?
    (b) What are two important properties of a rational expectation?

5. What is the difference between the equilibrium real wage rate and the money wage rate?

6. (a) Was inflation in Israel in the 1980s anticipated or unanticipated?
    (b) What happened during the 1980s to real GDP growth in Israel?

7. (a) What is arbitrage?
    (b) How long will arbitrage transpire?

8. From 1945 to the early 1970s, what exchange rate system was adopted by the
    (a) Canada?
    (b) rest of the world?

9. Explain why anticipated inflation affects the *IS* curve.

10. Explain how anticipated inflation affects the *LM* curve.

Problem Solving

How does it go?

You are given the following information about Silly Isle's short-run aggregate supply and aggregate demand curves:

$$y^s = -100 + 100P$$
$$y^d = 300 - 100P.$$

(a) Calculate real GDP.

Real GDP is determined at the intersection of aggregate demand and aggregate supply. That is, solving the equations to the *AD* and *SAS* curves for *y* gives real GDP equal to 100.

(b) The money supply increases by 5 percent and this increase is expected. Calculate the price level.

A 5 percent increase in the money supply shifts the *AD* curve upward by 5 percent. But the increase is expected, so money wages increase by 5 percent, shifting the *SAS* curve upward by 5 percent. The price level increases by 5 percent to 2.1.

(c) Calculate the equation to the new short-run aggregate supply curve.

The short-run aggregate supply curve shifts upward by 5 percent. To calculate the equation to the new *SAS* curve, notice that any level of real GDP will now be supplied only at a price level that is 5 percent higher. Begin by writing the equation to the original *SAS* curve as

$$P = (y^s + 100)/100.$$

The money supply has increased, so the price level at which any value of *y* will now be supplied is 5 percent higher. That is,

$$P = 1.05(y^s + 100)/100.$$

Re-arranging, the equation to the new *SAS* curve is

$$y^s = -100 + 95.24P.$$

2. The money supply growth rate is 6 percent a year and inflation is also 6 percent a year. The money supply growth rate increases to 10 percent a year. The increase is expected. What is the effect of an increase in the money supply growth rate on the *LM* and *IS* curves.

The money supply growth rate is initially 6 percent a year. The inflation rate is also 6 percent a year. The *LM* curve is stationary and the *IS* curve is stationary.

(a) An increase in the growth rate of the money supply to 6 percent a year causes the *LM* curve to start shifting to the right at 2 percent a year. But the increase in the growth rate of the money supply is expected, so the inflation rate increases. If the inflation rate is less than 10 percent a year, the *LM* curve is shifting to the right; and if the inflation rate exceeds 10 percent a year the *LM* curve is shifting to the left. When the inflation rate equals 10 percent a year, the *LM* curve is stationary.

The *IS* curve shifts to the right. Firms expect that the higher prices will increase their profits, so they increase investment. The increase in investment shifts the *IS* curve to the right. If inflation is expected to remain at 10 percent a year, the size of the shift of the *IS* curve, measured in the vertical direction, is 4 percentage points.

(b) What is the path of inflation?

The inflation rate increases from 6 percent a year to above 10 percent a year, but then decreases to 10 percent a year.

(c) What is the change in interest rates?

Interest rates rise by 4 percentage points a year.

Now try these

1. The money supply is increasing at 5 percent a year and anticipated inflation is 5 percent a year. What is happening to

   (a) real GDP?
   (b) the price level?
   (b) aggregate demand?
   (c) short-run aggregate supply?

2. When the inflation rate is expected to be zero, an investment project is just profitable at an interest rate of 5 percent a year. Would this investment project still be profitable when the interest rate is 10 percent a year and prices are expected to rise by 5 percent a year?

3. Initially the anticipated inflation rate is 5 percent a year. If then expectations are revised—the money supply growth rate is anticipated to be cut by 5 percentage points a year. Explain what happens to the interest rate?

4. Windy Isle adopts a fixed exchange rate. Explain what determines the inflation rate on Windy Isle. Explain the effect of its inflation on the money supply growth rate on Windy Isle.

5. What is the effect on inflation of an anticipated change in the money supply growth rate of 10 percent.

6. The inflation rate is expected to be 10 percent a year. What is the effect on the *LM* curve of this expected inflation rate.

Fact 11.1 Shark Island's real income growth rate is constant at 4 percent a year. Its inflation rate is constant at 4 percent a year, and its velocity of circulation is constant at 10.

7. Use Fact 11.1. Calculate the growth rate of Shark Island's money supply.

8. Use Fact 11.1. Shark Island doubles its money supply growth rate and the increase is anticipated. Calculate Shark Island's new long-run inflation rate.

9. Use Fact 11.1. Shark Island doubles its money supply growth rate and the increase is anticipated. Describe the path of Shark Island's inflation rate back to equilibrium.

10. Snake Island is an open economy and its exchange rate is flexible. It has the following short-run aggregate supply and aggregate demand:

$$y^s = -3500 + 250P$$
$$y^d = 5000 - 250P.$$

The government of Snake Island increases its money supply by 6 percent and this increase is expected. What are the effects of this policy change on its

(a) *AD* curve?
(b) *SAS* curves?

✓ Answers

Concept Review

1) velocity of circulation
2) actual inflation. anticipated inflation
3) actual
4) rational expectation
5) forecasted inflation rate
6) Plaza Agreement
7) equal percentage, the inflation rate
8) System, fix exchange rates
9) eliminated
10) equation of exchange, velocity of circulation, independent, money supply growth rate

True or False

1) T	5) F	9) T	13) T	17) F
2) F	6) T	10) F	14) F	18) T
3) T	7) F	11) F	15) T	19) F
4) T	8) F	12) F	16) F	20) F

Multiple Choice

1) e	5) b	9) a	13) d	17) d
2) d	6) d	10) d	14) e	18) d
3) a	7) d	11) e	15) a	19) d
4) d	8) d	12) a	16) b	20) e

Short Answer Questions

1. The European Monetary System is a system of fixed exchange rates between some of the members of the European Community. The main members of the European Monetary System are France, Germany, and Belgium, the Netherlands and Luxembourg (Benelux).

2. (a) When a country has a fixed exchange rate, its inflation is determined by world inflation and its growth rate of the money supply adjusts to accommodate that inflation.

    (b) When a country has a flexible exchange rate, this country is free to determine its monetary policy and inflation rate.

3. Anticipated inflation is a process in which prices are increasing at a rate equal to the rate forecasted by economic agents. With anticipated inflation, the actual inflation rate is equal to the expected inflation rate. Unanticipated inflation is a process in which prices increase at a rate that is differs from that forecasted by economic agents. With unanticipated inflation, the actual rate of inflation is not equal to the expected rate of inflation.

4. (a) A rational expectation is a forecast about the future value of an economic variable made using all available information.

    (b) First, it is unbiased. The expected forecast error is zero. There is as much chance of being wrong on the upside as on the downside and by an equal amount. Second, the forecast has the minimum range of error. This does not mean that it might be wildly wrong, but there is no way to reduce the range of error in the forecast.

5. The equilibrium real wage rate is the real wage rate at which the quantity of labor demanded equals the quantity of labor supplied.
    The money wage rate is the real wage rate multiplied by the price level.

6. (a) Inflation in Israel in the 1980s was anticipated. From 1983 to 1986, inflation accelerated. After 1985, inflation was brought under control. Both the increase and decrease in inflation were anticipated and strongly correlated with the change in the money supply growth rate.

   (b) Real GDP growth was virtually unaffected by these changes in inflation.

7. (a) If goods are cheaper in one country than in another country, it will pay people to buy goods in the country where they are cheap and sell them in the country where the goods are more expensive. This is a process called arbitrage.

   (b) Arbitrage will occur until there are no profit opportunities remaining from buying at the low price and selling at a high price. At that point, the price of internationally traded goods will be the same in all countries.

8. (a) From 1945 to 1950 and form 1962 to 1970, Canada was part of a fixed exchange rate system. From 1950 to 1962, Canada adopted a flexible exchange rate.

   (b) During this time period, the rest of the world also operated a fixed exchange rate system.

9. Anticipated inflation increases the cutoff point for any investment project. Investment increases at any given interest rate, so the *IS* curve shifts to the right.

10. Anticipated inflation does not affect the *LM* curve because its position depends on the real money supply. With anticipated inflation, the real money supply is constant—the price

level increases at the same rate as the money supply does.

Problems

1. (a) Real GDP remains the same.
   (b) The price level increases by 5 percent.
   (c) The aggregate demand curve shifts upward by 5 percent.
   (d) The short-run aggregate supply curve shifts upward by 5 percent.

2. That same project will just break even.

3. The interest rate will fall by 5 percent.

4. (a) Its inflation rate is determined by the inflation rate of the world.

   (b) Its money supply growth rate adjusts to accommodate that inflation rate.

5. The inflation rate increases by 10 percent.

6. Expected inflation does not shift the *LM* curve.

7. 8 percent a year.

8. 12 percent a year.

9. Inflation increases initially above 12 percent a year, but then decreases to 12 percent a year.

10. (a) $y^d = 5000 - 238.85P$.
    (b) $y^s = -3500 + 235.85P$.

CHAPTER 12

Inflation and the Business Cycle

Perspective and Focus

This chapter examines how inflation and the business cycle interact with each other. It studies the fluctuations in the inflation rate and the level of economic activity that occur simultaneously as the economy ebbs and flows over the course of the business cycle.

Learning Objectives

After studying this chapter, you will be able to:

- Describe the main features of inflation over the business cycle
- Explain the effects on unanticipated changes in aggregate demand on inflation
- Explain how an unanticipated decrease in aggregate demand brought inflation under control in the early 1980s but also brought recession
- Explain the effects of supply shocks on inflation
- Explain how oil price shocks influenced inflation in the 1970s
- Define the Phillips curve and explain the Phillips curve theory
- Describe the shifts in the Canadian Phillips curve since 1960

Increasing Your Productivity

The key thing to pay attention to in this chapter is the fact that in order to generate fluctuations in real GDP around its full-employment level and simultaneous fluctuations in the inflation rate, aggregate demand must change in an unanticipated way. Anticipated changes in aggregate demand have the effects that we studied in the Chapter 11—they change the price level (or inflation rate), leaving real GDP unaffected.

The second thing to pay attention to in this chapter is the equivalence of two alternative ways of looking at the determination of real economic activity and the inflation rate. One of these is the *AD-AS* model, with which you now very familiar, and the other is the Phillips curve approach. Figure 12.9 on page 345 is a crucial one showing you how the *AD-AS* model and the Phillips curve framework are really two ways of looking at the same thing. Be sure to spend a good deal of time working through that figure and the text description and explanation of it. Once you understanding how that figure works and are thoroughly familiar with the equivalence of the *AD-AS* and Phillips curve approaches you will have no difficulty in handling any of the material in this chapter.

The "trickiest" thing in this chapter is the analysis of the effects of the shift in the production function on the short-run and long-run aggregate supply curves. This material is contained on pages 338-341 and summarized in Figure 12.4. Work hard to thoroughly understand this figure.

Self Test

Concept Review

1. The simultaneous occurrence of inflation and recession is called
   _____.

2. The _____
   is the relationship between the inflation rate and unemployment rate for a particular expected inflation rate, holding constant the natural rate of unemployment.

3. The _____
   is the relationship between the inflation rate and unemployment rate for a particular natural rate of unemployment, when inflation is anticipated.

4. A Phillips curve whose position depends on the expected inflation rate is _____
   _____.

5. The short-run Phillips curve and the long-run Phillips curve intersect at
   _____
   and _____.

True or False

1. A process of rising prices and falling real GDP is known as stagflation.

2. A short-run Phillips curve, the position of which depends on the expected inflation rate is known as expected-augmented Phillips curve.

3. With a high correlation between wage change and inflation, the original Phillips curve evolved from the relationship between wage change and unemployment to one between inflation and unemployment.

4. The Phillips curve is a theory of inflation that is quite different from the one based on the aggregate demand-aggregate supply model.

5. The change in the expected inflation rate does not shift the short-run Phillips curve.

6. Between 1966 and 1970, Canadian unemployment was steady and inflation increased. Then, in 1972, unemployment began to increase.

7. Disruptions to the supply of key raw materials from the remainder of the world or large increases in the world price of such materials have a positive impact on aggregate supply.

8. In 1973, oil imported from Saudi Arabia was $2.70 a barrel. By 1975, the same oil had increased to $27.00 a barrel.

9. The Phillips curve provides another way of looking at the relationship between inflation and the business cycle.

10. The long-run Phillips curve is horizontal at the natural rate of unemployment.

11. An unanticipated increase in the money supply increases the price level by the same percentage amount.

12. A negative shock to technology decreases long-run and short-run aggregate supply.

13. A positive technology shock increases the demand for labor and increases the real wage rate.

14. An unanticipated slowdown in the rate of inflation increases the real wage rate.

15. An unanticipated increase in the inflation rate shifts the short-run Phillips curve upward.

16. An unanticipated increase in the inflation rate shifts the aggregate demand curve to the right, causes a movement along the short-run aggregate supply curve, and causes a movement along the short-run Phillips curve. Real GDP increases and the unemployment rate decreases.

17. An increase in the natural rate of unemployment decreases the inflation rate.

18. The Canadian Phillips curve has been stable since the 1960s.

19. When inflation expectations increase both inflation and unemployment rise.

20. When inflation expectations increase, the short-run Phillips curve shifts upwards, but the long-run Phillips curve does not change.

Multiple Choice

1. When an increase in aggregate demand is not anticipated, wages
   (a) rise in anticipation of rising prices.
   (b) remain constant in anticipation of rising prices.
   (c) do not rise in anticipation of rising prices.
   (d) wages may either rise or fall in anticipation of rising prices.
   (e) none of the above.

2. Capital accumulation and technological advancement
   (a) decrease aggregate supply at a constant pace.
   (b) do not affect aggregate supply.
   (c) decrease aggregate supply.
   (d) increase aggregate supply, but their pace is variable.
   (e) decrease aggregate demand, but their pace is variable.

3. When the production function shifts down, the long-run aggregate supply curve shifts to the left,
   (a) increasing the marginal product of labor and shifting the demand for labor curve to the right.
   (b) reducing the marginal product of labor and shifting the demand for labor curve to the right.
   (c) increasing the marginal product of labor and shifting the demand for labor curve to the left.
   (d) leaving the marginal product of labor constant and the demand for labor curve unchanged.
   (e) reducing the marginal product of labor and shifting the demand for labor curve to the left.

4. Choose the best statement.
   (a) The steeper the supply of labor curve, the greater is the shift in the long-run aggregate supply curve.
   (b) The flatter the supply of labor curve, the greater is the shift in the long-run aggregate supply curve.
   (c) The flatter the supply of labor curve, the greater is the shift in the short-run aggregate supply curve.
   (d) The steeper the supply of labor curve, the less is the shift in the short-run aggregate supply curve.
   (e) None of the above.

5. Which of the following is a short-run Phillips curve, the position of which depends on the expected inflation rate? The
   (a) original Phillips curve.
   (b) natural-rate Phillips curve.
   (c) auction Phillips curve.
   (d) expectations-augmented Phillips curve.
   (e) rules-augmented Phillips curve.

6. Which of the following will shift a short-run Phillips curve?
   (a) A change in the expected inflation rate.
   (b) Unanticipated inflation.
   (c) The real interest rate.
   (d) The market interest rate.
   (e) The long-run Phillips curve.

7. Technological change itself
   (a) can result in a permanent decrease in aggregate supply when it has a strong sectoral bias.
   (b) can bring a temporary decrease in aggregate supply when it has a strong sectoral bias.
   (c) has no impact on aggregate supply.

   (d) always increases aggregate supply when it has a strong sectoral bias.
   (e) none of the above are correct.

8. When a decrease in aggregate demand is not anticipated, real GDP
   (a) moves above its full-employment level and inflation accelerates.
   (b) moves below its full-employment level and inflation slows.
   (c) remains at its full-employment level and inflation accelerates.
   (d) remains at its full-employment level and inflation slows down.
   (e) moves below its full-employment level and inflation accelerates.

9. The long-run Phillips curve is intersected at any point by which of the following? The
   (a) supply of labor curve.
   (b) demand for labor curve.
   (c) aggregate demand curve.
   (d) expectations-augmented Phillips curve.
   (e) none of the above.

10. Between 1973 and 1975, massive oil price increases shifted
    (a) both the short-run and long-run aggregate supply curves to the right.
    (b) both the short-run and long-run aggregate supply curves to the left.
    (c) only the short-run aggregate supply curve to the left.
    (d) only the long-run aggregate supply curve to the right.
    (e) only the short-run aggregate supply curve to the right.

11. A 10 percent unanticipated increase in the money supply
    (a) increases aggregate demand to the point at which the new *AD* curve intersects the *LAS* curve at a price level 10 percent higher than the original one.
    (b) increases the price level by 10 percent.
    (c) increases the price level and real GDP because aggregate supply increases.
    (d) results in a movement along the short-run aggregate supply curve increasing both the price level and real GDP.
    (e) both (a) and (d).

12. A 20 percent increase in factor prices combined with a 5 percent increase in the money supply, both of which are unanticipated
    (a) increases aggregate supply.
    (b) decreases real GDP and increases the price level.
    (c) increases real GDP and increases the price level.
    (d) decreases both real GDP and the price level.
    (e) results in inflation but no change in real GDP.

13. A decrease in labor productivity that shifts the short-run production function downward
    (a) increases the demand for labor because the existing labor force is less productive.
    (b) decreases short-run aggregate supply but not long-run aggregate supply.
    (c) decreases long-run aggregate supply but not short-run aggregate supply.
    (d) decreases both long-run and short-run aggregate supply by the same amount.
    (e) decreases both long-run and short-run aggregate supply but decreases short-run aggregate supply by more than the decrease in long-run aggregate supply.

14. A technological change that increases the marginal productivity of labor
    (a) increases the level of employment, increases the real wage rate and increases long-run and short-run aggregate supply.
    (b) increases the real wage rate leading to an increase in the supply of labor and an increase in long-run aggregate supply.
    (c) increases long-run aggregate supply but does not change short-run aggregate supply.
    (d) increases the level of employment but does not change real wages.
    (e) extends the economies potential output level but does not change real GDP in the short run.

15. An increase in factor prices of 10 percent that is unexpected
    (a) increases the price level by 10 percent.
    (b) decreases real GDP by 10 percent.
    (c) increases the price level and decreases real GDP but each by less than 10 percent.
    (d) increases short-run aggregate supply.
    (e) decreases long-run aggregate supply.

16. As the economy moves down a short-run Phillips curve,
    (a) unemployment increases and expected inflation decreases.
    (b) unemployment increases and actual inflation decreases but expected inflation remains constant.
    (c) actual inflation falls and the natural rate of unemployment increases.
    (d) the expected inflation rate falls and the natural rate of unemployment rate increases.
    (e) inflation decreases, unemployment increases, but it is not possible to say what happens to either the expected inflation rate or the natural rate of unemployment.

17. Initially the short-run Phillips curve intersects the long-run Phillips curve at an inflation rate of 10 percent a year and an unemployment rate of 5 percent. A change then takes place that results in the short-run Phillips curve intersecting the long-run Phillips curve at the same unemployment rate but at an inflation rate of 5 percent a year.
    (a) The natural rate of unemployment has fallen.
    (b) The natural rate of unemployment has risen.
    (c) The expected inflation rate has fallen.
    (d) The expected inflation rate has risen.
    (e) The actual inflation rate has fallen.

18. An unexpected increase in the growth rate of the money supply
    (a) causes a movement down the short-run Phillips curve increasing the unemployment rate and lowering the inflation rate.
    (b) causes a movement up the short-run Phillips curve lowering the unemployment rate and increasing the inflation rate.
    (c) shifts the short-run Phillips curve increasing the expected inflation rate.
    (d) have no effect on the Phillips curve or the position on the Phillips curve at which the economy operates.
    (e) always results in the economy moving to an above full-employment equilibrium.

19. An economy is initially on its long-run and short-run Phillips curve. Then both inflation and unemployment increase. We can infer that
    (a) the natural rate of unemployment is increased.
    (b) the expected inflation rate has increased.
    (c) the natural rate of unemployment has not changed nor has the expected inflation rate.
    (d) either the natural rate of unemployment rate has increased or the expected inflation rate has increase but not both.
    (e) either the natural rate of unemployment has increased or the expected inflation rate has increased, or both have increased.

20. During the 1960's
    (a) the natural rate of unemployment decreased.
    (b) the expected inflation rate increased.
    (c) inflation expectations in the natural unemployment rate were constant and there was a movement along the fixed short-run Phillips curve.
    (d) the natural rate of unemployment decreased making it possible to keep prices stable even though unemployment was falling.
    (e) the short-run Phillips curve and the long-run Phillips curve were one of the same curve.

Short Answers Questions

1. Explain the following Phillips curves.

    (a) An expectations-augmented Phillips curve.
    (b) A long-run Phillips curve.
    (c) A short-run Phillips curve.

2. Briefly summarize the recession of 1981-1982.

3. When looking at inflation, does the Phillips curve have an advantage over the *AD-AS* model? Explain.

4. Is there a correlation between inflation and the business cycle? Explain.

    What happens to the Phillips curve(s) if there is a decrease in the natural rate of unemployment?

6. How did the original Phillips curve evolve?

7. What is the effect of an unanticipated increase in the growth rate of the money supply?

8. What caused the 1981-1982 recession?

9. How does stagflation arise?

10. (a) What is held constant along the short-run Phillips curve?
    (b) What is held constant along the long-run Phillips curve?

Problem Solving

How does it go?

1. Sun State has the following production function, demand for labor, and supply of labor:

    $$y = 20n - 0.1n^2$$
    $$nd = 100 - 5(W/P)$$
    $$n^s = 5(W/P).$$

    (a) What is the full-employment level of employment? Full-employment level of employment occurs at the intersection of the demand and supply of labor curves. Substitute $5(W/P)$ for n in the demand for labor curve. Full-employment level of employment is 50.

    (b) What is the full-employment real wage rate?

    At full employment, the level of employment is 50. Substitute 50 for n in either the demand for labor or the supply of labor curves. the full-employment real wage rate is 10.

(c) What is full-employment output?

At full employment, the level of employment is 50. Substitute 50 for n in the production function. Full-employment output is 750.

2. You are given the following data about the economy of Lizard Island:

$$y^d = 300/P$$
$$y^s = 250 - 250/P^2.$$

Aggregate demand on Lizard Island unexpectedly increases by 10 percent.

(a) Calculate the price level.

The price level is determined at the intersection of the aggregate demand curve and the long-run aggregate supply curve. Real GDP demanded at any price level increases by 10 percent. The aggregate demand curve is

$$y^d = 1.1(300/P).$$

The increase in aggregate demand is not expected, so wages remain the same and so too does the short-run aggregate supply curve. That is,

$$y^s = 250 - 250/P^2.$$

The price level is determined at the intersection of aggregate demand and aggregate supply curves. The price level is 1.86.

(b) Calculate real GDP.

Substitute 1.86 for the price level in either the equation to the aggregate demand or the aggregate supply curves. Real GDP is 177.59.

Now try these

Fact 12.1 For an economy has the following aggregate demand and short-run aggregate supply:

$$y^d = 1,000 - P$$
$$y^s = 4P.$$

1. Use Fact 12.1. Find the equilibrium level of real GDP.

2. Use Fact 12.2. Find the equilibrium price level.

Fact 12.2 Given Fact 12.1 aggregate demand now increases unexpectedly by 20 percent.

3. Use Fact 12.2. What is the percentage increase in real GDP?

4. Use Fact 12.2. What is the percentage increase in the price level?

Fact 12.3 An economy's production function, demand for labor, and supply of labor is described by the following equations:

$$y = 100n - 0.2n^2$$
$$n^d = 250 - 2.5(W_0/P)$$
$$n^s = 100 + 7.5(W_0/P).$$

5. Use Fact 12.3. Calculate full-employment real GDP.

6. Use Fact 12.3. Calculate full-employment real wage rate.

7. Use Fact 12.3. Calculate the equation for the long-run aggregate supply curve.

8. Use Fact 12.3. Calculate the equation for the short-run aggregate supply curve.

Fact 12.4 The economy described in Fact 12.3 experiences a 20 percent increase in labor productivity.

9. Use Fact 12.4. Find the new long-run equilibrium real wage.

10. Use Fact 12.4. Find the equation for the new long-run aggregate supply curve.

11. Use Fact 12.4. Find the equation for the new short-run aggregate supply curve.

12. Use Fact 12.4. Find the equilibrium level of unemployment.

Fact 12.5 All the variables are logarithms: y is the log of real GDP, p is the log of the price level and m is the log of the nominal money supply.

You were given the following facts about an economy:

$$y_t^s = 10 + 3(p_t - p_t^e)$$

$$y_t^d = 50 + 1.5(m_t - p_t)$$

$$m_t^e = 10.$$

13. Use Fact 12.5. Calculate the rational expectation of the price level.

14. Use Fact 12.5. Calculate full-employment level of real GDP.

Fact 12.6 Refer to Fact 12.5. Suppose there is an unexpected 20 percent increase in the money supply.

15. Use Fact 12.6. Calculate the new rational expectation of the price level.

16. Use Fact 12.6. Calculate the equilibrium price level.

17. Use Fact 12.6. Calculate the equilibrium level of real GDP.

✓ Answers

Concept Review

1) stagflation
2) short-run Phillips curve
3) long-run Phillips curve
4) expectations-augmented Phillips curve
5) expected inflation rate, the natural rate of unemployment

True or False

1) T	5) F	9) T	13) T	17) F
2) T	6) F	10) F	14) T	18) F
3) T	7) F	11) F	15) F	19) F
4) F	8) F	12) T	16) T	20) T

Multiple Choice

1) c	5) d	9) d	13) e	17) c
2) d	6) a	10) b	14) a	18) b
3) e	7) b	11) e	15) c	19) e
4) b	8) b	12) b	16) b	20) c

Short Answer Questions

1. (a) An expectations-augmented Phillips curve is a short-run Phillips curve and its position depends on the expected inflation rate.

(b) A long-run Phillips curve depicts the relationship between the rate of inflation and the rate of unemployment when inflation is fully anticipated.

(c) A short-run Phillips curve is a Phillips curve drawn for a particular, given, expected rate of inflation.

2. In the early 1980s, the economy experienced an unanticipated slowdown in the growth of aggregate demand. Wages and other costs increased, shifting the short-run aggregate supply curve to the left (and upward) at a faster pace than the growth of aggregate demand resulting in stagflation. Furthermore, real GDP fell below its full-employment level and inflation slowed.

3. Yes, because one can keep track of an inflating economy without using curves that constantly shift as the price level increases.

4. No strong, simple correlation exists between inflation and the business cycle, but there is an important pattern. Inflation tends to increase when real GDP is above trend and decrease when real GDP is below trend. Also, the turning points in inflation do not coincide with the points at which real GDP switches from being on one side of trend to the other. Inflation tends to keep on increasing for a while after real GDP falls below trend and begins to increase again before real GDP gets back above trend.

5. A decrease in the natural rate of unemployment shifts both the long-run and short-run Phillips curves to the left.

6. The original Phillips curve evolved from the relationship between wage change and unemployment to one between inflation and unemployment.

7. Aggregate demand increases but long-run and short-run aggregate supply remain the same. With higher aggregate demand, there is a movement along the short-run aggregate supply curve and both real GDP and the price level rise.

8. Aggregate demand growth slowed below its expected growth rate. Short-run aggregate supply decreased by more than aggregate demand increased hence the price level rose but real GDP fell.

9. Stagflation arises when short-run aggregate supply decreases by more than aggregate demand increases.

10. (a) The expected inflation rate and the natural rate of unemployment.
    (b) The natural rate of unemployment.

Problems

1. 80
2. 200
3. 15.39 percent
4. 15.39 percent
5. 12,218.75
6. 15
7. $y = 12,218.75$
8. $y = 12,500 - 281.25(P^e/P)^2$
9. 15.66
10. $y = 12,288.01$
11. $y = 15,000 - 15,00(P^e/P)^2$
12. 217.44
13. 36.67
14. 10
15. 36.67
16. 37.33
17. 12

CHAPTER 13

Public and Private Deficits and Debts

Perspective and Focus

This chapter focuses on one particular aspect of macroeconomic problems and policy issues—deficits and debts of the government and private sectors. You have met these concepts before when we studied the national income accounts in Chapter 2. There you learnt how the deficit of the government sector is connected with the deficits or surpluses of the private sector and the foreign sector. That is, you learnt that the government deficit (government purchases minus taxes) equals the private sector surplus (saving minus investment) plus the foreign sector deficit (imports minus exports).

The goal of this chapter is to focus more detailed attention on these deficits and the way in which they result in the accumulation of debt. The chapter focuses on the dynamic relationships between deficits and debts.

Learning Objectives

After studying this chapter, you will be able to:

- Describe Canadian deficits and debts and place them in their historical and international context
- Explain the relationships between stocks and flows, receipts and payments, and borrowing and lending
- Describe the main sources of Canadian government deficits in the 1980s
- Explain how inflation distorts the deficit
- Explain the limits to the amount that can be borrowed
- Explain how deficits can lead to inflation
- Compare the deficits in Canada, Bolivia and Israel in the 1980s
- Explain the burden debt places on future generations

Increasing Your Productivity

The heart of this chapter is the connection between debts and deficits. The key to understanding this connection is the realization that a deficit is a flow while a debt is a stock. Flows change stocks. An ongoing deficit leads to the perpetual accumulation of debt; an ongoing surplus leads to a perpetual accumulation of assets.

The critical feature of the dynamic relationship between deficits and debts is the fact that interest is paid on borrowing or earned on lending. An ongoing deficit not only leads to a rising debt but to an increasing interest burden. Thus an ongoing deficit leads to the accumulation of debt that mushrooms as a result of interest payments.

But if the borrowing is put to productive use, it leads to growth in productive resources and growth in income. Growing incomes enable debt burdens to be carried more readily. Thus the key question that this chapter helps you understand is that of determining how much someone (or a government or a firm) can borrow without running into an ever bigger debt problem and ever larger debt burden in relation to its ability to service the debt.

This chapter uses some simple algebra in the section on budget constraints, borrowing, and lending. The chapter derives those basic relationships especially in Tables 13.1 and 13.2. You do need to spend some time studying this algebra and becoming thoroughly comfortable with it.

Self Test

Concept Review

1. The budget deficit minus the basic deficit is equal to _____.

2. The limits to expenditure is called the _____.

3. The change in the real value of outstanding government debt is the _____.

4. Debt owed by the private sector and the government sector to the rest of the world is _____.

5. The deficit of the federal government is the _____.

6. Inflation in excess of _____ per month is called hyperinflation.

7. _____ is the deficit of all levels of government.

8. An _____ is an implicit tax that people pay as a result of a decrease in the value of the money and government debt that they hold.

9. Ricardian equivalence theorem is the proposition that _____ and _____ are equivalent to each other and have on effect on _____.

10. The limits to expenditure at each point in time and the links between spending, _____, and _____ is the _____.

True or False

1. A budget constraint defines the limits of expenditure—the maximum that can be spent given the resources available to finance that spending.

2. Net foreign assets in Canada are equal to government debt minus private debt.

3. The inflation tax is the tax that people implicitly pay when the real value of money and the government debt they hold increases because of rising prices.

4. The government sector's basic deficit is its budget deficit plus debt interest.

5. From the end of World War II through 1974, the debt of the Canadian federal government as a percentage of GDP steadily increased.

6. The balance on the rest of the world's transactions with Canada (viewed from the perspective of residents of the rest of the world) is equal to Canadian imports of goods and services plus Canadian exports of goods and services.

7. People can smooth their expenditure by borrowing when incomes are low and repaying their loans when incomes are high.

8. In the United States, the government sector deficit is entirely a federal government deficit.

9. Canada has experienced a good deal of inflation through the 1970s and 1980s. As a consequence, the real deficit has been larger than the nominal deficit.

10. The proposition that government debt and taxes are equivalent to each other and have no effect on interest rates is known as the Ricardian equivalence theorem.

11. Canada has had a federal government budget deficit every year since 1970.

12. Governments can smooth expenditure by borrowing more when revenue is low and borrowing less when revenue is high. On the average, its deficit is zero and it has no debt.

13. The more a household saves, the faster can its consumption expenditure grow.

14. The government deficit exploded in the 1980s because government expenditure on goods and services as a percentage of GDP grew every year.

15. The presence of inflation makes the government deficit look larger than it really is.

16. If the economy grows at a rate higher than the real interest rate, then there exits a steady-state debt-GDP ratio.

17. If the economy grows at a rate equal to the real interest rate and the government runs a deficit, then the debtGDP ratio grows without limit.

18. Deficits always lead to inflation.

19. Deficits burden future generations only if the present generation ignores the future tax liability created by the present deficit.

20. Inflation reduces the size of the real deficit, making it smaller than the nominal deficit.

Multiple Choice

1. The sum of the government balance, the private sector balance, and the rest of the world balance equals
   (a) a positive sum.
   (b) a negative sum.
   (c) zero.
   (d) either a positive or a negative sum.
   (e) none of the above.

2. Net foreign assets in Canada are equal to
   (a) Canadian government debt minus Canadian private debt.
   (b) the ratio of Canadian government debt to Canadian private debt.
   (c) Canadian government debt multiplied by Canadian private debt.
   (d) Canadian government debt plus private debt.
   (e) none of the above.

3. Which of the following states the limits of expenditure at each point in time and the links between spending, borrowing, and lending? A(n)
   (a) interdimensional budget constraint.
   (b) multitemporal budget constraint.
   (c) intertemporal budget constraint.
   (d) two-dimensional budget constraint.
   (e) none of the above.

4. The equation that states that the change in assets from one year to the next equals income minus expenditure plus interest income is
   (a) $A_{t+1} - A_t = Y_t + E_t + r_t A_t$.
   (b) $A_{t+1} - A_t = Y_t - E_t + r_t A_t$.
   (c) $A_{t+1} - A_t = Y_t - E_t - r_t A_t$.
   (d) $A_{t+1} - A_t = Y_t + E_t - r_t A_t$.
   (e) $A_{t+1} - A_t = Y_t - E_t - r_t A_t$.

5. Which of the following equations represents the government's intertemporal budget constraint?
   (a) $(D_{t+1} - D_t) = G_t + r_t D_t - T_t$.
   (b) $(D_{t-1} - D_t) = G_t + r_t D_t - T_t$.
   (c) $(D_{t-1} - D_t) = G_t - r_t D_t - T_t$.
   (d) $(D_{t-1} + D_t) = G_t - r_t D_t - T_t$.
   (e) $(D_{t-1} + D_t) = G_t + r_t D_t + T_t$.

6. Which of the following represent motives for borrowing and lending?
   (a) Expenditure smoothing.
   (b) Consumption growth.
   (c) Saving growth.

(d) Both (a) and (b).
(e) All of the above.

7. An intertemporal budget constraint can be written as
   (a) $E_t + A_{t+1} = (1 + r_t)A_t - Y_t$.
   (b) $E_t + A_{t+1} = (1 + r_t)A_t/Y_t$.
   (c) $E_t + A_{t+1} = (1 + r_t)A_t + Y_t$.
   (d) $E_t + A_{t+1} = (1 - r_t)A_t + Y_t$.
   (e) $E_t + A_{t+1} = (1/r_t)A_t + Y_t$.

8. The value of debt outstanding expressed as a percentage of GDP is known as the
   (a) debt-GDP accelerator.
   (b) debt-GDP multiplier.
   (c) debt-GDP inflator.
   (d) debt-GDP ratio.
   (e) debt-GDP deflator.

9. The debt owed by the private and government sectors of an economy to the remainder of the world is known as
   (a) internal debt.
   (b) autonomous debt.
   (c) global debt.
   (d) endogenous debt.
   (e) external debt.

10. In studying debts and deficits and their effects on the macroeconomy, which of the following sectors are distinguished? The
    (a) government.
    (b) private.
    (c) rest of the world.
    (d) both (a) and (c).
    (e) (a), (b), and (c).

11. The government budget balance is equal to
    (a) $T + G$.
    (b) $T - G$.
    (c) $G - T$.
    (d) T/G.
    (e) G/T.

12. A persistent government budget deficit during the 1980s
    (a) decreased the debt-GDP accelerator.
    (b) increased the debt-GDP ratio.
    (c) decreased the debt-GDP ratio.
    (d) increased the debt-GDP accelerator.
    (e) left the debt-GDP ratio unchanged.

13. The federal government's debt as a percentage of GDP has been
    (a) growing every year since World War II.
    (b) at a higher level during the 1980s than at any other time in history.
    (c) on an upward trend since the middle 1970s.
    (d) on a declining trend since World War II.
    (e) higher in the 1980s than it was in the 1940s.

14. Household has assets of $100, an income from employment of $100, and earns interest at 5 percent a year on its assets. The maximum amount the household can consume in the next time period is
    (a) $105.
    (b) $100.
    (c) $500.
    (d) $205.
    (e) $200.

15. A government has a debt in year 1 of $1 trillion. Its current years expenditure is $150 billion (excluding interest) and its current period tax receipts are $250 billion. The interest rate is 15 percent a year and the inflation rate is 10 percent a year.
    (a) The government has a real surplus but a nominal deficit.
    (b) A real surplus and a real deficit.
    (c) A nominal surplus and a nominal deficit.
    (d) A nominal surplus and a real deficit.
    (e) Not enough information to say.

16. The government has a deficit equal to 10 percent of GDP. Real GDP is growing at 5 percent a year and the real interest rate is 4 percent a year. The steady-state debt-GDP ratio is
    (a) greater than 20.
    (b) less than or equal to 20 but greater than 10.
    (c) less than or equal to 10 but greater than 5.
    (d) less than or equal to 5 but greater than 2.
    (e) less than or equal to 2.

17. A government that has a budget deficit can finance its deficit, no matter how large it is,
    (a) by issuing debt.
    (b) by printing money.
    (c) by any combination of debt issue and money printing it chooses.
    (d) by only raising taxes.
    (e) by only cutting expenditure.

18. A government that is running a budget deficit and that faces a real interest rate in excess of the economy's growth rate
    (a) can keep inflation under control by restricting the rate of money growth.
    (b) can keep inflation under control by issuing debt.
    (c) cannot keep inflation under control and must accept inflation as an inevitable consequence of its deficit.
    (d) will be forced to create a new monetary standard every few years.
    (e) will eventually run out of money.

19. The government budget deficit
    (a) inevitably poses a burden on future generations.
    (b) imposes a burden on foreigners.
    (c) imposes a burden on only the current generation.
    (d) imposes no burden because the interest payments are somebody's income.
    (e) imposes a burden on future generations if capital accumulation is crowded out.

20. Sandy Island has a basic deficit of 5 percent of GDP. The interest rate onn Sandy Island is 2 percent per year. Government debt at the beginning of the 1992 is $2.5 million. GDP in 1992 is $10 million. GDP growth rate is 2.5 percent a year. In 1993, Sandy Island's debt-GDP ratio is
    (a) 5 percent.
    (b) 10 percent.
    (c) 19 percent.
    (d) 30 percent.
    (e) 50 percent.

Short Answers Questions

1. Define the two deficits.

2. Explain the difference between flows and stocks.

3. Define the budget balance of businesses.

4. Does external debt impose a burden on future generations? Explain.

5. What is a budget constraint?

6. What caused the persistent federal government deficit of the 1980s?

7. What is meant by an intertemporal budget constraint?

8. (a) What is meant by expenditure smoothing?
   (b) How do governments smooth expenditure?
   (c) How do households smooth expenditure?

9. (a) What is an inflation tax?
   (b) Is this tax a legislated tax?

10. By what amount does the government debt change each year?

11. Set out the main trends and turning points in federal government debt since 1900.

12. What is the relationship between the government budget deficit, the private sector budget balance, and the rest of the world balance?

13. What is the intertemporal budget constraint? Set out an equation describing this constraint.

14. How is the real deficit calculated?

15. Explain why there is a steady-state debt-GDP ratio if the economic growth rate exceeds the real interest rate.

Problem Solving

How does it go?

You are given the following information about Big Wave Island:

GDP	$68 million
Consumer expenditure	$36 million
Government purchases of goods and services	$12 million
Government transfer payments and subsidies	$4 million
Total taxes paid	$18 million
Exports to the rest of the world	$24 million
Imports from the rest of the world	$28 million

(a) What is the government sector balance?

Government sector balance is equal to $T - G$, where T is total taxes paid minus transfer payments and G is government purchases of goods and services:

$$T - G = (18 - 4) - 36$$
$$= -22.$$

(b) What is the private sector balance?

The private sector balance is equal to $S - I$, where S is saving and I is private investment. Neither S nor I is given in the information supplied, but we can calculate $S - I$ as follows:

$$(S - I) = -(T - G) + (EX - IM) (13.1)$$
$$= 22 + (24 - 28)$$
$$= 18.$$

(c) What is the rest of the world's balance with Big Wave Island?

The rest of the world's balance with Big Wave Island is equal to $IM - EX$, which is

$$IM - EX = 28 - 24$$
$$= 4.$$

2. An economy has an interest rate of 3 percent a year and no inflation. The economy's real growth rate is 6 percent a year. Its current debt is $0.25 million and

its current GDP is $5 million. The government's basic deficit is equal to 5 percent of GDP.

(a) Calculate its current debt-GDP ratio.

The current debt-GDP ratio is $0.25 million/$5 million, which is 0.05.

(b) Calculate its debt-GDP ratio after one year.

The growth rate is 6 percent a year, so GDP at the end of the year is 1.06 × $5 million, which is $5.3 million. Its debt at the end of one year equals $(1.03 × 0.25 + 0.05 × 5)million, which is $0.51 million. Therefore its debt-GDP ratio at the end of one year is (0.51/5.3), which is 0.096.

(c) Calculate the steady-state debt-GDP ratio.

The steady-state debt-GDP ratio is 0.05/(0.06 - 0.03), which is 1.67 (167 percent of GDP).

(d) Calculate the steady-state deficit.

The steady-state deficit is equal to

(0.03 × 1.67)GDP + 0.05GDP,

which is 0.1GDP.

Now try these

Fact 13.1 Given the following information about an economy:

GDP	$340 billion
Consumer expenditure	$180 billion
Government purchases of goods and services	$60 billion
Government transfer payments and subsidies	$20 billion
Total taxes paid	$90 billion
Exports to the rest of the world	$120 billion
Imports from the rest of the world	$140 billion

1. What is the government sector balance?

2. What is the private sector balance?

3. What is the rest of the world's balance with this economy?

4. Which of the above balances is a surplus and which is a deficit?

5. Is this economy a net lender or to or a net borrower from the rest of the world?

6. If the interest rate at which this economy can borrow or lend is 10 percent a year, what is the equation for the government's intertemporal budget constraint in the current year.

Fact 13.2 An economy has an interest rate of 10 percent a year and an inflation rate of 6 percent a year. The economy's real growth rate is 5 percent a year. Its current debt is $1 trillion and its current GDP is $10 trillion. The government increases spending creating a basic deficit equal to 10 percent of GDP.

7. Calculate the current debt-GDP ratio.

8. Calculate the debt-GDP ratio to the end of one year.

9. Calculate the steady-state debt-GDP ratio.

10. Calculate the steady-state deficit.

11. If the growth rate of real GDP falls to 1 percent a year, what problems does the economy described in Fact 13.2 face?

✓ Answers

Concept Review

1) debt interest
2) budget constraint
3) real deficit
4) external debt
5) federal deficit
6) 50
7) total government deficit
8) inflation tax
9) debt, taxes, interest rates
10) borrowing, lending, intertemporal budget constraint

True or False

1) T	5) F	9) F	13) T	17) T
2) F	6) F	10) T	14) F	18) F
3) F	7) T	11) F	15) T	19) T
4) F	8) T	12) F	16) T	20) T

Multiple Choice

1) c	5) a	9) e	13) c	17) b
2) d	6) d	10) e	14) d	18) c
3) c	7) c	11) b	15) a	19) e
4) b	8) d	12) b	16) c	20) d

Short Answer Questions

1. The federal deficit is the deficit of the federal government. The total government deficit are the combined deficits of federal, province, and local governments.

2. A deficit is a flow, measured in dollars per unit of time. A debt is a stock, measured as dollars at a point in time.

3. The budget balance of businesses equals business saving minus business investment.
   Business saving = business profits – taxes – dividends and interest payments to households.
   Business investment is the purchase of new plant, equipment, and buildings by firms as well as net changes in inventories.

4. Whether external debt imposes a burden on future generations depends on the rate of return and the rate of economic growth achieved with the borrowed resources.

5. A budget constraint defines the limits of expenditure, that is the maximum that can be spent given the resources available to finance that spending.

6. The persistent federal government deficit of the 1980s has arisen from increases in expenditure, especially increases in transfer payments and subsidies and net interest.

7. An intertemporal budget constraint states the limits of expenditure at each point in time and the links between spending, borrowing, and lending.

8. (a) As a rule, people dislike expenditure to fluctuate. They prefer to smooth their expenditure over time.

(b) Governments smooth their spending by borrowing more in recessions and less in booms.
(c) Households smooth their expenditure (consumption) by saving less in recessions and more in booms.

9. (a) The inflation tax is the tax that people implicitly pay when the real value of money and the government debt they hold declines because of rising prices.
(b) No, this tax is not a legislated tax.

10. The government debt changes each year by an amount equal to the interest rate paid on the debt held by the public plus the basic deficit.

11. The debt-GDP ratio grew until the Great Depression. It dipped slightly in the 1930s and then climbed to an all time peak during World War 2. Following World War 2, the debt-GDP ratio declined until the middle of the 1970s. Since that time the ratio has increased.

12. The Government budgets surplus plus the private sector budget surplus plus the rest of world surplus equals zero.

13. The intertemporal budget constraint states the limit of expenditure at each point in time and the links between spending, borrowing and lending. The equation for the intertemporal budget constraints states that current expenditure plus assets of the beginning of the next period equals current period income plus initial assets at the beginning of the current period. Current period income equals income from assets (interest rate times the value of assets plus income from other sources such as labor income.

14. The real deficit is calculated by deflating current debt by the current price level and then calculating the first difference of change in real debt.

15. If the growth rate exceeds the real interest rate, real GDP grows at a faster rate than the outstanding debt interest. So eventually there is a stable relationship between debt and income.

Problems

1. $10 billion
2. −$30 billion
3. $20 billion
4. Private sector has a deficit and the other two sectors have surpluses
5. Borrower
6. $(D_{t+1} - D_t) = 0.1D_t - 10$
7. 0.1
8. 0.099
9. 10
10. 0.5 GDP

CHAPTER 14

Why Macroeconomists Disagree About Policy

Perspective and Focus

You have now completed your study of macroeconomic theory. You have studied the forces that determine the level of real GDP and its main expenditure components—consumer expenditure, investment, government purchases, and net exports. You have also studied what determines labor market variables—employment, unemployment, and real wages. You've studied what determines financial market variables, such as the quantity of money supplied and demanded and the interest rate. You've also studied how this all comes together to determine real GDP and the price level, both in the short run and the long run. Finally, you've studied the way in which debts accumulate as a result of an ongoing deficit and the dynamic relationships between deficits and debts.

You are now ready to tackle some policy questions. These questions center on the role of government in the macroeconomy and the influence of changes in physical policy and monetary policy on the main macroeconomic variables.

This first policy chapter sets the broad scene by examining the range of opinion among macroeconomists about the potential effects of policy on the economy.

Learning Objectives

After studying this chapter, you will be able to:

- Describe the conflicting policy advice given by macroeconomists and others
- Distinguish among targets, instruments, and indicators of macroeconomics policy.
- Distinguish between rules and discretion
- Explain the content and consequences of monetarist policy advice
- Describe Japan's experience with monetarist policies since 1978
- Explain the content and consequences of activist policies
- Describe the consequences pursuing activist policies in the 1960s
- Explain why monetarists and activists offer conflicting advice
- Explain the consensus policy of targetting nominal GDP

Increasing Your Productivity

This chapter is not a heavy one in terms of analysis but your understanding and appreciation of it will be greatly enhanced if you are completely familiar with the *IS-LM* analysis developed in Chapter 6 for the closed economy and Chapter 7 for the open economy. If you are not thoroughly familiar with this material, go back to Chapters 6 and 7 and refresh your understanding of that material before embarking on the present chapter.

The second thing to keep in mind as you work through this chapter is that the analysis abstracts from ongoing inflation and economic growth. This abstraction does not mean that the analysis is irrelevant to an economy with inflation and economic growth. It means simply that in studying the central issues involved in economic *fluctuations*, a clearer picture and a sharper focus can be obtained by ignoring the ongoing inflation and growth trends. Thus the diagrammatic analysis of the consequences of each alternative stabilization policy studies movements in real GDP and the price level around their trends.

The final part of this chapter studies nominal GDP targetting and summaries an emerging consensus about macroeconomic policy. Be sure that you understand the figure depicting the nominal GDP target, Figure 14.11. Such a target is a band and the goal is to place the price level and real GDP in a giving year inside this band. In a sense nominal GDP targetting is a recognition that demand management policies can do no more than stabilize aggregate demand. They have no ability to stabilize aggregate supply. Controversy may exist but there is no disagreement on this proposition.

As you work through the material in this chapter, try to form your own critically and carefully arrived at position on the appropriateness of alternative stabilization policies. Repeatedly ask yourself the question, to what extent is my conclusion driven by my preferences about inflation, unemployment, and real growth and to what extent is it driven by my best assessment of the way the economy works?

Self Test

Concept Review

1. Nominal GDP targetting is a policy of targetting a pre-determined growth path for _____.

2. The objectives that macroeconomic policy seeks to achieve are macroeconomic _____.

3. The variables the macroeconomics seeks to influence are _____.

4. Variables manipulated by the government or the monetary authorities to influence the macroeconomic policy targets are macroeconomic _____.

5. Variables that provide information, on a frequent basis, about the current state of the economy are called _____.

6. A fixed rule is a prescription of behavior that is _____ of the circumstances.

7. A policy that reacts to the state of the economy is a _____ policy.

8. A discretionary macroeconomic policy is a policy that _____ the state of the economy.

9. A macroeconomic policy rule is one that operates _____.

10. A statistical description of the economy is called _____ _____.

True or False

1. Macroeconomic indicators are variables that provide information, on a frequent basis, about the current state and direction of the economy.

2. A macroeconomic policy rule is a macroeconomic policy that reacts to changing economic conditions.

3. A discretionary macroeconomic policy is a policy that does not react to the current state of the economy.

4. Following monetarist policy advice in the face of an aggregate supply shock leads to movements in real GDP and the price level in the same directions.

5. Nominal GDP targetting is based on the presumption that it is possible to make aggregate demand more stable than it would be in the absence of activist policy.

6. Nominal GDP equals real GDP multiplied by the price level.

7. Calculations with statistical models of the Canadian economy suggest that nominal GDP targetting could indeed by used to decrease the variability of real GDP and inflation, keeping the economy closer to its full-employment level and avoiding excesses of inflation and deflation.

8. Monetarists advocate feedback rules for the money supply and fiscal policy.

9. Target variables are variables that macroeconomic policy seeks to influence.

10. Monetary policy instruments are the monetary base and bank's reserve requirements.

11. Macroeconomists agree about policy objectives but not about the way the economy works.

12. Monetarists advocate feed-back rules while activists advocate stable rules.

13. Monetarists policy advice, if followed results in no fluctuations arising from aggregate demand shocks.

14. Monetarist policies can avoid stagflation.

15. Activist policies can avoid demand shocks only if the policy maker has perfect foresight.

16. Activist policies can limit stagflation.

17. If policy makers to not have perfect foresight, activists policies lead to bigger price level fluctuations than those arising from monetarist policies.

18. Successful nominal GDP targetting stabilizes real GDP and the price level when demand shocks occur.

19. Random temporary shocks hit the economy from time to time. Monetarist advice is based on the fact that policy makers can forecast these shocks.

20. For a negative random shock to aggregate demand, activist advice is to increase the money supply.

Multiple Choice

1. A macroeconomic policy that does not react to changing economic conditions is known as
   (a) a variable rule.
   (b) an activist rule.
   (c) a feedback policy rule.
   (d) a discretionary rule.
   (e) a fixed rule.

2. Variables the provide information about the state of the economy
   (a) include interest rates and exchange rates.
   (b) include the money supply and unemployment.
   (c) are called macroeconomic indicators.
   (d) include stock prices and consumer prices.
   (e) all of the above.

3. The following schools of thought advocate the use of fixed rules, especially for the growth rate of the money supply,
   (a) Keynesians.
   (b) supply siders.
   (c) new classical economists.
   (d) monetarists.
   (e) classical economists.

4. The consequences of following monetarist policy advice when the economy is hit by aggregate demand shocks are
   (a) nominal GDP deviating from its long-run level and the price level deviating from its actual level.
   (b) real GDP deviating from its long-run level and the price level deviating from its actual level.
   (c) real GDP deviating from its long-run level and the price level deviating from its expected level.

   (d) nominal GDP deviating from its long-run level and the price level deviating from its expected level.
   (e) real GDP deviating from its long-run level but the price level remaining constant.

5. A monetarist policy in the face of a negative aggregate supply shock results in
   (a) inflation.
   (b) disinflation.
   (c) stagflation.
   (d) hyperinflation.
   (e) none of the above.

6. The macroeconomic policy targets are the objectives that macroeconomic policy seeks to achieve. The main target variables are
   (a) unemployment.
   (b) real GDP.
   (c) the current account balance.
   (d) inflation.
   (e) all of the above.

7. Fiscal policy instruments are
   (a) government purchases of goods and services.
   (b) the monetary base.
   (c) transfer payments.
   (d) taxes.
   (e) (a), (c), and (d).

8. A feedback policy is a policy that reacts to the current state of the economy. It is also known as
   (a) an activist macroeconomic policy.
   (b) a non-discretionary macroeconomic policy.
   (c) a fixed policy.
   (d) a variable policy.
   (e) a discretionary macroeconomic policy.

9. If real GDP is (or is forecasted to be) below its full-employment equilibrium level, then an increase in aggregate demand by increasing the money supply, increasing government purchases of goods and services or cutting taxes is known as
   (a) fixed policy rule advice.
   (b) activist policy advice.
   (c) variable policy advice.
   (d) conflicting policy advice.
   (e) monetarist policy advice.

10. In recent years, opinion has converged on the nature of a desirable and possible macroeconomic stabilization policy. It is
    (a) real GDP targetting.
    (b) real GDP targetting.
    (c) nominal GDP targetting.
    (d) nominal GDP targetting.
    (e) real national income targetting.

11. Stabilizing the economy is beyond our reach because
    (a) there are too many policy disagreements.
    (b) we do not have sufficient knowledge of how the economy works.
    (c) politicians and central bankers are ignorant of the knowledge about how the economy works that is available to economists.
    (d) we do not spend enough resources on economic research.
    (e) monetary and fiscal policy are always operating in opposite directions to each other.

12. An economy is subject only to temporary aggregate demand shocks and policy affects aggregate demand with a one period time lag.
    (a) Monetarist policy achieves greater stability of real GDP than activist policy.
    (b) Activist policy achieves greater stability of real GDP than monetarist policy.
    (c) Activist and monetarist policy have the same effect on real GDP.
    (d) Not possible to say which of these two policies have the larger or smaller effect on real GDP.
    (e) Long-run aggregate supply responds more with activist policies than with monetarist policies.

13. An economy is subject a permanent aggregate demand shock and policy affects aggregate demand with a one period time lag.
    (a) The price level fluctuates more with monetarist policy than with activist policy.
    (b) The price level fluctuates more with activist policy than with monetarist policy.
    (c) The price level fluctuates the same regardless of the policy.
    (d) It is not possible to say under which policy the price fluctuates more.
    (e) The average inflation rate is higher with monetarist policy.

14. An economy experiences a negative, temporary shock to long-run aggregate supply.
    (a) Monetarist policy achieves greater stability of real GDP than activist policy.
    (b) Activist policy achieves greater stability of real GDP than monetarist policy.
    (c) Activist and monetarist policy have the same effect on real GDP.
    (d) Not possible to say which of these two policies have the larger or smaller effect on real GDP.
    (e) Long-run aggregate supply responds more with activist policies than with monetarist policies.

15. An economy experiences a negative, permanent shock to long-run aggregate supply.
    (a) The price level fluctuates more with monetarist policy than with activist policy.
    (b) The price level fluctuates more with activist policy than with monetarist policy.
    (c) The price level fluctuates the same regardless of the policy.
    (d) It is not possible to say under which policy the price fluctuates more.
    (e) The average inflation rate is higher with monetarist policy.

16. When monetarist policies were pursued in Japan during the 1980s,
    (a) inflation accelerated.
    (b) real GDP growth collapsed.
    (c) inflation gradually moderated and real GDP growth remained steady.
    (d) inflation moderated and real GDP growth accelerated.
    (e) the policy had no effect on inflation.

17. Real GDP targeting prevents
    (a) real GDP from falling when there is an aggregate supply shock.
    (b) real GDP from falling when there is an aggregate demand shock.
    (c) short-run aggregate supply from fluctuating when long-run aggregate supply is stable.
    (d) long-run aggregate supply from fluctuating.
    (e) both (b) and (c).

18. For a positive random shock to aggregate demand,
    (a) activist advice is to hold the money supply constant.
    (b) monetarist advice is to hold the money supply constant.
    (c) activist advice is to decrease taxes.
    (d) activist advice is increase government purchases.
    (e) all of the above.

19. A positive aggregate supply shock hits the economy and a policy lag exits. In the period of the shock, the economy experiences
    (a) inflation if monetarist advice is followed but not if activist advice is followed.
    (b) inflation but not an increase in unemployment.
    (c) inflation and an increase in unemployment.
    (d) stagflation if activist advice is followed but not if monetarist advice is followed.
    (e) none of the above.

20. A temporary decrease in investment that is unexpected leads to
    (a) an permanent decrease in the price level if a feedback policy if adopted.
    (b) a temporary decrease in the price level if a fixed rule policy is adopted.
    (c) a temporary decrease in unemployment if a fixed rule policy is adopted.
    (d) a permanent increase in unemployment if a fixed rule policy is adopted.
    (e) (b) and (c).

Short Answers Questions

1. What is a macroeconomic indicator? Give some examples.

2. (a) What are macroeconomic policy instruments?
   (b) What are fiscal policy instruments?
   (c) What are monetary policy instruments?

3. (a) Explain the policy advise of the monetarist.
   (b) What is the main instrument of macroeconomic policy for the monetarist? Explain.

4. What type of monetarist policy has been pursued by the Bank of Japan since 1978?

5. Explain the policy advice of activists.

6. The essence of the dispute between activists and monetarists turns on the question of information and the use that may be made of new information. Explain these assertions.

7. Why is nominal GDP targetting most useful for coping with aggregate supply shocks?

8. What are econometric models?

9. What are the consequences of following an activist policy in the face of an aggregate supply shock?

10. What are the three steps involved in macroeconomic stabilization policy?

11. What is the theory of aggregate demand based on?

12. (a) How did the U.S. economy perform during the Kennedy years?
    (b) What happened to GDP?
    (c) Did unemployment rise or decline?
    (d) Did inflation accelerate, remain stable, or go lower?

13. What are the main targets of macroeconomics stabilization policy?

14. What are the main ingredients of monetarists policy advice?

15. What are the main ingredients of activist policy advice?

16. What is nominal GDP targetting?

17. What is the main argument against nominal GDP targetting?

Problem Solving

How does it go?

You are given the following information about Hibiscus Island's long-run aggregate supply, short-run aggregate supply, and aggregate demand:

$$y = 750 \tag{14.1}$$
$$y^s = 150P \tag{14.2}$$
$$y^d = 150M/P + e. \tag{14.3}$$

The expected value of e is zero.

(a) Calculate the long-run level of real GDP.

> In the long run, the economy is on its long-run aggregate supply curve. So, the long-run level of real GDP is 750.

(b) Calculate the rational expectation of the price level.

> The rational expectation of the price level is equal to the price level at which the *LAS* curve intersects the *SAS* curve. Therefore solving Equations (10.1) and (10.2) for P gives an expected price level of 5.

(c) Calculate equilibrium real GDP if the value of e is 25.

> Before the equilibrium value of real GDP can be found, it is necessary to calculate the expected money supply. The expected aggregate demand curve intersects the long-run aggregate supply curve at the expected price level.

> The expected price level is 5, long-run real GDP is 750 and the expected shock is 0. Substituting for P, y, and e in Equation (14.3) gives a money supply of 25.

> Therefore the equation to the aggregate demand curve before the shock hits is

$$y^d = 3,750/P.$$

> Once the shock hits the aggregate demand curve becomes

$$y^d = 3,750/P + 25. \tag{14.4}$$

Equilibrium real GDP is determined by the intersection of the aggregate demand and short-run aggregate supply curves. Solving Equations (14.4) and (14.2) for y gives the equilibrium real GDP equal to 762.6.

(d) Calculate the equilibrium price level if the value of e is 25.

> At the equilibrium, real GDP is 762.6. Substituting for y in either the aggregate demand or the aggregate supply curves gives a price level of 5.08.

Now try these

Fact 14.1 You are given the following information about Hibiscus Island's long-run aggregate supply, short-run aggregate supply, and expected aggregate demand:

$$y = 1000$$
$$y^s = 100P$$
$$y^d = 100M/P + e.$$

The expected value of e is zero.

1. Use Fact 14.1. Calculate long-run equilibrium real GDP.

2. Use Fact 14.1. Calculate the rational expectation of the price level.

3. Use Fact 14.1. Calculate equilibrium real GDP if the value of e is 50.

4. Use Fact 14.1. Calculate the equilibrium price level if the value of e is 50.

5. Use Fact 14.1. Calculate equilibrium real GDP if policy responds by decreasing the money supply so as to offset the effect of e on aggregate demand.

6. Use Fact 14.1. If monetary policy operates with a one period time lag, calculate equilibrium real GDP in the next period following the shock that increases *e* to 50 if the money supply is decreased to offset the effect of *e* on aggregate demand and if the shock to *e* is temporary and in the next period is equal to 0.

7. Use Fact 14.1. Calculate the equilibrium price level in the situation described in the Problem 6.

8. Does real GDP fluctuate most in Problems 5 and 6 or in the case in which the money supply is held constant.

9. Does the price level fluctuate most in Problems 5 and 6 or in the case in which the money supply is held constant.

10. In Problems 5 to 8, which policies are activist and which are monetarist?

✓ Answers

Concept Review

1) nominal GDP
2) policy targets
3) target variables
4) policy instruments
5) macroeconomic indicators
6) the same regardless
7) feedback
8) reacts to
9) according to a fixed formula
10) an econometric model

True or False

1) T	5) T	9) T	13) F	17) T
2) F	6) T	10) T	14) F	18) T
3) F	7) T	11) F	15) T	19) F
4) F	8) F	12) F	16) F	20) T

Multiple Choice

1) e	5) c	9) b	13) b	17) e
2) e	6) e	10) d	14) b	18) b
3) d	7) e	11) b	15) b	19) e
4) c	8) e	12) c	16) c	20) b

Short Answer Questions

1. Macroeconomic indicators are variables that provide information, on a frequent basis, about the current state and direction of the economy. The main daily indicators are interest rates, stock prices, and exchange rates. The main monthly indicators include the money supply, unemployment, consumer prices, industrial production, new housing starts, and retail sales.

2. (a) Macroeconomic policy instruments are variables manipulated by the government or the Bank of Canada to influence macroeconomic policy targets.
(b) Fiscal policy instruments are government purchases of goods and services, transfer payments, and taxes.
(c) Monetary policy instruments are the monetary base and bank's reserve requirements.

3. (a) Monetarists offer the following policy advise. First, to set government purchases, transfer payments, and taxes at levels that achieve an efficient allocation of resources and a fair distribution of income and wealth. (Fairness, an

ethical concept, has to be determined by an economic analyst.) Second, to let the foreign exchange rate be flexible and pay no attention to the current account balance. Third, to make the money supply grow at a constant rate.

(b) The main instrument of macroeconomic policy for the monetarist is the money supply. Monetarists advocate setting the growth rate of a monetary aggregate (either the monetary base or one of the broader monetary aggregates such as M1 or M2) so that, on the average, the inflation rate will be zero. This money supply growth rate can be computed as the growth rate of real GDP multiplied by the income elasticity of the demand for money minus the long-term growth in the velocity of circulation of money. Once calculated, monetarists advocate, the chosen monetary aggregate should be made to grow at the predetermined rate with no deviation from it, regardless of the state of the economy, the state of the government's budget, or any other economic factor.

4. Since 1978, the Bank of Japan has pursued a monetarist policy of targetting the growth rate of a monetary aggregate and keeping its actual growth rate close to the target. The particular monetary aggregate targetted is a broad one, it is M2 plus certificates of deposit (CDs).

5. Activists advice states that if real GDP is (or is forecasted to be) below its full-employment equilibrium level, increase aggregate demand by increasing the money supply, increasing government purchasing of goods and services, or cutting taxes. Alternatively, if real GDP is (or is forecasted to be) above its

full-employment level, decrease aggregate demand by decreasing the money supply, decreasing government purchases of goods and services, or increasing taxes.

6. The monetarist asserts that the Bank of Canada has no information advantage over private agents and that it can do nothing that private agents will not do for themselves. Any attempt by the Bank of Canada to fine-tune or stabilize the economy by making the money supply react to previous shocks everybody knows about will not keep real GDP any closer to its full-employment level and will make the price level more variable.

Activists assert that the Bank of Canada has an effective informational advantage. They agree that individuals form their expectations rationally, using all the information available to them. But they also assert that individuals get locked into contracts based on expectations of the price level that, after an aggregate demand shock, turn out to be wrong. The Bank of Canada can act after private agents have tied themselves into contractual arrangements based on a wrong price level expectation to compensate for and offset the effects of those random shocks.

7. Nominal GDP targetting is most useful for coping with aggregate supply shocks because it imposes discipline on the capacity of the economy to respond without an unending burst of inflation.

8. Econometric models are statistical descriptions of the economy that could be used to study the effects of alternative policies before they were implemented.

9. Initially, policy leads to inflation but no decrease in real GDP or employment. Subsequently, if the shock is temporary, the economy returns to its initial equilibrium. If the shock is permanent, prices rise further. At some point, once it has been recognized that the shock is permanent, real GDP will be permitted to decrease to its new long-run equilibrium level but at a higher price level.

10. First, formulating the objectives as the values of the policy target variables. Second, undertaking research to discover stable policy-invariant relationship among the variables. Third, choosing the setting and the rules governing changes in the policy instrument.

11. The theory of aggregate demand is based on theories of consumption, investment, the demand for money, and international trade and capital flows.

13. Low and stable unemployment, high and stable real GDP growth, the moderate current account balance, and low and steady inflation.

14. 1. Set government purchases, transfer payments and taxes at levels that achieve an efficient allocation of resources and a fair distribution of income and wealth.
    2. Let the foreign exchange rate adjust and pay no attention to the current account balance.
    3. Make the money supply grow at a constant rate.

3. 1. If real GDP is forecasted to be below its full-employment level, increase aggregate demand by increasing the money supply, increasing government purchases, or cutting taxes.

2. If real GDP is forecasted to be above its full-employment level, decrease aggregate demand by decreasing the money supply, decreasing government purchases, or increasing taxes.

4. Seeking to keep nominal GDP growth inside a predetermined target range.

5. The time lags in the operation of monetary are believed by some economists to be too long for effective nominal GDP targetting to be undertaken.

Problems

1. 1,000.
2. 10.
3. 1052.31.
4. 10.25.
5. 1,000.
6. 975.31.
7. 9.75.
8. Problem 6 and monetarist policy give the same fluctuations in real GDP.
9. Problem 6 gives the largest fluctuations in the price level.
10. Problems 5 and 6 are activist.

CHAPTER 15

Stabilizing the Canadian Economy

Perspective and Focus

The previous chapter studies some general issues concerning stabilization policy. This chapter focuses on the specific problems of stabilizing the Canadian economy. Its describes the Bank of Canada and the tools at its disposal. It then examines the alternative policies that can be pursued by the Bank of Canada so as to keep real GNP growth stable and inflation under control. And like previous chapters, it builds on the *IS-LM* framework.

Learning Objectives

After studying this chapter, you will be able to:

- Describe the balance sheet of the Bank of Canada and chartered banks and define various monetary aggregates
- Describe the policy instruments available to the Bank of Canada
- Explain how open market operations influence the money supply and interest rates
- Explain the difference between money supply targetting and interest rate targetting
- Explain the lags in the operations of the Bank of Canada's monetary policy
- Describe the Bank of Canada's evolving policies between 1962 and 1991

Increasing Your Productivity

This chapter, like the previous one, is not heavy on new analytical material. It applies and extends the *IS-LM* model of aggregate demand. It does so, however, with a new twist and being aware of the new twist will allow you to make progress more easily. The new twist is money supply targetting versus interest rate targetting.

If the central bank targets the interest rate, its action makes the supply of money perfectly elastic at its targetted interest rate. The effect of such an action is to make the *LM* curve irrelevant for the determination of equilibrium in the *IS-LM* framework. Instead, equilibrium is determined at the point of intersection of the *IS* curve and the target interest rate. Once you have understood this fact, the comparison of interest rate targetting and money supply targetting is very straightforward. In one case you are studying the predictions from the *IS-LM* model, and in the other case you are studying the predictions of a model in which only the *IS* curve and fixed interest rate are relevant. In effect, you are comparing the *IS-LM* model and the aggregate expenditure model of Chapter 4.

An implication of interest rate targetting is that the aggregate demand is vertical. To appreciate this outcome, just think about the effect on the money market of a change in the price level. Other things being equal, a change in the price level changes the real money supply and the interest rate. Since the Bank of Canada is pegging the interest at its target level, the money supply adjusts automatically to compensate for any change in the price level. As a result, the real money supply does not change. With no change in the real money supply, there is no change in the real GNP, so the *AD* curve is vertical. The *AD* curve shifts if there is a *change* in the target interest rate because the resulting change in the interest rate brings a change in aggregate expenditure.

Self Test

Concept Review

1. Impact effects are _____ effects of policy actions on _____ or _____.

2. Reserves held by the banks in excess of their required reserves and reserves borrowed from the Bank of Canada are called _____ _____.

3. The interest rate paid by banks when they borrow from the Bank of Canada is the _____ _____.

4. Bank reserves consist of deposits made by _____ at _____, together with _____ held by the banks.

5. Total bank reserves minus those borrowed from the Bank of Canada are called _____.

6. The money multiplier is equal to the change in _____ divided by the change in the monetary base.

7. Total bank reserves is the sum of _____, _____ and _____.

8. Monetary base is the sum of _____ and _____ held by _____.

9. The long drawn-out effects of a policy action are the _____ effects.

10. When the Bank of Canada buys or sells government securities to the public it undertakes _____ _____. As a result the _____ changes.

11. Note and coins held by households and firms is called _____ _____.

12. _____ are minimum percentage of deposits that _____ can hold.

13. The money supply that is the sum of currency held by the public plus demand deposits at the chartered banks is _____.

14. The money supply that is the sum of currency held by the public plus demand deposits, savings deposits, and personal notice deposits is _____.

True or False

1. An independent central banks is a national institution that formulates and conducts monetary policy within the legal framework that established it. Furthermore, it answers t the government on a day-to-day basis for its conduct of policy.

2. Bank rate is the interest rate paid by chartered banks when they borrow from the Bank of Canada.

3. The Bank of Canada can influence the money supply by influencing the supply of monetary base by adjusting reserve requirements.

4. Reserve requirements are rules stating the minimum percentages of bank deposits that banks must keep as reserves (as deposits at the Bank of Canada or as currency in its vault.

5. Effectiveness lags are the time lapses from the implementation of a policy action to its effects on the target variables.

6. Dynamic effects are the instantaneous effects of policy actions on indicators or targets.

7. The time lags in the operation of monetary policy are not only long but also variable.

8. The money multiplier is the change in the money supply per one-dollar change in the monetary base.

9. The act under which the Bank of Canada operates has not changed since the bank was created in 1935.

10. The Bank of Canada can increase the monetary base with an open market purchase of securities or by lowering the bank rate, thereby encouraging banks to borrow additional reserves.

11. Currency held by the public is part of M1 but not part of the monetary base.

12. An open market purchase of securities by the Bank of Canada decreases the monetary base.

13. The larger the percentage of the money supply held as currency, the smaller is the money multiplier.

14. By targetting interest rates rather than the money supply, the Bank of canada can prevent instability in the demand for money from effecting aggregate demand.

15. By targetting the interest rate rather than the money supply, the Bank of Canada can prevent fluctuations in investment from influencing aggregate demand.

16. By targetting the money supply rather than interest rates, the Bank of Canada can narrow the range of fluctuations in aggregate demand arising from instability in the demand for money function.

17. By targetting interest rates rather than the money supply, the Bank of Canada makes aggregate demand more elastic.

18. Interest rate targetting causes inflation if the interest rate target is set too low.

19. If the Bank of Canada could make its decision more quickly, then there would be no major time lags in the operation of monetary policy.

20. Financial innovation that decreases the demand for money increases aggregate demand.

Multiple Choice

1. The Bank of Canada was created in
   (a) 1925.
   (b) 1935.
   (c) 1945.
   (d) 1899.
   (e) 1933.

2. The monetary base consists of
   (a) bank deposits at the Bank of Canada.
   (b) the sum of bank reserves and currency held by the public.
   (c) the money supply.
   (d) government securities held by the Bank of Canada.
   (e) gold and special drawing rights (SDRs) held by the Bank of Canada.

3. Bank of Canada's main instruments for influencing the money supply include
   (a) printing money.
   (b) reserve requirements.
   (c) the purchasing and selling of government securities.
   (d) both (b) and (c).
   (e) all of the above.

4. The interest rate on short-term loans made by one bank to another banks is known as the
   (a) discount rate.
   (b) bank rate.
   (c) transactions rate.
   (d) reserve rate.
   (e) current rate.

5. The bank rate
   (a) is determined by the Finance Minister.
   (b) can be manipulated by the Bank of Canada in order to regulate the volume of loans to banks.
   (c) is administered by the government.
   (d) is the interest rate on short-term loans between banks.
   (e) none of the above.

6. Free reserves are equal to
   (a) total reserves − (required reserves + borrowed reserves).
   (b) total reserves − (required reserves − borrowed reserves).
   (c) required reserves + borrowed reserves.
   (d) total reserves − borrowed reserves.
   (e) total reserves − required reserves.

7. An increase in the bank rate
   (a) increases the demand for reserves.
   (b) increases the monetary base.
   (c) decreases the demand for reserves.
   (d) increases the money supply.
   (e) none of the above.

8. The Bank of Canada's most important assets include
   (a) gold.
   (b) Special Drawing Rights (SDRs).
   (c) government securities.
   (d) both (a) and (c).
   (e) all of the above.

9. The Bank of Canada can decrease the monetary base by
   (a) increasing the bank rate or making an open market purchase.
   (b) increasing the bank rate or making an open market sale.
   (c) decreasing the bank rate or making an open market purchase.
   (d) decreasing the bank rate or making an open market sale.
   (e) none of the above

10. If the Bank of Canada decreases required reserves, the
    (a) money supply increases.
    (b) money supply decreases.
    (c) monetary base increases.
    (d) neither the monetary base nor the money supply increases.
    (e) both the monetary base and the money supply increase.

11. The monetary base includes
    (a) demand deposits held by the public.
    (b) demand deposits held by the government.
    (c) currency held by the public.
    (d) government securities.
    (e) all the liabilities of the Bank of Canada.

12. All of the following actions by the bank of Canada will have the effect of increasing the monetary base *except*
    (a) an open market purchase of securities.
    (b) a decrease in the bank rate.
    (c) a decrease in reserve requirements.
    (d) the sale of government securities to chartered banks.
    (e) the purchase of government securities from chartered banks.

13. Other things being equal, the money multiplier is larger,
    (a) the larger is the currency to deposit ratio.
    (b) the larger is the banks required ratio.
    (c) the smaller is the currency to deposit ratio.
    (d) the larger is the sum of the currency to deposit ratio and the banks required reserve ratio.
    (e) the larger is an open market operation.

14. Targetting the interest rate
    (a) increases the fluctuations in the amount of money held.
    (b) increases fluctuations in investment.
    (c) decreases fluctuations in consumption.
    (d) increases fluctuations in aggregate demand.
    (e) both (a) and (b).

15. Shocks to the *IS* curve can be effectively reduced by
    (a) interest rate targetting.
    (b) money supply targetting.
    (c) increasing the money supply whenever there is a positive shock to investment.
    (d) cutting interest rates when spending increases.
    (e) none of the above.

16. With money supply targetting, a financial innovation that decreases the demand for money,
    (a) increases the interest rate and decreases real GDP.
    (b) decreases the interest rate and increases real GDP.
    (c) decreases the interest rate and increases real GDP.
    (d) increases the interest rate and increases real GDP.
    (e) has an ambiguous effect on the interest rate and real GDP.

17. With interest rate targetting, a decrease in the target interest rate
    (a) increases aggregate demand.
    (b) results in a movement along the aggregate demand curve.
    (c) increases aggregate supply.
    (d) increases short-run aggregate supply but not long-run aggregate supply.
    (e) increases investment but decreases consumption.

18. If the interest rate is targetted and the target interest rate is below its full-employment level
    (a) the price level begins to rise, decreasing aggregate demand and decreasing real GDP to its full-employment level.
    (b) the price level begins to increase but aggregate supply falls.
    (c) real GDP and the price level both decrease.
    (d) the price level increases without limit but real GDP returns to its long-run aggregate supply level.
    (e) the price level begins to increase without limit and real GDP remains above its long-run level.

19. With interest rate targetting,
    (a) an increase in the demand for money has a larger effect on real GDP and the price level than it does with money supply targetting.
    (b) a decrease in the demand for money has a smaller effect on real GDP and the price level than it does with money supply targeting.
    (c) an increase in investment demand has a smaller effect on real GDP and the price level than it does with money supply targetting.
    (d) an increase in consumption demand has a smaller effect on real GDP and price level than it does with money supply targetting.
    (e) a decrease in short-run aggregate supply has a larger effect on real GDP than it does with money supply targetting.

20. Double-digit inflation was eliminated in the early 1980s because the Bank of Canada
    (a) stuck to its money supply growth targets.
    (b) pursued interest rate targetting and brought interest rates down.
    (c) tightened monetary policy undershooting the money supply growth targets.
    (d) abandoned open market operations.
    (e) ordered the banks to stop lending.

Short Answers Questions

1. In what year was the Bank of Canada establish? In what year was the current Bank of Canada Act was passed by parliament?

2. What is the bank rate?

3. What are the two stages in the effectiveness lags. Explain each stage.

4. (a) What instruments does the Bank of Canada use for monetary control?
   (b) Which instrument is the most important one?

5. Explain what the size of the money supply depends on.

6. Explain the difference between nonborrowed reserves and free reserves.

7. Describe the effects resulting from an increase in the bank rate.

8. If the bank of Canada wants to adopt an expansionary monetary policy, what are its options?

9. Explain how an open market operation changes the money supply.

10. What is the money multiplier.

11. Why might interest rate targetting be superior to money supply targetting?

12. In what circumstances is money supply targetting superior to interest rate targetting?

13. What is the main danger in interest rate targetting?

14. What are the main time lags in the operation of monetary policy?

Problem Solving

How does it go?

You have the following information about Green Island in 1991:

Currency held by public	$10 million
Bank reserves	$5 million
M1	$110 million

(a) Calculate Green Island's monetary base in 1991.

> The monetary base is equal to the total liabilities of the Bank of Canada. Those liabilities are banks' deposits with the Bank of Canada plus the currency outside the Bank of Canada.
>
> Bank reserves consist of the banks' deposits with the Bank of Canada plus the currency that they hold. So bank reserves is the part of the monetary base that banks hold.
>
> But households and firms (the public) also hold part of the monetary base—the currency that they hold.

Therefore the monetary base is the sum of bank reserves and currency held by the public. It is equal to $10 million plus $5 million, which is $15 million.

(b) Calculate the amount of demand deposits in 1991.

> The currency held by the public plus demand deposits equals M1. Therefore the amount of demand deposits is $110 million minus $10 million, which is $100 million.

(c) Calculate the money multiplier.

> The money multiplier is $(1 + a)$ divided by $(1 + b)$, where a is the proportion of deposits that the public holds as currency and b is the proportion of deposits that banks hold as reserves. On Green Island, a is 0.1 and b is 0.05. The money multiplier is 1.1/1.05, which is 1.048.

Now try these

1. On Coral Island, the public holds $5,000 of currency, banks hold $10,000 of reserves, and the public holds $20,000 in demand deposits.
   (a) Calculate the money supply.
   (b) Calculate the monetary base.

2. You are given the following information about Space World:

Demand deposits	$20 million
Foreign exchange reserves	$1 million
Currency held by the public	$15 million
Gold reserves	$1 million
Savings deposits	$10 million
Eurodollar deposits	$1 million
Money market mutual fund shares	$2 million

(a) Calculate M1.
(b) Calculate M2.

Fact 15.1

| | Year | |
	1992	1993
Currency held by public	150	180
Bank reserves	50	60
M1	1150	1380

3. Use Fact 15.1.
   (a) Calculate the monetary base in 1992 and 1993.
   (b) Calculate the change in the monetary base.
   (c) Calculate the amount of demand deposits in 1992 and 1993.
   (d) Calculate the money multiplier.

4. Use Fact 15.1. The central bank conducts an open market purchase of government securities in 1994 of 50.

   Calculate the 1994 values of
   (a) M1.
   (b) the amount of currency held by the public.
   (c) The amount of demand deposits.
   (d) the amount of bank reserves.

Fact 15.2 You are given the following information about an economy:

$$c = 100 + 0.9(y - t)$$
$$i = 50 - 50r + e_1$$
$$g = 100$$
$$t = 100$$
$$M/P = 0.15y + 50 - 50r + e_2$$
$$M = 500$$
$$P = 1.$$

e_1 is a random shock to investment demand and e_2 is a random shock to the demand for money.

5. Use Fact 15.2. Calculate
   (a) the multiplier effect on aggregate demand of a random shock to investment demand with interest rate targetting.
   (b) of a random shock to investment demand with money supply targetting.
   (c) a random shock to the demand for money with money supply targetting.
   (d) a random shock to the demand for money with interest rate targetting.

6. Use Fact 15.2. Calculate
   (a) the slope of the aggregate demand curve at the equilibrium point with money supply targetting.
   (b) the slope of the aggregate demand curve at the equilibrium point with interest rate targetting

✓ Answers

Concept Review

1) instantaneous, indicators, targets
2) free reserves
3) bank rate
4) banks, the Bank of Canada, currency
5) nonborrowed reserves
6) money supply, monetary base
7) free reserves, borrowed reserves, required reserves
8) bank reserves, currency, the public
9) dynamic
10) an open market operation
11) currency in circulation
12) reserve requirements, banks
13) M1
14) M2

True or False

1) F	5) T	9) F	13) T	17) F
2) F	6) F	10) T	14) T	18) T
3) F	7) T	11) F	15) F	19) F
4) T	8) T	12) F	16) F	20) T

Multiple Choice

1) b	5) b	9) d	13) c	17) a
2) b	6) a	10) a	14) e	18) e
3) d	7) c	11) c	15) d	19) b
4) b	8) c	12) d	16) b	20) c

Short Answer Questions

1. The Bank of Canada was established in 1935. The current Bank of Canada Act was passed by parliament in 1967.

2. Bank rate is the interest paid by chartered banks when they borrow from the Bank of Canada.

3. The two stages are the impact effects and the dynamic effects. Impact effects are the instantaneous effects of policy actions on indicators or targets. Dynamic effects are the drawn-out effects that take place as households and firms respond to policy actions.

4. (a) The three main instruments of monetary control are open market operations, bank rate, and reserve requirements.

    (b) Open market operations are the most important and most frequently used instrument.

5. The size of the money supply depends partly on the actions of the Bank of Canada and partly on the response of the chartered banks as well as the general public.

6. Nonborrowed reserves are total bank reserves minus reserves borrowed from the bank of Canada. Free reserves are the reserves held by banks in excess of their required reserves and reserves borrowed from the Bank of Canada.

7. An increase in the bank rate influences the amount of borrowing from the Bank of Canada. Furthermore, if a bank borrows from the Bank of Canada, the monetary base increases by the amount borrowed.

8. The Bank of Canada can purchase government securities, lower reserve requirements, and lower the bank rate.

9. An open market purchase by the Bank of Canada increases the monetary base. Banks reserves increase and they increase lending. The increased lending increases the money supply and lowers interest rates. Lower interest rates stimulate spending, so aggregate demand increases. With higher aggregate demand real GDP and the price level rise. There are long and variable time lags in the effects of an open market operation on real GDP and the price level.

10. The money multiplier is the amount by which a change in the monetary base is multiplied to calculate the resulting change in the money supply. The money multiplier equals one plus the currency to deposit ratio divided by the sum of the currency to deposit ratio and the banks' reserve ratio.

11. If the instability in the demand for money is large and instability in investment demand is small, then fluctuations in aggregate demand can be reduced by targetting interest rates.

12. If most of the instability in aggregate demand arises from fluctuations in investment, these fluctuations can be moderated by controlling the money supply and permitting the interest rate to fluctuation to counter the fluctuations in investment.

13. The main danger in interest rate targetting is setting the interest rate too low. The consequence is runaway inflation.

14. The main time lags in the operation of monetary policy are an observation lag, an interpretation lag, a decision lag, an implementation lag, and an effectiveness lag.

Problems

1. (a) $25,000
   (b) $15,000

2. (a) $35 million
   (b) $48 million

3. (a) 200, 240
   (b) +40
   (c) 1,000, 1,200
   (d) 5.75

4. (a) 1,667.5
   (b) 217.5
   (c) 1,450.0
   (d) 72.5

5. (a) 10
   (b) 4
   (c) 10
   (d) 0

6. (a) −2,000
   (b) 0

CHAPTER 16

Stabilizing the World Economy

Perspective and Focus

This chapter broadens your vision away from the problems of the Canadian economy to the interactions among economies and the problems of the global economy.   This chapter builds on and makes use of the *IS-LM* model of the open economy that you studied in Chapter 7.

Learning Objectives

After studying this chapter, you will be able to:

- Describe the main trends and the global economy
- Describe the main features of the international monetary system
- Explain how exchange rates are determined
- Explain some of the major movements in the foreign exchange rates
- Explain how the balance of payments is determined
- Explain the main sources of balance of payments deficits and surpluses in recent years
- Explain the global business cycle and its international transmission

Increasing Your Productivity

One point in the analysis of this chapter that often causes students problems is the definition of the exchange rate. In this chapter, the exchange rate is defined as units of foreign currency per unit of domestic currency. The chapter uses yen and dollars, and the exchange rate is measured as yen per dollar. If the exchange rate goes down from 140 yen per dollar to 120 yen per dollar, the yen strengthens and the dollar weakens. A dollar costs a smaller number of yen and you get fewer yen for your dollar.

It is possible to define the exchange rate the other way around as dollars per yen. When the exchange rate is expressed as dollars per yen and its value increases, the dollar strengthens. When the exchange rate is expressed as dollars per yen and its value declines, the dollar weakens. (In an earlier printing of the textbook we inadvertently switched the definition of the exchange rate between Chapter 7 and this chapter. Be on your guard and always ask which way around is the exchange rate is being defined?)

Another potential stumbling block in this chapter has the concept *dollar denominated assets*. Financial assets can be denominated in any currency. The currency of denomination defines the units in which the asset will be repaid or redeemed. A Canadian dollar asset is one that is worth certain number of Canadian dollars. How much that asset will ultimately be worth in terms of Canadian dollars or Japanese yen depends on the exchange rate between the currencies. The currency of denomination defines the nature of the legal obligation being undertaken.

The third potential stumbling block in this chapter is the distinction between stocks and flows.

Dollars that flow across the foreign exchange market in either direction do not determine the price or value of the currency in terms of another currency. The demand for currency and the supply of currency are stock concepts. They are the demand for and supply of a stock of assets. Stocks are influenced by flows and flows result from changes in desired stocks. But it is the demand for a quantity of the dollar denominated assets to hold by domestic and foreign holders and the supply of dollar denominates assets that determine the equilibrium price of a dollar in the foreign exchange market.

With these concepts clear, you will have no difficulty with the analysis in this chapter.

Self Test

Concept Review

1. The time path of net exports following a major change in the exchange rate is a _____.

2. The set of institutional arrangements and institutions for governing the financial relations among countries is called _____.

3. A change in the value of a _____ exchange rate such that the currency is weaker is a _____.

4. A monetary system in which each currency is fixed in terms of gold and gold is freely traded between countries is called

    _____.

5. The _____
    is the quantity of _____
    _____ in
    Canadian dollars that people plan to
    hold at a given point in time.

6. The _____
    is the quantity of _____
    _____ in
    Canadian dollars that are available to
    be held at a given point in time.

7. An increase in the value of a _____ exchange rate such that the currency is stronger is a _____.

True or False

1. An international monetary system is a set of arrangements and institutions for governing the financial relations among countries.

2. Other things remaining constant, the lower the interest rate on dollar assets, the greater is the demand for dollar assets; the lower is the interest rate on yen assets, the lower is the demand for demand for dollar assets; the lower is the future exchange rate, the greater is the demand for dollar assets.

3. For a nation to make a credible revaluation of its currency, it must have a large enough stock of foreign exchange reserves to convince people that it can maintain the new higher value for its currency.

4. Under a managed float, speeding up or slowing down the growth rate of the money supply sets up the same dynamic overshooting adjustments as is done under flexible exchange rates.

5. A convenient method of taking into account the difference between U.S. and Japanese monetary policy is to define the monetary policy difference between Japan and the United States as (Japanese money growth + U.S. money growth) − (Japanese GDP growth + U.S. GDP growth).

6. Since a higher Canadian real exchange rate increases Canadian imports and decreases Canadian exports, Canadian net exports rise, resulting in a larger current account surplus or a smaller current account deficit.

7. A speed-up in the Canadian money supply growth will make the Canadian dollar depreciate, causing the real exchange rate to fall.

8. The International Monetary Fund provides assistance to countries with long-term balance of payment problems and the World Bank provides short-term financing to developing countries with intermittent shortages of foreign exchange.

9. The large net export deficit during the 1980s is well accounted for by the steady strengthening of the U.S. dollar in the first half of that decade. Continued increases in the net export deficit in 1986 subsequent to the beginning of the dollar depreciation is part of the *J*-curve phenomenon.

10. A decrease in the value of a fixed exchange rate is known a revaluation.

11. The Japanese yen depreciated more than most other currencies during the 1980s.

12. The international monetary system is based on fixed exchange rates.

13. Other things being equal, an increase in interest rates in the domestic economy causes an increase in the demand for a domestic currency.

14. With a fixed exchange rate, the supply of a currency is perfectly elastic.

15. Exchange rate fluctuations are smaller and balance of payments fluctuations larger with a fixed exchange rate than with a flexible exchange rate.

16. A depreciation of the domestic currency at first lowers net exports but eventually increases them resulting in a *J*-curve effect.

17. A decrease in income in the rest of the world has a larger effect on the domestic economy if the exchange rate is fixed than it does if the exchange rate is flexible.

18. A decrease in interest rates in the rest of the world increases real GDP in the domestic economy under flexible exchange rates but decreases real GDP in the domestic economy under fixed exchange rates.

19. A country can completely insulate itself from foreign supply shocks by having a flexible exchange rate.

20. The world business cycle became more synchronized in the 1970s and 1980s.

Multiple Choice

1. The global macroeconomy consists of some
   (a) four billion people residing in 300 countries.
   (b) five billion people living in 150 nations.
   (c) thirty billion people residing in 500 countries.
   (d) fifty billion people living in 100 countries.
   (e) one billion people residing in 50 countries.

2. The most important aspect of an international monetary system is its rules governing the determination of exchange rates. These include
   (a) fixed exchange rates.
   (b) flexible exchange rates.
   (c) managed-floating exchange rates.
   (d) both (a) and (b).
   (e) all the above.

3. Which of the following exchange rates does the monetary authority pay attention to in the foreign exchange market in an attempt to smooth out fluctuations in the exchange rate?   A
   (a) fixed exchange rate.
   (b) flexible exchange rate.
   (c) managed-floating exchange rate.
   (d) pegged exchange rate.
   (e) both (a) and (b).

4. With a flexible exchange rate, the quantity of dollar assets supplied
   (a) is independent of the actions of the Bank of Canada.
   (b) is not independent of the actions of the Bank of Canada.
   (c) may or may not be independent of the actions of the Bank of Canada.
   (d) is variable at any point in time.
   (e) none of the above.

5. Which of the following measures the price of domestic goods and services relative to foreign goods and services? The
   (a) Nominal Exchange Rate (NER).
   (b) Implicit Price Deflator (IPD).
   (c) Consumer Price Index (CPI).
   (d) Real Exchange Rate (RER).
   (e) none of the above.

6. Which of the following is the most important short-run influence on the real exchange rate? The
   (a) flexible exchange rate.
   (b) nominal exchange rate.
   (c) fixed exchange rate.
   (d) floating exchange rate.
   (e) pegged exchange rate.

7. The *IS* curve under
   (a) flexible exchange rates is steeper than under fixed exchange rates.
   (b) flexible exchange rates is less steep than under fixed exchange rates.
   (c) fixed exchange rates is less steep than under flexible exchange rates.
   (d) fixed exchange rates is as steep as under flexible exchange rates.
   (e) none of the above.

8. The time path followed by net exports following a major change in the exchange rate is depicted by the
   (a) *B*-curve.
   (b) *E*-curve.
   (c) *D*-curve.
   (d) *C*-curve.
   (e) *J*-curve.

9. The international monetary system of the 1990s is a
   (a) fixed exchange system.
   (b) flexible exchange system.
   (c) managed-floating system.
   (d) pegged exchange system.
   (e) gold standard system.

10. The supply curve under fixed exchange rates is
    (a) vertical at the chosen value for the exchange rate.
    (b) horizontal at the chosen value for the exchange rate.
    (c) upward sloping at the chosen value for the exchange rate.
    (d) downward sloping at the chosen value for the exchange rate.
    (e) none of the above.

11. If the domestic interest rate is 10 percent and the foreign interest rate is 5 percent, the domestic currency is expected to
    (a) appreciate.
    (b) depreciate.
    (c) remain constant.
    (d) rise at first but then fall.
    (e) fall at first but then rise.

12. Each of the following results in an increase in the demand for dollar-denominated assets *except*
    (a) an increase in the interest rate on dollar-denominated assets.
    (b) a decrease in the interest rate on yen-denominated assets.
    (c) an expectation that the dollar will strengthen against the yen.
    (d) an expectation that the interest rate on yen-denominated assets will increase.
    (e) a combination of the above factors.

13. The slope of the supply of dollar-denominated assets curve depends on the exchange rate regime and
    (a) is more elastic with a fixed exchange rate than a managed-floating exchange rate.
    (b) is more elastic with a flexible exchange rate than a managed-floating exchange rate.
    (c) is more elastic with a managed-floating exchange rate than a fixed exchange rate.

    (d) can sometimes be more elastic with a managed-floating exchange rate than with a fixed exchange rate.
    (e) varies from day to day depending on the actions on the central bank.

14. Compared with a fixed exchange rate, a managed-floating exchange rate regime results in
    (a) smaller fluctuations in the exchange rate.
    (b) smaller fluctuations in the quantity of dollar-denominated assets.
    (c) larger fluctuations in the exchange rate.
    (d) larger fluctuations in the supply of dollar-denominated assets.
    (e) both (b) and (c).

15. Compared with a flexible exchange rate regime, under a managed-floating exchange rate regime
    (a) the exchange rate fluctuates by more.
    (b) the exchange rate fluctuates by less.
    (c) it is not possible to say whether the exchange rate fluctuates by more or less.
    (d) there are large fluctuations in the quantity of dollar-denominated assets outstanding.
    (e) both (b) and (d).

16. If the supply of dollar-denominated assets decreases, then with a flexible exchange rate system, the currency
    (a) appreciates but initially by less than it eventually appreciates.
    (b) does not change until the balance of payments adjusts.
    (c) depreciates but initially by more than it eventually depreciates.
    (d) appreciates but initially by more than it eventually appreciates.
    (e) could appreciate or depreciate depending on expectations.

17. Under flexible exchange rates with perfect capital mobility, a decrease in income in the rest of the world
    (a) does not decrease domestic income because the exchange rate adjusts.
    (b) results in a lower domestic interest rates.
    (c) results in permanently lower domestic interest rates but no change in real GDP.
    (d) results in a permanent decrease in domestic interest rates and decrease in real GDP.
    (e) results in a temporary decrease in domestic interest rates and a fall in real GDP.

18. With perfect international capital mobility, a decrease in world interest rates
    (a) decreases real GDP under flexible exchange rates and increases real GDP under fixed exchange rates.
    (b) decreases domestic real GDP under fixed exchanges and increases domestic real GDP under flexible exchange rates.
    (c) increases domestic real GDP under flexible exchange rates and increases it under fixed exchange rates.
    (d) has no effect on domestic real GDP regardless of the exchange rate regime.
    (e) decreases domestic real GDP under flexible exchange rates and decreases it under fixed exchange rates.

19. The international business cycle
    (a) was more synchronized under the fixed exchange rate period of the 1960s than in later decades.
    (b) was more synchronized in the 1970s when exchange rates were flexible.
    (c) was more synchronized in the 1980s when exchange rates were flexible.
    (d) converged to a single cycle by 1990.
    (e) demonstrates the power of flexible exchange rates to isolate economies from the problems of others.

20. With a fixed exchange rate, the quantity of Canadian dollar assets supplied
    (a) is independent of the actions of the Bank of Canada.
    (b) is not independent of the actions of the Bank of Canada.
    (c) may or may not be independent of the actions of the Bank of Canada.
    (d) is variable at any point in time.
    (e) none of the above.

Short Answers Questions

1. Distinguish between devaluation and revaluation of a currency?

2. What are Canadian dollar-denominated assets? Give some examples.

3. What is one of the most important influences on the demand for dollar assets?

4. Explain the role of the monetary authority with a
   (a) fixed exchange rate.
   (b) flexible exchange rate.
   (c) managed-floating exchange rate.

5. (a) What is meant by the quantity of dollar assets supplied?
   (b) What is meant by the supply of dollar assets?

6. The official settlements account of the balance of payments records the transactions by the monetary authority in the foreign exchange market. That is, it records the net intervention by the monetary authority in the foreign exchange market.

   How does the monetary authority influence the balance of payments by its intervention?

7. Why is it possible that the world economy will be less stable under flexible exchange rates than under fixed exchange rates?

8. What was the Bretton Woods system?

9. What have been the main trends in world exports between 1960 and 1990?

10. What is interest rate parity?

11. What is the *J*-curve?.

12. Explain how a flexible exchange rate limits the effects of foreign aggregate demand shocks on the domestic economy.

Problem Solving

How does it go?

Jodi has $1,000. By holding dollar assets, she can get a return of 8 percent a year. At the same time, the interest rate on yen assets is 3 percent a year. The exchange rate is 230 yen per dollar today and is expected to be 219 yen per dollar one year from today.

(a) What is Jodi's rate of return if she holds her $1,000 in dollar assets for one year?

   If she holds her $1,000 in dollar assets her rate of return will be 8 percent a year.

(b) What is her expected rate of return on yen assets if she holds her $1,000 in yen assets for one year?

   If she holds her $1,000 in yen for the year, she must initially convert her dollars at the spot exchange rate. Doing this gives her 230,000 yen. At the end of the year she will have 230,000(1 + 0.03), or 236,900 yen. But she will then have to convert the yen back into dollars. She expects that when she does this she will have 236,900/219, or 1,081.74 dollars. Her expected rate of return is (1.081.74 − 1.000)/1,000, which is 8.174 percent a year.

Now try these

1. Assuming that you have $100. By holding dollar assets, you can get a return of 10 percent a year. At the same time, the interest rate on yen assets is 5 percent a year. The exchange rate is 130 yen per dollar today and is expected to be 120 yen per dollar one year from today.
   (a) What is your rate of return if you hold $100 in dollar assets for one year from now?
   (b) What is your expected rate of return on yen assets one year from now if you hold $100 in yen assets for one year from today?

2. When the number of yen per dollar decreases, what effect does it have on the
   (a) dollar?
   (b) yen?

3. Random fluctuations in the demand for dollar assets lead to random fluctuations in the exchange rate and/or in the quantity of dollar assets in existence.
   How do fluctuations in the exchange rate and the quantity of dollar assets in existence compare under a
   (a) fixed exchange rate regime?
   (b) flexible exchange rate regime?
   (c) managed-floating exchange rate regime?

4. (a) How does the exchange rate influence the balance of payments?
   (b) How does the balance of payments influence the exchange rate?

Fact 16.1 You are given the following information:

Interest rate in Japan   3 percent a year
Interest rate in Canada   10 percent a year
Exchange rate   150 yen per dollar

5. Use Fact 16.1. Calculate
   (a) the expected exchange rate one year in the future.
   (b) the expected rate of return for a Canadian investing in Japan when the yen are converted to dollars.
   (c) the expected rate of return for a Japanese investing in Canada when the dollars are converted into Japanese yen.
   (d) the expected rate of appreciation or depreciation of the dollar against the yen.

6. If Canada tries to establish a fixed exchange rate at a rate higher than what the market believes can be sustained, what will happen to the exchange rate and to Canadian foreign exchange reserves?

7. Explain why an increase in the stock of dollar-denominated assets leads to a depreciation of the currency under flexible exchange rates and why, in the process, the exchange rate undershoots its long-run equilibrium value.

8. What is the *J*-curve effect and why does it occur?

9. Explain how an increase in world real GDP is transmitted to the domestic economy
   (a) Under fixed exchange rates.
   (b) Under flexible exchange rates.

✓ Answers

Concept Review

1) *J*-curve
2) international monetary system
3) fixed, devaluation
4) international gold standard
5) quantity of dollar assets demanded
6) quantity of dollar assets supplied
7) fixed, revaluation

True or False

1) T	5) F	9) T	13) T	17) T
2) F	6) F	10) F	14) T	18) F
3) T	7) F	11) T	15) T	19) F
4) T	8) F	12) F	16) T	20) T

Multiple Choice

1) b	5) d	9) c	13) a	17) a
2) e	6) b	10) b	14) e	18) a
3) c	7) b	11) b	15) e	19) b
4) b	8) e	12) d	16) d	20) a

Short Answer Questions

1. A devaluation is the decrease in the fixed exchange rate of a currency and a revaluation is the increase in the fixed exchange rate of a currency.

2. Canadian dollar-denominated assets are promises to pay so many Canadian dollars under given circumstance on a given date. Bank of Canada notes, the monetary base, M1, M2, M3, and Canadian government debt held by the public.

3. One of the most important influences on the demand for dollar assets is the expected future exchange rate.

4. (a) Under a fixed exchange rate, the monetary authority pegs the foreign currency price of the domestic currency and stands ready to buy or sell foreign assets in exchange for domestic assets.
    (b) Under a flexible exchange rate, the monetary authority pays no attention to the foreign exchange value of its currency. There is a given quantity of dollar assets in existence and this quantity is independent of the exchange rate.
    (c) Under a managed-floating exchange rate, the monetary authority pays attention to the foreign exchange market and attempts to smooth out fluctuations in the exchange rate. To do this, it increases the quantity of dollar assets supplied when the dollar appreciates and decreases the quantity supplied when the dollar depreciates.

5. (a) The quantity of Canadian dollar assets supplied is the quantity of net financial assets denominated in Canadian dollars available to be held at a point in time.
    (b) The supply of Canadian dollar assets is the relationship between the quantity of dollar assets supplied and the exchange rate.

6. A decision to use foreign reserves to buy dollar assets worsens the balance of payments. A decision to use dollar assets to buy foreign reserves improves the balance of payments.

7. Under flexible exchange rates, the exchange rate can overshoot changes in the real exchange rate. Such changes in the real exchange rate bring fluctuations in net exports. These fluctuations, in turn, disturb real economic activity. In a fixed exchange world this source of macroeconomic disturbance is absent.

8. The Bretton Wood system was a world monetary system based on fixed exchange rates. It was the outgrowth of World War II.

9. World exports increased sharply in the 1970s and reached a peak in 1980. They then declined until 1985. Between 1985 and 1990 they increased strongly again surpassing their previous peak value. Export growth in industrial countries has been much stronger than in the developing countries.

10. Interest rate parity is the equality of interest rates in assets denominated in different currencies once expectations of the change in the exchange rate are taken into account.

11. The *J*-curve gives the response of the current account (or net exports) to a devaluation or depreciation of a currency. Initially, net exports decline (the current account deteriorates) but eventually net exports increase (the current account improves).

12. A flexible exchange rate limits the effects of foreign shock by changing the real exchange rate and thereby changing aggregate expenditure. A decrease in world income results in a depreciation of the domestic currency and stimulation of exports.

Problems

1. (a) 10 percent
   (b) 13.75 percent

2. (a) The dollar depreciates
   (b) The yen appreciates

3. (a) With fixed exchange rates, the exchange rate remains constant but fluctuations in the quantity of dollar assets in existence are greatest
   (b) With flexible exchange rates, the quantity of dollar assets in existence is fixed and fluctuations in the exchange rate are greatest
   (c) With managed-floating exchange rates, the fluctuations in the exchange rate are smaller than under a flexible exchange rate, and the fluctuations in the quantity of dollar assets are smaller than in the case of a fixed exchange rate

4. (a) The exchange rate influences the balance of payments through its effects on international relative prices—real exchange rates
   (b) The balance of payments influences the exchange rate through expectations and intervention

5. (a) 140.45
   (b) 10 percent
   (c) 3 percent
   (d) -7 percent (approx.)

6. To answer this question draw a diagram similar to that in Figure 16.8(b) in the textbook (page 458). The unsustainable revaluation sets up an expectation of the future devaluation (depreciation). The demand for dollar-denominated assets decreases and foreign exchange reserves have to be used to maintain the exchange rate. The reserves keep falling until they reach a point below which they can fall no further. At this point the new higher unsustainable exchange rate is abandoned and the currency depreciates, probably to a level lower than that from which it started.

7. To answer this question use Figure 16.9 and Figure 16.10 in the textbook (pages 461 and 462). The detailed answer is contained in the extended caption to these two figures.

8.   To answer this question use Figure 16.12 in the textbook (page 470). The caption to the figure and the discussion in the *TESTCASE* on the payments imbalances in the 1980s gives a detailed answer.

9.   Use Figure 16.13 in the textbook (page 472) to answer this question but do the analysis in the figure in the opposite direction.

For a fixed exchange rate, the *IS* curve shifts to the right and interest rates increase. Higher interest rates bring a balance of payments surplus and the money supply increases. The *LM* curve shifts to the right initially. Interest rates increase and real GDP begins to increase. Eventually, interest rates return to their original level but real GDP continues to increase further.

Under flexible exchange rates, the *IS* curve shifts rightward increasing the interest rate and real GDP. There is no change in the money supply.

CHAPTER 17

Consumption and Saving

Perspective and Focus

The chapters that appear in this part of the book, take a deeper look at the determination of the components of aggregate expenditure and aggregate demand. This chapter looks at consumption and saving. It digs more deeply behind the consumption function that you studied in Chapter 4. You may be studying this chapter in sequence or you may be studying it immediately after you've studied Chapter 4. It works well either way, so you should not be alarmed whichever of these orders you've been asked to study the chapter in.

Learning Objectives

After studying this chapter, you will be able to:

- Describe the main facts about consumption, saving, and income, both overtime and across income groups
- Describe the household's intertemporal and lifetime budget constraints
- Explain how consumption and saving decisions are made
- Define permanent income and explain the permanent income hypothesis
- Explain the life-cycle hypothesis
- Explain the behavior of consumption and saving in Canada and other countries in the 1980s
- Explain the effect of taxes on consumption and saving
- Explain the effects of money and credit on consumption and saving

Increasing Your Productivity

This chapter contains an analysis of the household's choice of the timing of its consumption. The basic analysis is an application of the microeconomic theory of indifference curves and the determination of substitution and wealth effects. (The wealth effect is the intertemporal analog of the income effect in a choice made at a given point in time). If you are studying microeconomics at the same time as macroeconomics, then now is a good opportunity to cross fertilize the two parts of the discipline.

The core of the chapter is contained in section 17.3 on pages 489-492. The permanent income hypothesis in section 17.4 and the life-cycle hypothesis in section 17.5 are extensions of this basic model. There is no point in moving forward to these parts until you are thoroughly familiar with the basic model in section 17.3.

This chapter is a good one for illustrating the method of scientific analysis in economics. It shows you how economists develop models to interpret data and, how theories result from this process.

Self Test

Concept Review

1. _____ is the difference between the current period's actual income and the previous period's permanent income.

2. _____ is the average income that the household expects to receive from the present over the rest of its life.

3. _____is the maximum amount of current consumption that can be financed by borrowing against future labor income.

4. The present value of current and future labor income is called

   _____.

5. A household's endowment is equal to what it has to _____ over its lifetime.

6. The permanent income hypothesis is the proposition that _____ _____ is proportional to permanent income.

7. The value today of a future sum of money is its _____.

8. The life-cycle hypothesis is the proposition that households _____ _____ over their lifetimes.

9. The _____ is the amount of future consumption that a household is willing to give up in order to have one more unit of consumption today.

10. The _____ is the limit to a household's consumption over its lifetime.

True or False

1. Cross-sectional data record the values of variables over time, that is from one quarter or year to the next.

2. The long-run consumption function is the average relationship between real personal consumer expenditure and real personal disposable income over a long period of time.

3. In the household's intertemporal budget constraint, its income is its labor income, YL_t, and its income from assets, rA_t.

4. Human capital is another name for the present value of current and future labor income.

5. The effect of interest rate changes on consumption choices has two components. They are an income effect and a saving effect.

6. The percentage of personal disposable income saved in Canada decreased from almost 18 percent in 1982 to 9 percent in 1987.

7. A permanent tax change influences permanent disposable income and has a large effect on consumer expenditure.

8. Temporary changes in the money supply change the nominal interest rate and the expected inflation rate.

9. Transitory income, the difference between permanent income and actual income, has a small and perhaps zero effect on consumer expenditure.

10. According to the permanent income hypothesis, households smooth their consumption over their lifetimes, accumulating assets while they are working and consuming out of assets in their retirement years.

11. The short-run marginal propensity to consume is higher than the long-run marginal propensity to consume.

12. In cross-section data, the marginal propensity to consume decreases as disposable income increases.

13. Wealth is equal to the present value of future income.

14. An increase in the interest rate decreases the amount of consumption that can be undertaken.

15. Permanent income is always greater than current income.

16. The marginal propensity to consume out of transitory income is smaller than to consume out of permanent income.

17. According to the life cycle hypothesis, the propensity to consume out of labor income increases with age.

18. According to the life cycle hypothesis, the marginal propensity to consume out of assets increases with age.

19. A country with the highest saving rate is Japan.

20. The saving rate in Canada is lower than that in the United States and lower than the world average.

21. The intertemporal budget constraint is effected by the real interest rate, not the nominal interest rate.

Multiple Choice

1. Which of the following constraints represents the intertemporal budget constraint?
    (a) $C_t + A_{t-1} \leq YL_t - (1 + r)A_t$.
    (b) $C_t + A_{t-1} \leq YL_t + (1 + r)A_t$.
    (c) $C_t - A_{t-1} \leq YL_t + (1 + r)A_t$.
    (d) $C_t - A_{t-1} \leq YL_t - (1 - r)A_t$.
    (e) $C_t + A_{t-1} \leq YL_t + (1 - r)A_t$.

2. In the household's intertemporal budget constraint, (YL_t) is its labor income and (rA_t) is its
    (a) returns from durable goods.
    (b) returns from equities.
    (c) income from assets.
    (d) interest from capital.
    (e) economic profits.

3. The household's saving is the change in the value of its assets. That is
    (a) $S_t = A_{t-1} + A_t$.
    (b) $S_t = A_{t-1} - A_t$.
    (c) $S_t = A_{t+1} + A_t$.
    (d) $S_t = A_{t+1} - A_t$.
    (e) $S_t = A_t - A_{t-1}$.

4. A household's wealth is equal to
    (a) $YL_1 + YL_2/(1 - r)$.
    (b) $YL_1 - YL_2/(1 - r)$.
    (c) $YL_1 + YL_2/(1 + r)$.
    (d) $YL_2 - YL_1/(1 + r)$.
    (e) $YL_2 + YL_1/(1 - r)$.

5. The slope of the household's indifference curve equals the household's
(a) marginal rate of technical substitution.
(b) marginal rate of utility substitution.
(c) average rate of technical substitution.
(d) average rate of utility substitution.
(e) marginal rate of intertemporal substitution.

6. The two components of the effect of interest rate changes on consumption choices are
(a) a substitution effect and an income effect.
(b) a substitution effect and a wealth effect.
(c) an income effect and a wealth effect.
(d) an income effect and a saving effect.
(e) a substitution effect and a saving effect.

7. Assuming that the government budget starts out balanced and the government cuts taxes. Furthermore, it borrows to cover the deficit. At some time in the future the debt plus the interest on it has to be repaid. Rational households recognize this fact and realize that the tax cut has not changed their permanent income. It has simply changed the timing of their tax payments and the timing of their net-of-tax income receipts, but it has not changed their permanent income or shifted their lifetime budget constraint. This is known as the
(a) Ricardo-Barro hypothesis.
(b) Ricardo-Malthus hypothesis.
(c) Ricardo-Sargent hypothesis.
(d) Ricardo-Lucas hypothesis.
(e) Keynes-Barro hypothesis.

8. There have been some occasions when there was no doubt that tax changes enacted were indeed temporary. Two temporary tax changes were
(a) the 1986 imposition of a temporary 10 percent surcharge on personal income taxes.
(b) a 1970 imposition of a temporary 25 percent surcharge on personal income taxes.
(c) the 1975 one-time tax rebate and Social Security bonus of $9.4 billion.
(d) both (a) and (c).
(e) both (b) and (c).

9. The intertemporal theories of consumption and saving recognize only one constraint on the household's consumption choice, which is its
(a) one pay period budget constraint.
(b) lifetime budget constraint.
(c) one year budget constraint.
(d) liquidity budget constraint.
(e) investment budget constraint.

10. The maximum amount that a household can borrow to finance current consumption out of future labor income is an additional constraint on consumption, known as
(a) credit constraint.
(b) liquidity constraint.
(c) capital constraint.
(d) saving constraint.
(e) none of the above.

11. All of the following are true about the consumption function *except*
   (a) the long-run marginal propensity to consume is greater than the short-run marginal propensity to consume.
   (b) the short run consumption function shifts upward over time.
   (c) the marginal propensity to consume diminishes in the cross-section data as income increases.
   (d) consumption expenditure is highly unpredictable and volatile.
   (e) in some years during the great depression consumption expenditure exceeded disposable income.

12. Other things being equal, the higher the interest rate,
   (a) the greater the level of wealth.
   (b) the lower the level of wealth.
   (c) the more the household can consume in the current period.
   (d) the less the household can consume in the current period.
   (e) the more consumption will fluctuate over time.

13. Permanent income is
   (a) the part of a household's income that it will always be able to rely on.
   (b) income from a job that is secure.
   (c) interest from bonds that is guaranteed.
   (d) household average income.
   (e) the average income that the household expects to receive over the rest of its life.

14. According to the permanent income hypothesis,
   (a) the higher a household's measured income the higher is its level of consumption.
   (b) the higher is the household's permanent income the higher is its consumption.
   (c) the higher a household's transitory income the higher its consumption.
   (d) the higher a household's transitory income the lower its consumption.
   (e) the long-run marginal propensity to consume is the same as the short-run marginal propensity to consume.

15. According to the life-cycle hypothesis,
   (a) households consume more when their incomes higher.
   (b) households smooth their income over their working lives.
   (c) the marginal propensity to consume out of disposable labor income increases as the household gets older.
   (d) the marginal propensity to consume out of assets increases as the household gets older.
   (e) those who are retired save most.

16. Choose the best statement.
   (a) Liquidity-constrained households consume more than other households.
   (b) Liquidity-constrained households consume less than other households.
   (c) A liquidity-constrained household could consume more or less than an unconstrained household.
   (d) Liquidity constraints make the consumption function highly unpredictable.
   (e) Liquidity constraints are more important than disposable income in determining consumption expenditure.

17. According to the Ricardo-Barro hypothesis,
  (a) consumption depends on disposable income not aggregate income.
  (b) consumption depends on aggregate income not disposable income.
  (c) consumption depends on net of tax wealth.
  (d) consumption depends on pre-tax wealth.
  (e) consumption does not depend on taxes at all.

18. Inflation
  (a) increases interest rates and decreases current consumption.
  (b) increases interest rates and increases current consumption.
  (c) increases interest rates and has no effect on current consumption.
  (d) increases interest rates and has an ambiguous effect on current consumption.
  (e) has no effect on interest rates.

19. Other things being equal, a one dollar increase in the government deficit is predicted to
  (a) increase household consumption by more than one dollar.
  (b) decrease household consumption by one dollar.
  (c) decrease household consumption by less than one dollar.
  (d) increase household consumption one dollar.
  (e) neither increase or decrease consumption.

20. The maximum amount that a household can borrow to finance current consumption out of future labor income is an additional constraint on consumption, known as a(n)
  (a) intertemporal budget constraint.
  (b) human capital constraint.
  (c) liquidity constraint.
  (d) permanent income constraint.

  (e) transitory income constraint.

Short Answers Questions

1. Briefly explain the distinction between time-series data and cross-sectional data.

2. What does aggregate consumer expenditure depend on?

3. Wealth has previously been defined as the difference between total assets and total liabilities. What is another way of defining wealth?

4. What two variables influence the lifetime budget constraint?

5. What is meant by a liquidity constraint?

6. With the presence of a liquidity constraint there are two important influences on consumer expenditure other than the interest rate and the household's endowment. What are these two important influences on consumer expenditure?

7. What does the term *present value* mean?

8. What happens to household saving when the government increases its deficit by one dollar?.

9. What is the distinction between the long-run and the short-run consumption function?

10. Explain and distinguish the intertemporal budget constraint and the lifetime budget constraint.

11. Explain how an increase in the interest rate changes the lifetime budget constraint.

12. What is the permanent income hypothesis?

13. What is the life cycle hypothesis?

Problem Solving

How does it go?

Suppose that the Dundee Family's life runs from age 20 to age 80 and that its retirement age is 60. During the working years, its income is $50,000 each year and the interest rate is zero. Furthermore, the Dundee Family prefers constant consumption of $35,000 each year over its entire lifetime. It has $100,000 of assets at age 20.

(a) Calculate the Dundee Family human capital.

The Dundee Family's human capital is the sum of its lifetime labor income, which is $2,500,000.

(b) Calculate the Dundee Family's assets at age 65.

The Dundee Family's assets at age 65 are given by the following formula:

$$A_t = A_0 + (YL - C)(t - 20)$$

where A_0 represents assets at age 20, YL is labor income each year, C is yearly consumption, and t is current age.

Substituting into the formula gives

$$A_t = \$100,000 + \$15,000 \times (65 - 40),$$
which equals $475,000.

(c) Calculate the Dundee Family's saving when it is 30 years.

The Dundee Family's income is $50,000 a year and its current consumption is $35,000, so its saving is $50,000 minus $35,000, which equals $15,000.

(d) Calculate the Dundee Family's marginal propensity to consume out of labor income when the Dundee Family is 40 years.

The marginal propensity to consume out of labor income, when $t = 40$ (25 years before the Dundee Family retires):

$$b = (R - t)/(L - t).$$

where R is the age at retirement (65), L is the age at death (80), and t is the current age.

Substituting into the formula, gives b equal to 1.25.

Now try these

Fact 17.1 The Lee Family receives a labor income of $50,000 in year 1 and $55,000 in year 2. It can borrow and lend at an interest rate of 10 percent a year.

1. Use Fact 17.1. According to the lifetime budget constraint,
   (a) if the household consumes zero income in year 1, how much can be consumed in year 2?
   (b) if the household borrows all available funds against its labor income in year 2, how much could be consumed in year 1?
   (c) how much would the household have to repay in (b)?

2. Use Fact 17.1. The Lee Family's labor income increases by 10 percent in year 1 and year 2. According to the lifetime budget constraint,
(a) by how much does labor income increase in year 1 and year 2?
(b) what is maximum consumption in year 2?
(c) what is maximum consumption in year 1?

Fact 17.2 You are given the following information about an economy:

A marginal propensity to consume out of permanent income if 0.8. The speed of adjustment of permanent income to actual income is 0.4.

3. Use Fact 17.2. Calculate the marginal propensity to consume in the short run.
4. Use Fact 17.2. Calculate the marginal propensity to consume in the long run.
5. Use Fact 17.2. Calculate the effects of a $100 million windfall—increase in income—on consumption in the period in which the windfall occurs.
6. Use Fact 17.2. Calculate the effect of the windfall in Problem 5 on consumption in the long run.

Fact 17.3 A household consists of two 50 years old people. They have assets valued at $1 million and they plan to retire at age 60. They expect to live to 80 years.

7. Use Fact 17.3. Calculate the household's lifetime consumption constraint.

8. Use Fact 17.3. Calculate the household's marginal propensity to consume out of assets.

9. Use Fact 17.3. Calculate the household's marginal propensity to consume out of labor income.

10. Use Fact 17.3. What is the household's marginal propensity to consume out of assets in the year in which it retires.

11. Use Fact 17.3. What is the household's marginal propensity to consume out of labor income at the beginning of its last year at work.

✓ Answers

Concept Review

1) transitory income
2) permanent income
3) liquidity constraint
4) human capital
5) spend
6) consumer expenditure
7) present value
8) smooth, consumption
9) marginal rate of intertemporal substitution
10) lifetime budget constraint

True or False

1) F 5) F   9) T 13) T 17) T   21) T
2) T 6) F 10) F 14) F 18) F
3) T 7) T 11) F 15) F 19) T
4) T 8) F 12) T 16) F 20) T

Multiple Choice

1) b 5) e   9) b 13) e 17) c
2) c 6) c 10) b 14) b 18) d
3) b 7) a 11) d 15) b 19) d
4) c 8) d 12) b 16) c 20) c

Short Answer Questions

1. Time-series data record the values of variables over time (i.e., from one quarter or year to the next). Time-series data can be utilized to calculate a consumption function which is the relationship between personal consumer expenditure and personal disposable income.

   Cross-sectional data record the level of consumer expenditure at each level of income at a point in time. When families with different income levels are studied, the relationship between the consumer expenditure and disposable income of these different families gives rise to a cross-sectional consumption function.

2. Aggregate consumer expenditure depends on permanent income (or lifetime average income), the interest rate, current disposable income, and available credit.

3. Another way of defining wealth is that it is the maximum amount that can be consumed in the current period if nothing is consumed in later periods.

4. The lifetime budget constraint is influenced by the interest rate and labor income.

5. A liquidity constraint is the maximum amount that a household can borrow to finance current consumption out of future labor income.

6. The other two important influences on consumer expenditure other than the interest rate and the household's endowment are disposable income and available credit.

7. The present value of a future sum of money is the amount that, if invested now at the interest rate r, would accumulate to the future sum over a given number of years.

8. If the government increases its deficit by one dollar, that action creates a liability for households to pay interest on that dollar in perpetuity. The value of the liability created is equivalent to the dollar the government has spent. Other things being equal, a one-dollar increase in the government deficit is predicted to increase household saving by one dollar.

9. The short run consumption function shows how consumption expenditure responds to a change in disposal income over a short period such as a year. The long run consumption shows the average relationship between consumption and disposable income over a long period of time.

10. The intertemporal budget constraint states how current consumption and next periods assets are related to current assets and current income. The lifetime budget constraint describes the connection between lifetime consumption and wealth.

11. An increase in the interest rate rotates the lifetime budget constraint on the endowment point. It decreases consumption possibilities for cases where the household wishes to consume more than its endowment in early periods and less than its endowment in later periods.

12. The permanent income hypothesis is the proposition that consumption expenditure is proportional to permanent income. Permanent income is the level of income that could be consumed on an ongoing basis.

13. The life-cycle hypothesis is the proposition that households consume out of assets and labor income and that the marginal propensity to consume out of assets while that to consume out of labor income decreases over the household's life-cycle.

Problems

1. (a) $110,000.
   (b) $100,000.
   (c) $55,000.

2. (a) $5,000 and $5,500 respectively.
   (b) $121,000.
   (c) $110,000.

3. 0.32.

4. 0.8.

5. $32,000 increase.

6. 0 increase.

7. $C(80 - t) = \$1m. + (60 - t)YL.$

8. 1/30.

9. 10/30 or 1/3.

10. 1/20.

11. 1/21.

CHAPTER 18

Investment

Perspective and Focus

Like Chapter 17, this chapter also digs more deeply into one of the components behind aggregate expenditure—investment. You first encountered investment in Chapter 6 and here we study it more deeply. Chapter 18 may be studied in sequence or immediately following Chapter 6. Either way, the chapter contains everything that you need to make good progress with the material. You do not need to be concerned if you have not studied Chapters 7 to 17 before beginning this chapter.

The core to the chapter is sections 18.2 and 18.4.

Learning Objectives

After studying this chapter, you will be able to:

- Describe the volatility of investment in Canada and other countries
- Explain the accelerator theory of investment
- Explain how the rental rate of capital is determined
- Explain why investment responds to interest rates
- Explain how monetary policy effects investment
- Explain how taxes effect investment
- Explain why there are alternative waves of optimism and pessimism
- Explain how fluctuations in investment bring fluctuating output and interest rates

Increasing Your Productivity

Focus most of your attention in this chapter initially on section 18.2 (capital, investment, and the accelerator theory) and section 18.4 (investment and the rental rate of capital).

The accelerator theory is an analysis of the connection between the desired capital stock and the current capital stock and the influence that the gap between the desired and actual capital stocks has on investment. It is not a theory of the desired capital stock. The desired capital stock depends on the rental rate of capital, which in turn depends on the interest rate.

It is also worth spending some time studying investment in Canada to see how the accelerator and interest rate mechanisms work. The key point of this chapter is that the investment demand curve fluctuates a great deal.

Self Test

Concept Review

1. The user cost of capital is the cost of using capital, expressed _____.

2. An alternative name of the user cost of capital is _____ of capital.

3. _____ is a situation in which no reallocation of assets will increase the return on a combination of assets with the same amount of risk.

4. A technique that uses a lot of capital is called a _____ _____.

5. An accelerator mechanism is a mechanism that links the _____ of _____ to the _____ in _____ .

6. Residential fixed investment is expenditure by _____ on _____.

7. Nonresidential fixed investment is expenditure by _____ on _____.

8. Tobin's q is the _____ of the _____ of a firm to _____ of its _____.

9. A technique that uses a large amount of labor is called a _____ _____.

True or False

1. Investment is the least volatile component of aggregate demand.

2. Investment includes changes in inventories, residential fixed investment, and nonresidential fixed investment.

3. In order to see the connection between the stock of capital and the flow of investment, investment may be divided into net investment and replacement investment.

4. In the national income and product accounts, replacement investment is called capital consumption allowances.

5. A technique that uses a large amount of capital and a small amount of labor is called a labor-intensive technique.

6. Capital is a flow. It is measured as the rate of purchase of new plant, buildings, and equipment over a particular period of time.

7. Other things being equal, the higher the real interest rate, the higher is the level of gross investment.

8. A permanent change in the money supply growth rate that brings a permanent change in the inflation rate leaves the real interest rate unaffected and, in the long run, has no effect on the desired capital stock or investment.

9. Monetary policy can have an important effect on the desired capital stock and investment by influencing the after-tax rental rate.

10. Despite the fact that tax changes appear to affect investment, they are not regarded as a reliable tool for stabilizing fluctuations in investment and aggregate demand.

11. Investment is one of the most volatile components of aggregate expenditure

12. Net investment fluctuates more than replacement investment

13. The level of investment is related to the change in real GDP because of the accelerator mechanism

14. The higher is the inflation rate, other things being equal, the higher is the real rental rate of capital

15. The higher the depreciation rate the higher is the rental rate of capital

16. The faster our assets prices expected to increase relative to inflation the higher is the rental rate

17. If the marginal product of capital exceeds the rental rate firms have got too much capital

18. Investment only increases when the real interest rate declines

19. An increase in the corporate income tax rate increases the rental rate of capital

20. An investment tax credit decreases the rental rate of capital.

Multiple Choice

1. Which of the following represents the second largest component of gross private domestic investment?
   (a) Nonresidential fixed investment.
   (b) Residential fixed investment.
   (c) Inventory changes.
   (d) Replacement investment.
   (e) Net investment.

2. The mechanism linking the level of net investment to the change in output is known as
   (a) internal funds mechanism.
   (b) accelerator mechanism.
   (c) classical mechanism.
   (d) Tobin's q.
   (e) Tobin's r.

3. An alternative name for the rental rate of capital is
   (a) rental cost of capital.
   (b) purchase price of capital.
   (c) marginal product of capital.
   (d) user cost of capital.
   (e) wear and tear cost of capital.

4. Which of the following represents Tobin's q?
   (a) $q = MPK/P_k$.
   (b) $q = SMV/P_k$.
   (c) $q = MPK/SMV$.
   (d) $q = P_k/SMV$.
   (e) $q = R/MPK$.

5. The accelerator mechanism must be modified in order to take account of the dependency of the desired capital-sales ratio on
   (a) income.
   (b) rental income.
   (c) labor income.
   (d) interest rate.
   (e) economic profits.

6. Monetary policy can influence investment through
   (a) the interest rate effect.
   (b) the exchange rate effect.
   (c) the real balance effect.
   (d) the income effect.
   (e) (a), (b), and (c).

7. Three main sources of tax effects on the after-tax rental rate are
   (a) corporate income taxes, social security taxes, and investment tax credits.
   (b) depreciation deductions, investment tax credits, and personal income taxes.
   (c) corporate income taxes, depreciation deductions, and investment tax credits.
   (d) personal income taxes, corporate income taxes, and social security taxes.
   (e) depreciation deductions, corporate income taxes, and personal income taxes.

8. Even so investment tax credits were abolished in 1986, an investment tax credit is a decrease in a firm's taxable profit, determined by the scale of the firm's investment in
   (a) year $t - 1$.
   (b) year $t - 2$.
   (c) year $t + 1$.
   (d) the current year.
   (e) the last five years.

9. If one ignores changes in the price of capital, the rental rate is equal to
   (a) $P_k(\delta - r)$.
   (b) $P/k(\delta + r)$.
   (c) $P_k(\delta - r)$.
   (d) $P_k(\delta/r)$.
   (e) $P_k(\delta \times r)$.

10. When investment tax credits were introduced in 1962, they permitted firms a tax reduction of
    (a) 25 percent of most of their business fixed investment.
    (b) 7 percent of most of their business fixed investment.
    (c) 10 percent of all of their business fixed investment.
    (d) up to 30 percent of some of their business fixed investment.
    (e) 5 percent of all of their business fixed investment.

11. Net investment
    (a) equals the change in the capital stock plus depreciation.
    (b) gross investment equals the replacement of worn out capital.
    (c) net investment equals the replacement of worn out capital.
    (d) net investment equals the change in the capital stock.
    (e) replacement investment equals additions to the capital stock.

12. The accelerator mechanism means that
    (a) when real GDP is high investment is high.
    (b) when real GDP is rising investment is rising.
    (c) when real GDP is rising investment is high.
    (d) when investment is rising real GDP is high.
    (e) the change in investment is correlated with the level of real GDP.

13. The rental rate of capital is
    (a) only relevant if a firm actually rents its capital equipment.
    (b) a theoretical price of no practical importance.
    (c) expressed an a percentage of the price of capital.
    (d) is equal to the price of a capital asset multiplied by the interest rate.
    (e) is the cost of using a piece of capital equipment regardless of whether the capital is actually rented.

14. The rental rate of capital is higher,
    (a) the higher is the price of capital.
    (b) the higher is the rate of depreciation.
    (c) the higher is the rate of inflation.
    (d) the higher is the real interest rate.
    (e) all of the above except (c).

15. If the marginal product of capital exceeds the real interest rate firms can lower their costs by
    (a) increasing their capital stock.
    (b) decreasing their capital stock.
    (c) renting more capital.
    (d) renting less capital.
    (e) none of the above.

16. If the marginal product of capital exceeds the real rental rate firms can lower their costs by
    (a) buying or renting more capital equipment.
    (b) buying or renting less capital equipment.
    (c) buying some capital and renting it out.
    (d) decreasing the amount of capital they own.
    (e) financing their capital investment by selling bonds.

17. If a firm has a marginal product of capital that exceeds the rental rate of capital, then
    (a) it pays to buy shares in that firm.
    (b) it pays to sell shares in that firm.
    (c) it pays to take a bank loan and buy bonds.
    (d) it pays to buy stock in the firm only if the economy is expanding.
    (e) it pays to sell stock in the firm if the economy is contracting.

18. If we observe a positive correlation between interest rates and investment we must conclude that
    (a) the amount of investment is wrong.
    (b) there have been fluctuations in inflation.
    (c) the accelerator mechanism does not operate.
    (d) shifts in the investment demand curve have been more important than movements along the investment demand curve.
    (e) investment is completely random.

Short Answer Questions

1. (a) What are the three components of gross private domestic investment?
   (b) Rank these components in terms of the largest, and so forth.

2. What is meant by the accelerator mechanism?

3. How is investment influenced by monetary policy?

4. Fiscal policy can have an important effect on the desired capital stock and investment by influencing the after-tax rental rate.

   What are the three main sources of tax effects on the after-tax rental rate?

5. (a) What is meant by the rental rate of capital?
   (b) What is meant by the user cost of capital?

6. What are *animal spirits*?

7. (a) How do modern macro theorists explain sunspots?
   (b) How do sunspot effects operate in reality?

8. Which components of investment fluctuate most?

9. What is the accelerator mechanism?

10. Does the accelerator mechanism operate in practice?

11. What determines a firms optimal capital stock?

12. How is the rental rate of capital related to the interest rate?

13. How do taxes affect investment?

Problem Solving

How does it go?

La Bella Pizza is considering buying a new pizza oven for $3,000. If it buys the oven it has to borrow form the bank and the interest rate on the loan is 8 percent a year. Zippy Rentals is willing to rent La Bella Pizza an oven for $500 a year. The price of pizza ovens is expected to increase by 5 percent a year, and they depreciate at 15 percent a year.

(a) Calculate the highest price that La Bella Pizza is willing to pay for a pizza oven.

The highest price that La Bella Pizza is willing to pay for the oven is the price that makes the implicit rental rate equal to $3,000.

$$\text{Rental rate} = P_k(\delta + r_m - \Delta P_k^e/P_k)$$

$$500 = P_k(0.15 + 0.08 - 0.05)$$

That is,

$$P_k = \$2,777.78.$$

Now you try these

Fact 18.1 An earthmover costs a $100,000 and has a five year life after which it is worthless. The interest rate is 5 percent a year and there is no inflation.

1. Use Fact 18.1. What is the (approx.) rate of depreciation of the earthmover?

2. Use Fact 18.1. What is the expected rate of appreciation of earthmover prices?

3. Use Fact 18.1. What is the real interest rate?

4. Use Fact 18.1. What is the rental rate of such an earthmover?

5. Use Fact 18.1. Suppose an earthmover of this type can be rented for $30,000 per year does it pay to buy or to rent?

6. Use Fact 18.1. Whichever it pays to do in your answer to Problem 5, does the firm do it?

Fact 18.2 XYZ Inc. owns 10 earthmovers of the type described in Fact 18.1. They are all brand new. Also the firm has made wise investment decisions and this quantity of earthmovers exactly minimizes its cost. The stock market value of the firm is $900,000.

7. Use Fact 18.2. What is the value of the firms Tobin's q?

8. Use Fact 18.2. Will people buy of sell shares in this firm?

Fact 18.3 Refer to Fact 18.2. The government introduces a 25 percent corporate income tax rate.

9. Use Fact 18.3. How does this income tax rate affect the firms rental rate?

10. Does the firm now buy more earthmovers or sell some?

Fact 18.4 Refer to Fact 18.2. The government introduces an investment tax credit permitting firms to deduct 10 percent of the purchase price of new capital against their income when computing their income tax liability.

11. Use Fact 18.4. How does this investment tax affect the rental rate of capital?

12. Use Fact 18.4. Does the firm now acquire more capital or less?

13. You are thinking of buying a big screen Magnavox television set for $2,000. The price of such televisions is expected to decrease by 20 percent a year. If you did purchase this television set you would have to borrow the money from the bank at 10 percent interest per year. Furthermore, the television depreciates at 10 percent per year. A friend owns exactly the same television set and you can rent it from him for $20 per month.

   (a) What is the implicit rental rate if you purchase the television set?
   (b) Is it cheaper to rent the television from your colleague for one year or purchase it from the store?

14. You are trying to decide whether to buy a condominium or rent one. The price of the condominium is $100,000 and the mortgage interest is 10 percent a year. Furthermore, condominium prices are expected to increase by 5 percent a year and depreciate by 2 percent a year.

   (a) What is the maximum rent you would pay for such a condominium?
   (b) What is the implicit rental rate?

15. ABC Rentals has capital that cost $1,000,000. Its marginal product of a capital is $90,000, and the interest rate on bonds is 10 percent.

   Calculate
   (a) the stock market value of the firm.
   (b) Tobin's q.
   (c) the rental rate of capital.

✓ Answers

Concept Review

1) in terms of dollars
2) rental rate
3) portfolio equilibrium
4) capital-intensive technique
5) level, net investment, change, output
6) households and firms, new houses and apartments
7) firms, new plant, buildings, and equipment
8) ratio, stock market value, price, capital assets
9) labor-intensive technique

True or False

1) F	5) F	9) F	13) T	17) F
2) T	6) F	10) T	14) F	18) F
3) T	7) F	11) T	15) T	19) T
4) F	8) T	12) T	16) F	20) T

Multiple Choice

1) b	5) d	9) c	13) e	17) a
2) b	6) e	10) b	14) e	18) d
3) d	7) c	11) d	15) e	19)
4) b	8) d	12) c	16) a	20)

Short Answer Questions

1. (a) The three components of gross private domestic investment include changes in inventories, residential fixed investment, and nonresidential fixed investment.

   (b) The largest component of gross private domestic investment comprises nonresidential fixed investment; the second largest component consists of residential fixed investment; and changes in inventory are the smallest component.

2. The accelerator mechanism is the mechanism linking the level of net investment to the change in output. The mechanism arises from the fact that firms desire to maintain a particular relationship between the level of their sales and the level of their capital stock.
   Because the change in the capital stock is net investment, a change in sales leads to a temporary increase in net investment.

3. Monetary policy can influence investment through the interest rate effect, the exchange rate effect, and the real balance effect.

4. The three main sources are corporate income taxes, depreciation deductions, and investment tax credits.

5. (a) The rental rate of capital is the cost of using a piece of capital equipment, expressed in terms of dollars per hour.

   (b) The user cost of capital is an alternative name for the rental rate of capital since most capital equipment is not rented, it is bought and used by its owners.

6. Keynes's *animal spirits* describe the forces at work generating swings in mood and changes in expectations. The name conjures up the idea of instinctive reactions to collective swings of moods rather than rational responses to changes in the objective environment.

7. (a) Modern theorists have used the term sunspot to denote any variable that in fact has no effect but that people believe has an effect on the economy.

   (b) So far, it is not known whether sunspot effects operate in reality. Sunspot effects are the subject of a great deal of current research.

8. The short-run consumption function shows how consumption expenditure responds to a change in disposal income over a short period such as a year. The long-run consumption shows the average relationship between consumption and disposable income over a long period of time.

9. The intertemporal budget constraint states how current consumption and next periods assets are related to current assets and current income. The lifetime budget constraint describes the connection between lifetime consumption and wealth.

10. An increase in the interest rate rotates the lifetime budget constraint on the endowment point. It decreases consumption possibilities for cases where the household wishes to consume more than its endowment in early periods and less than its endowment in later periods.

11. The permanent income hypothesis is the proposition that consumption expenditure is proportional to permanent income. Permanent income is the level of income that could be consumed on an ongoing basis.

12. The life-cycle hypothesis is the proposition that households consume out of assets and labor income and that the marginal propensity to consume out of assets increases while the marginal propensity to consume out of labor income decreases over the household's life-cycle.

Problems

1. 0.2
2. 0
3. 0.05
4. $25,000 per year
5. Buy
6. Cannot tell because the firm needs to know the marginal product of capital
7. 0.9
8. Buy
9. With a 25 percent tax rate, the rental rate increases by 25 percent
10. Sell
11. The rental rate decreases by 10 percent
12. It pays to buy more capital (but not very much because the allowance applies only to new investment not to existing capital stock)

13 (a) $250
    (b) It is cheaper to rent

14. (a) $7,000
    (b) $7,000

15. (a) $900,000
    (b) 0.9
    (c) $100,000

CHAPTER 19

Money and Asset Holding

Perspective and Focus

This chapter also probes more deeply behind the determinants of aggregate demand. This chapter focuses on the microeconomic foundations of the demand for money that lies behind the *LM* curve.

Learning Objectives

After studying this chapter, you will be able to:

- Describe the trends and velocity of circulation of various monetary aggregates
- Explain the inventory theory of the demand for money
- Explain the precautionary theory of the demand for money
- Explain the speculative theory of the demand for money
- Explain the modern quantity theory of money
- Explain the main influences on the amount of money held in Canada during the 1970s and 1980s
- Explain the effect of the demand for money on aggregate economic fluctuations
- Explain the implications of the demand for money for stabilization policy

Increasing Your Productivity

The key to understanding what is going on in this chapter is the concept of opportunity cost. You first encountered this concept in your very first lecture in economic principles. The concept pays handsome dividends in this chapter. It is the concept applied to holding money. The concept of the opportunity cost of holding money is summarized in Table 19.1 and explained on pages 542-544 once you have understood the concept of the opportunity cost of holding money and what constitutes that opportunity cost for different monetary aggregates you will have no difficulty with the rest of the chapter. You will race through the material on financial innovation and the influence of financial innovation on the velocity of circulation of the various monetary aggregates.

A potential stumbling block for students not familiar with the calculus is the material on the inventory theory of the demand for money. The diagrammatic analysis of this theory, summarized in Figures 19.2 and 19.3 are adequate. It would though be a good idea to try and understand the square root formula for this explains why the demand for money has economies of scale.

Self Test

Concept Review

1. The average number of times one dollar of money finances transactions in a given period of time is called the

_____.

2. The speculative theory of the demand for money is a theory that is based on the idea that people hold

_____
_____ that gives the best available _____.

3 _____ of the demand for money is a theory based on the idea that money, in part, is held as a general _____-_____ against _____.

4. GDP divided by the quantity of money is the _____
_____.

5. M2 is equal to M1 plus _____
_____ and
_____.

6. M2 is equal to M3 minus _____
_____
_____.

7. Inventory velocity of circulation is a theory of the demand for money based on _____ the cost of _____ of money.

True or False

1. M2 consists of M1 plus personal savings deposits and non-personal fixed-term deposits at chartered banks.

2. The velocity of circulation of money is the average number of times one dollar of money finances transactions during a given time period.

3. The inventory theory does not appear to be a good theory in so far as it does not account for the variations in the amount of money held as income and interest rates vary, but it does account for the absolute level of money holding.

4. The modern quantity theory of the demand for money, in effect, combines the elements of the inventory, precautionary, and speculative theories systematically into a unified theory of asset allocation.

5. The income velocity of circulation of money is GDP multiplied by the quantity of money.

6. The precautionary theory of the demand for money is based on the idea that money is held, in part, as a kind of general insurance against an uncertain future.

7. Money market mutual funds are financial institutions that issue shares redeemable at variable prices against which cheques can be written.

8. The quantity of money demanded fluctuates when the interest rate changes, but changes in the interest rate caused by some other factor do not change the demand for money.

9. M3 consists of M2 plus non-personal fixed-term deposits of residents booked at chartered banks.

10. The opportunity cost of holding long-term deposits is the interest rate on bonds and stocks plus the interest rate on long-term deposits.

11. The velocity of circulation of M1 money increased during the 1970s and 1980s and that of M2 money decreased.

12. The opportunity cost of holding money is the goods that are foregone by not making a purchase.

13. The opportunity cost of holding currency is zero.

14. The opportunity cost of holding a savings deposit is the interest rate on higher yielding assets.

15. Money holding is subject to economies of scale. An increase in the scale of expenditure does not, in general, lead to a proportional increase in the amount of money held.

16. Fluctuations in the demand for money are well explained by fluctuations in interest rates and financial innovation.

17. The amount of money held is so volatile that it is not possible to predict how interest rate changes will effect the quantity of money held.

18. The transactions theory of the demand for money explains why people, on the average, hold such a large quantity of money.

19. There is no reason to believe that the amount of money held depends on wealth. It only depends on income.

20. Fluctuations in the velocity of circulation are simply a reflection of movements up and down the demand for money curve.

Multiple Choice

1. M1 includes
   (a) currency in circulation.
   (b) savings deposits at chartered banks.
   (c) demand deposits at chartered banks.
   (d) non-personal notice deposits at chartered banks.
   (e) both (a) and (c).

2. The theory that is based on the idea that people minimize the cost of managing their inventories of money is called the
   (a) speculative theory of the demand for money.
   (b) precautionary theory of the demand for money.
   (c) transactions theory of the demand for money.
   (d) time theory of the demand for money.
   (e) inventory theory of the demand for money.

3. The total cost of managing a household's cash inventory is equal to
   (a) $bn + rY/n$.
   (b) $bn + rY/2n$.
   (c) $bn - rY/2n$.
   (d) $bn \times rY/2n$.
   (e) $bn + 2n/rY$.

4. The modern theory of the demand for money systematically combines elements of the
   (a) inventory theory.
   (b) precautionary theory.
   (c) speculative theory.
   (d) both (b) and (c).
   (e) all the above.

5. The modern quantity theory states that households allocate their given stock of wealth across
   (a) money.
   (b) bonds.
   (c) real capital.
   (d) human capital.
   (e) all of the above.

6. Bank deposits denominated in U.S. dollars held outside the United States are known as
   (a) Eurodollars.
   (b) British dollars.
   (c) European dollars.
   (d) German dollars.
   (e) none of the above.

7. Cash management accounts
   (a) include daily interest chequing accounts.
   (b) are available only to large corporate customers of chartered banks.
   (c) include sweep accounts.
   (d) includes non-personal savings accounts.
   (e) include money market mutual funds as well as (a) and (d).

8. Fluctuations in the velocity of circulation induced by changes in the interest rates do not cause fluctuations in aggregate economy activity. These fluctuations in velocity are a consequence of a
   (a) change in the demand for money.
   (b) movement along the demand for money curve.
   (c) counterclockwise movement in the demand for money curve.
   (d) clockwise movement in the demand for money curve.
   (e) either (c) or (d).

9. Financial innovation that decreases the demand for money and
   (a) shifts the *LM* curve to the right.
   (b) shifts the *LM* curve to the left.

   (c) decreases interest rates.
   (d) increases real GDP.
   (e) all the above except (b).

10. Fluctuations in aggregate economic activity can result from fluctuations in the velocity of circulation resulting from
    (a) changes in interest rates.
    (b) changes in the supply of money.
    (c) financial innovation.
    (d) investment.
    (e) all the above except (a).

11. The broader the definition of money
    (a) the smaller are the fluctuations in the velocity of circulation.
    (b) the larger of its fluctuations in the velocity of circulation.
    (c) the more likely it is to be used for transaction purposes.
    (d) the more its opportunity cost fluctuates.
    (e) the less rational it is to hold large quantities of it.

12. The opportunity cost of holding currency is equal to
    (a) zero.
    (b) the inflation rate.
    (c) the interest rate on bonds.
    (d) the interest rate on demand deposits.
    (e) the interest rate on credit cards.

13. The opportunity cost of holding a fixed-term deposit is
    (a) the interest rate on savings deposits.
    (b) the interest rate on bonds.
    (c) the inflation rate.
    (d) the interest rate on fixed-term deposits.
    (e) the interest rate on bonds minus the interest rate on fixed-term deposits.

14. According to the inventory theory of the demand for money
    (a) the higher the interest rate, the smaller is the number of trips to the bank.
    (b) the higher the level of income, the smaller is the number of trips to the bank.
    (c) the larger the number of trips to the bank, the larger is the amount of money held on the average.
    (d) as income increases, the amount of money held on the average increases and by the same percentage as the increase in the interest rate.
    (e) as the interest rises, the amount of money held on the average falls and by a smaller percentage than the increase in the interest rate.

15. According to the modern quantity theory of money, the amount of money held depends on all of the following *except*
    (a) human capital.
    (b) wealth.
    (c) the interest rate.
    (d) income.
    (e) the rate of return of real capital.

16. The expansion of credit cards have had the following effect on the demand for money.
    (a) The demand for M1 has increased but M2 has decreased.
    (b) The demand for M1 has decreased and the demand for M2 has increased.
    (c) The demand for all types of money has decreased.
    (d) The effect on the demand for money is ambiguous.
    (e) There has been no effect on the demand for money.

17. The velocity of circulation increases when
    (a) interest rates rise.
    (b) interest rates fall.
    (c) financial innovation leads to a decrease in the demand for money.
    (d) financial innovation leads to an increase in the demand for money.
    (e) both (a) and (c).

18. The demand for real money increases and the demand for nominal money increases, if the price level _____ and the inflation _____.
    (a) increases, increases.
    (b) increases, decreases.
    (c) decreases, increases.
    (d) decreases, decreases.
    (e) none of the above.

19. An increase in the demand for money
    (a) shifts the *LM* curve to the left, lowers the interest rate, and increases real GDP.
    (b) shifts the *LM* curve to the right, increases the interest rate, and increases real GDP.
    (c) has no effect on the *LM* curve.
    (d) shifts the *LM* curve to the left, increases the interest rate, and decreases real GDP.
    (e) shifts the *LM* curve to the right, decreases the interest rate, and increases real GDP.

20. The demand for real money _____ and the demand for nominal money _____, if the price level increases and inflation decreases.
    (a) increases, increases.
    (b) increases, decreases.
    (c) decreases, increases.
    (d) decreases, decreases.
    (e) none of the above.

Short Answers Questions

1. On what idea is the speculative theory of the demand for money based?

2. What did Milton Friedman suggest in his formulation of the modern quantity theory of money?

3. What does the proposition that the quantity of money demanded depends on permanent income imply?

4. (a) What are Eurodollars?
   (b) Why are Eurodollars attractive to banks?
   (c) How were Eurodollars invented?

5. What are cash management accounts?

6. Define the narrowest definition of money in Canada.

7. State the two reasons for the importance of the square root formula.

8. Briefly summarize the trends in the velocity of circulation of the various monetary aggregates.

9. What is meant by financial innovation.

10. What is the opportunity cost of holding money?

11. What is the tradeoff in managing an inventory?

12. What determines the optimal inventory of money?

13. What is the speculative theory of the demand for money?

14. What are the major financial innovations of the 1970s and 1980s?

15. How does a change in the demand for money effect equilibrium real GDP?

Problem Solving

How does it go?

Sammy earns $1,800 a month and he spends $400 on rent and other monthly expenses as soon as he is paid. He keeps the rest in cash and in an interest-earning chequing account and spends it at an even pace over the month. It costs Sammy $1.75 each time he goes to the bank. His bank pays 1 percent interest each month.

(a) How many times does Sammy go to the bank each month?

Sammy's cash expenditure in a month is equal to $1,800 – $400, which is $1,400.

Sammy makes n trips to the bank where

$$n = (rY/2b)^{1/2}. \qquad (19.1)$$

The interest rate, r, is 0.01 a month, his monthly cash expenditure, Y, is $1,400, and the cost of a trip to the bank, b, is 2. Substituting into Equation (19.1) gives

$$n = [(0.01 \times 1,400)/(1.75 \times 2)]^{1/2}$$
$$= 2.$$

Sammy makes 2 trips a month.

(b) How much does Sammy withdraw each time he goes to the bank?

On each occasion he withdraws $1,400 ÷ 2, which equals $700.

(c) What is Sammy's average currency holding?

Sammy's average currency holding is $1,400 ÷ (2 × 2), which is $350.

(d) What is Sammy's average holding of chequing deposits?

Sammy's average holding of chequing deposits is equal to his average cash expenditure minus his average currency holding. That is, $1,400/2 – $350, which equals $350.

(e) What is Sammy's average holding of M2?

Sammy's average holding of M2 is his average holding of cash plus chequing deposits. That is equal to his average monthly cash expenditure, which is $700.

(f) What does it cost Sammy to manage his inventory of cash?

Sammy's total cost of managing his cash holding is

$$TC = bn + (rY/2n)$$

$$= (1.75 \times 2) + \frac{(0.01 \times 1400)}{(2 \times 2)}$$

$$= \$10.5.$$

(g) How much of Sammy's cost of managing his cash inventory is the opportunity cost of holding cash and how much is the cost of transactions?

Sammy's opportunity cost of holding cash, $rY/2n$, equals $3.50, and his transactions costs, bn, equal $10.50 – $3.50, which is $7.00.

Now try these

1. Wei Ming receives a cash income of $2,000 per month and spends it uniformly throughout the month.
   (a) What is Wei Ming's average cash holding.
   (b) What is Wei Ming's average cash holding when she uses half of the income to buy bonds?

2. The Sukkar Family gets paid once a month and immediately writes cheques to pay all the bills. It then has $1,600 left to deposit into its interest-bearing bank account which pays an interest rate of 1 percent a month. Furthermore, the Sukkar Family spends its cash in equal amounts over the month.
   (a) The Sukkar Family makes two trips to the bank each month to withdraw cash. Calculate the Sukkar Family's average cash holding?
   (h) The Sukkar Family makes four trips to the bank each month to withdraw cash. Calculate the Sukkar Family's average cash holding?

3. Professor Ho earns $4,000 per month, each month of the year. As soon as she receives her income each month she pays the rent of $1,400 and puts $200 into a retirement account. The remainder of the income is spent evenly throughout the month.
   (a) What is Professor Ho's demand for money?
   (b) What is Professor Ho's average holding of money?

4. Sally earns $3,900 a month and she spends $600 on rent and other monthly expenses as soon as she is paid. She keeps the rest in cash and in an interest-earning chequing account and spends it at an even pace over the month. It costs Sally $2.75 each time she goes to the bank. Her bank pays 1.5 percent interest each month.

    (a) How many times does Sally go to the bank each month?
    (b) How much does Sally withdraw each time he goes to the bank?
    (c) What is Sally's average currency holding?
    (d) What is Sally's average holding of M2?
    (e) What does it cost Sally to manage her inventory of cash?
    (f) How much of Sally's cost of managing her cash inventory is the opportunity cost of holding cash and how much is the cost of transactions?

✓ Answers

Concept Review

1) velocity of circulation
2) mixture of money and other assets, combination of risk and return
3) precautionary theory, insurance, an uncertain future
4) income velocity of circulation
5) savings deposits, personal notice deposits at chartered banks
6) non-personal fixed-term deposits at chartered banks
7) minimizing, managing an inventory

True or False

1) T	5) F	9) F	13) F	17) F
2) T	6) T	10) F	14) F	18) F
3) F	7) F	11) T	15) T	19) F
4) T	8) T	12) F	16) T	20) F

Multiple Choice

1) e	5) e	9) e	13) e	17) e
2) e	6) a	10) e	14) e	18) b
3) b	7) c	11) a	15) b	19) e
4) e	8) b	12) d	16) c	20) a

Short Answer Questions

1. The speculative theory of the demand for money is based on the idea that people hold their wealth in a variety of assets that give different combinations of risk and return.

2. Milton Friedman suggested that wealth could be measured as permanent income. The key proposition in the modern quantity theory of money is that the quantity of money demanded depends inversely on the nominal rate and positively on permanent income.

3. It immediately implies that there will be time lags in the relationship between the quantity of money demanded and current income. Because permanent income responds gradually to changes in current actual income, the quantity of money demanded will respond only gradually to changes in current income. Thus there will be a time lag between a change in income and the change in the quantity of money demanded.

4. (a) Eurodollars are bank deposits denominated in U.S. dollars held outside the United States.

(b) They are attractive to banks because there are no required reserves on these deposits so banks can lend the entire amount deposited, thereby increasing their profits.

(c) They were invented when the Soviet Union wanted to hold the proceeds of its international trade in U.S. dollars but did not want to put the money in the United States.

5. Cash management accounts are a financial innovation that is available to corporations and other large customers of banks. one such account is the sweep account—at the end of the business day, the bank sweeps the balances from chequing deposits and places them in overnight investments. Cash management accounts have the effect of decreasing the demand for money and increasing the velocity of circulation of all types of money.

6. M1, the narrowest definition of money, consists of currency (Bank of Canada notes and coins) in circulation and demand deposit balances at chartered banks.

7. First, it makes a very precise prediction about the demand for cash. It predicts that as the amount of expenditure undertaken using cash increases, the amount of cash held increases, but only by the square root of the increase in expenditure. In other words, there is an economy of scale of holding cash. If spending increases fourfold, cash holdings increase only twofold. Furthermore, it predicts that the higher the interest rate on the next convenient asset, the smaller is the amount of currency held. Again, the responsiveness is very precise. A 1 percent increase in interest rates bring a one-half per-

cent decrease in the amount of currency held.
Second, the formula easily generalizes to deal with other components of money.

8. The velocity of circulation of M1 increased during the 1970s but has remained fairly constant since 1981. Since 1970, the velocity of circulation of M2 has trended downward.

9. Financial innovation is the development of new financial products, items such as credit cards and types of bank deposits and other securities.

10. The opportunity cost of holding money is the interest foregone on the next best alternative asset that could have been held instead. It is the nominal interest rate not the real interest rate.

11. The tradeoff in managing an inventory are the cost of replenishing the inventory versus the cost of holding the inventory. The more frequently it is replenished, the smaller the inventory can be and the smaller the cost of holding it.

12. The optimal inventory of money is determined by balancing the cost of replenishing the inventory against the cost of holding it.

13. The speculative theory of the demand for money is based on the fact that people hold a portfolio of assets of varying degrees of risks and expected return. Money is part of such a portfolio because, although it gives a low return, it has a lower risk.

14. The major financial innovations were the development of credit cards, the expansion of Eurodollars, the development of cash management accounts, such as sweep accounts, and the emergence of money market mutual funds.

16. A change in the demand for money has an equivalent but opposite effect to a change to the supply of money. A decrease in the demand for money shifts the *LM* curve to the right. The result is a higher level of real GDP and a lower interest rate (at a given price level).

Problems

1. (a) $1,000
   (b) $500

2. (a) $400
   (b) $200

3. (a) $1,200
   (b) $1,200

4. (a) 3
   (b) $1,100
   (c) $550
   (d) $1,100
   (e) $16.50
   (f) $8.25, $8.25 respectively

CHAPTER 20

New Classical Macroeconomics

Perspective and Focus

The final part of the book contains two chapters that study the microeconomic foundations of aggregate supply and the microeconomic decisions that lie behind the short-run aggregate supply curve. There are two chapters not because the material is divided into two parts but because there are two alternative approaches to this part of the subject.

Macroeconomics is a living science and is in a constant state of change. Most of the research of the past decade has concentrated on the aggregate supply side of the economy and, naturally, economists have tried a variety of alternative approaches. This chapter describes the new classical research program.

Learning Objectives

After studying this chapter, you will be able to:

- Explain the new classical theory of the labor market
- Explain the Lucas aggregate supply curve
- Explain how surprise changes in aggregate demand produce an output-inflation tradeoff
- Explain the policy implications of Lucas's new classical macroeconomic model
- Describe the ability of the Lucas model to account for aggregate economic fluctuations
- Explain real business cycle theory
- Describe the ability of real business cycle theory to explain the business cycle in the post-war years
- Explain how new classical macroeconomics accounts for unemployment
- Describe the new classical account of unemployment over the business cycle in the post-war years
- Describe the research agenda of new classical macroeconomics

Increasing Your Productivity

You will make most progress with this chapter if you focus on understanding the idea of rational expectations and the extension of the neoclassical growth model for the determination of aggregate fluctuations.

The idea of rational expectations lies at the heart of the whole of economics. It was first developed, however, in the context of the new classical theory of business cycles and the output-inflation tradeoff. However, do not get hung up on the lack of realism of the concept of rational expectations. At one level, it is the only realistic theory there is. People simply do not throw away information. They use information as efficiently as they use any other scarce resource. At another level, the theory is unrealistic. People do not go through the mental processes that you as a student of economics are capable of going through to predict the macroeconomic equilibrium and the price level. But performing that exercise is just the economists way of attempting to *build a model* of the process of expectations formation. A model is a conscious abstraction from reality.

Self Test

Concept Review

1. _____
   is a theory that bases its explanation
   of aggregate fluctuations on
   exogenous, random technological
   change.

2. The output-inflation tradeoff is the
   relationship between _____
   of _____ from _____
   _____ and _____
   from _____.

3. _____ is making one
   set of measurements correspond to
   another set.

4. When all inputs are increased by the
   same percentage and output also
   increases by the same percentage,
   _____ exit.

5. The _____ aggregate supply
   curve show the maximum real GDP
   that can be supplied at each price
   level, when the labor market is in
   equilibrium at a given expected price
   level.

6. The policy effectiveness proposition
   is the proposition that _____
   changes in _____
   have no effect on any _____
   variables.

7. If a 1 percent increase in
   employment increases output by 20
   percent and a 1 percent increase in
   capital increases output by 80
   percent, then the production function
   is a

   _____

   production function.

True or False

1. The output-inflation tradeoff is the
   relationship between deviations of
   real GDP from full employment and
   inflation from its expected level.

2. The relevant price for calculating the
   real wage rate is the same on both
   the supply side and demand side of
   the market.

3. Once incomplete information is
   introduced, equilibrium in the labor
   market depends on the price level
   relative to the expected price level.

4. The Lucas aggregate supply curve
   shows the maximum real GDP
   supplied at each price level when the
   labor market is in equilibrium at a
   given expected price level.

5. Real business cycle theory assumes
   that everyone has different
   preferences.

6. Technological change usually takes
   the form of progress.

7. The heart of real business cycle theory is the idea that the production function shifts because of technological change.

8. New classical macroeconomics presumes that the essence of aggregate fluctuations is intertemporal substitution.

9. The rational expectation of the price level is the price level that is expected on the basis of all relevant information available at the time the expectation is formed.

10. New classical macroeconomics was initially a theory of aggregate supply.

11. The output-inflation tradeoff is the loss of real GDP resulting from a given percentage increase in inflation.

12. If output increases by 1 percent when all inputs increase by 1 percent, then such a production function has constant returns to scale. An example of such as production function is the Cobb-Douglas production function.

13. According to real business cycle theory, the twin deficits are the main variables that generate real business cycles.

14. In the new classical labor market, the money wage depends only on the expected price level.

15. If the actual price level is less than the expected price level, then in a new classical labor market, employment exceeds full employment.

16. In the new classical labor market, price level expectations that turn out to be wrong cease are immediately changes to keep the labor market at a full-employment equilibrium.

17. Along the Lucas aggregate supply curve, the labor market is in equilibrium, given the expected price level.

18. As an economy moves up along its Lucas aggregate supply curve, the actual real wage decreases and the expected real wage increases.

19. As an economy moves down along its Lucas aggregate supply curve, the money wage rate decreases and the actual real wage increases.

20. The Lucas aggregate supply curve would be vertical if drawing up new labor contracts were costless and agents had rational expectations.

Multiple Choice

1. The new classical theory of the labor market assumes that the
   (a) quantity of labor demanded depends on the actual real wage rate.
   (b) quantity of labor supplied depends on the expected real wage rate.
   (c) average money wage rate continually adjusts to achieve labor market equilibrium.
   (d) both (a) and (b).
   (e) all the above.

2. The perception that anticipated changes in monetary policy do not have an effect on employment, output, or any other variable is known as the policy
   (a) effectiveness proposition.
   (b) anticipation proposition.
   (c) ineffectiveness proposition.
   (d) defect proposition.
   (e) diversion proposition.

3. Real business cycle theory predicts that real wages are
   (a) countercyclical—real wages increase when the economy moves into a boom.
   (b) procyclical—real wages decrease when the economy moves into a boom.
   (c) countercyclical—real wages decrease when the economy moves into a boom.
   (d) procyclical—real wages increase when the economy moves into a boom.
   (e) either procyclical or countercyclical—real wages either increase or decrease when the economy moves into a boom.

4. A Cobb-Douglas production function is one in which a 1 percent increase in employment increases output by a percent and a 1 percent increase in the capital stock
   (a) decreases output by $(1 - a)$ percent.
   (b) increases output by $(1 - a)$ percent.
   (c) decreases output by $(a - 1)$ percent.
   (d) increases output by $(a - 1)$ percent.
   (e) decreases output by $(1/a)$ percent.

5. If output increases by 1 percent when all inputs increase by 1 percent, then such a production function has
   (a) constant returns to size or scale.

   (b) decreasing returns to size or scale.
   (c) increasing returns to size or scale.
   (d) variable returns to size or scale.
   (e) none of the above.

6. The Cobb-Douglas production may be written as
   (a) $y = znk^{(1 - a)}$.
   (b) $y = zn^a k^{(1 - a)}$.
   (c) $y = zn^a k^{(a - 1)}$.
   (d) $y = zn^{(1 - a)} k^{(a)}$.
   (e) $y = znka^{(1 - a)}$.

7. The production function is Cobb Douglas and markets are competitive. Labor's share and capital's share of GDP are
   (a) a and $(1 - a)$, respectively.
   (b) $(1 - a)$ and a, respectively.
   (c) $(1/a)$ and a, respectively.
   (d) $(a/1)$ and a, respectively.
   (e) (a) and $(1 + a)$, respectively.

8. The key variable generating real business cycles according to real business cycle theory is
   (a) a change in consumption.
   (b) a change in investment.
   (c) the twin deficits.
   (d) the trade deficit.
   (e) technological change.

9. Which of the following is a measure of technological change? The
   (a) Prescott residual.
   (b) Solow residual.
   (c) Volcker residual.
   (d) Kydland residual.
   (e) Hercowitz residual.

10. There are three approaches to explaining unemployment that are consistent with real business cycle theory. They are
    (a) indivisible labor, sectoral reallocation, and job creation and job destruction.
    (b) indivisible labor, sectoral allocation, and job destruction.
    (c) visible labor, sectoral allocation, and job creation.
    (d) job creation, job destruction, and visible labor.
    (e) sectoral reallocation, job creation, and job destruction.

Fact 20.1 Consider an economy with a new classical labor market. Its production function is

$$y = 50 + 13n - 0.1n^2$$

Its demand for and supply of labor are given by

$$n^d = 65 - 5 \ (W/P)$$

$$n^s = 15 + 7(W/P^e).$$

11. Use Fact 20.1. Full-employment output is
    (a) less than 100.
    (b) between 101 and 200.
    (c) between 201 and 300.
    (d) between 301 and 400.
    (e) more than 400.

12. Use Fact 20.1. Full-employment level of employment is
    (a) less than 15.
    (b) between 16 and 25.
    (c) between 26 and 40.
    (d) between 41 and 50.
    (e) more than 50.

13. Use Fact 20.1. The expected price level is 2 and the actual price level is 1. The money wage rate is
    (a) less than $2.00.
    (b) between $2.10 and $4.00.

    (c) between $4.10 and $5.50.
    (d) between $5.51 and $6.50.
    (e) more than $6.50.

14. Use Fact 20.1. The expected price level is 2 and the actual price level is 1. Employment is
    (a) less than 20.
    (b) between 21 and 35.
    (c) between 36 and 45.
    (d) between 46 and 50.
    (e) more than 50.

15. Use Fact 20.1. The expected price level is 2 and the actual price level is 1. The expected real wage is
    (a) less than 3.
    (b) between 4 and 6.
    (c) between 7 and 10.
    (d) between 11 and 15.
    (e) more than 15.

16. The slope of the output-inflation tradeoff
    (a) is the same in all countries.
    (b) shows little variation from country to country.
    (c) does not vary from one time period to another.
    (d) varies from one time period to another.
    (e) (a), (b), and (d).

Fact 20.2 Caribou Country has a labor market that is new classical and described by the following equations:

$$n^d = 2,000 - 60(W/P)$$
$$n^s = 1,000 + 60(W/P).$$

17. Use Fact 20.2. Workers expect the price level to be 2 and the actual price level is 2.5. The money wage rate is
    (a) between $10.00 and $12.00.
    (b) between $12.00 and $14.00.
    (c) between $14.00 and $16.00.
    (d) between $16.00 and $18.00.
    (e) above $18.00.

18. Use Fact 20.2. Workers expect the price level to be 2 and the actual price level is 2.5. The employment level is
    (a) less than 1,400.
    (b) between 1,400 and 2,000.
    (c) between 2,000 and 2,600.
    (d) between 2,600 and 3,400.
    (e) more than 3,400.

19. Use Fact 20.2. Workers expect the price level to be 2 and the actual price level is 2.5. The unemployment rate
    (a) equals the natural rate of unemployment.
    (b) exceeds the natural rate of unemployment.
    (c) less than the natural rate of unemployment.
    (d) zero.
    (e) not enough information to know.

20. Use Fact 20.2. Workers expect the price level to be 2 and the actual price level is 2.5. The real wage rate
    (a) equals its full-employment level.
    (b) exceeds its full-employment level.
    (c) less than its full-employment level.
    (d) exceeds the expected real wage rate.
    (e) both (c) and (d),

Short Answers Questions

1. What is assumed by the new classical theory of the labor market?

2. What are the three approaches to explaining unemployment that are consistent with real business cycle theory?

3. What is meant by the job destruction rate?

4. Briefly provide an assessment of new classical macroeconomics.

5. How was the Kydland-Prescott model tested and what results were recorded?

6. What is the policy ineffectiveness proposition?

7. Explain how new classical theory of the labor market accounts for unemployment.

8. Explain why the Lucas aggregate supply curve is upward sloping.

9. Explain how an output-inflation tradeoff is generated.

Problem Solving

How does it go?

Sandy Island has a new classical labor market, as described by the following equations:

$$n^d = 200 - 2.5(W/P)$$
$$n^s = 100 + 2.5(W/P).$$

The actual price level is 1 and the expected price level is 0.5.

(a) Calculate the money wage rate.

Each firm's demand for labor depends on the actual price of its output. As a consequence the aggregate demand for labor depends on the actual price level. The supply of labor depends on the expected price level. The equilibrium money wage rate (W) is determined by the demand for and supply of labor. That is, it is the money wage rate determined at the intersection of:

$n^d = 200 - 2.5(W/P)$ (20.1)
$n^s = 100 + 2.5(W/P^e)$, (20.2)

where P is the actual price level, and P^e is the expected price level.

But the actual price level is 1, and the expected price level is 0.5. Substituting these values into Equations (20.1) and (20.2) gives

$n^d = 200 - 2.5(W)$ (20.3)
$n^s = 100 + 2.5(W/0.5)$, (20.4)

Solving Equations (20.3) and (20.4) gives

$W = \$13.33$.

(b) Calculate the number of people employed.

To calculate the number of people employed (n), substitute 13.33 for W in the demand for labor curve—Equation (20.3). That is,

$n = 166.67$.

(c) Calculate the expected real wage rate.

The expected real wage rate equals the money wage rate divided by the expected price level. That is,

Expected real wage rate $= W/P^e$
$= \$13.33/0.5$
$= 26.67$.

Now try these

1. Sail Island has a new classical labor market, as described by the following equations:

$n^d = 250 - 2.5(W/P)$
$n^s = 100 + 2.5(W/P)$.

The actual price level is 1.5 and the expected price level is 1.

Calculate the
(a) money wage rate.
(b) expected real wage.
(c) actual real wage.
(d) number of people employed.

2. Big Wave Island has a new classical labor market, as described by the following equations:

$n^d = 100 - 5(W/P)$
$n^s = 5(W/P)$.

The actual price level is 1.2 and the expected price level is 1.

Calculate the
(a) money wage rate.
(b) expected real wage.
(c) actual real wage.
(d) number of persons employed.

3. Silly Isle's Lucas aggregate supply curve is

$y^s = 800 - 250(P^e/P)^2$

and its aggregate demand curve is

$y^d = M/P$.

Calculate
(a) the rational expectation of the price level if the expected money supply is 1,512.5.
(b) the actual price level if the money supply turns out to be 1,769.80.

4. Heron Island's Lucas aggregate supply curve is

$y^s = 1250 - 50(P^e/P)^2$

and its aggregate demand curve is

$y^d = 500 + M/P$.

Calculate

(a) the rational expectation of the price level if the expected money supply is 500.

(b) the actual real GDP if the money supply turns out to be 400.

Fact 20.3 Sunny Island has a new classical labor market. It production function is

$$y = 100n - 0.2n^2.$$

Its supply of labor is

$$n^s = 200 + 2.5(W/P).$$

The expected price level is 2.

5. Use Fact 20.3. What is the equation to the demand for labor curve?

6. Use Fact 20.3. Calculate money wage rate and the level of employment if the actual price level is 1.5.

7. Use Fact 20.3. Calculate real GDP if the actual price level is 1.5.

8. Use Fact 20.3. What is the equation to the short-run aggregate supply curve?

9. Use Fact 20.3. Sunny Island is hit by a technology shock that shifts the production function upwards by 10 percent. What is the equation to the new production function?

10. In problem 9, what is the increase in labor productivity?

11. In problem 9, what is the equation to the new demand for labor?

✓ Answers

Concept Review

1) real business cycle theory
2) deviations, real GDP, full employment, inflation, its expected level.
3) calibration
4) constant returns to scale
5) Lucas
6) anticipated, monetary policy, real
8) Cobb-Douglas

True or False

1) T	5) F	9) T	13) F	17) T
2) F	6) T	10) T	14) F	18) T
3) T	7) T	11) F	15) F	19) T
4) T	8) T	12) T	16) F	20) F

Multiple Choice

1) e	5) a	9) b	13) d	17) e
2) c	6) b	10) a	14) c	18) b
3) d	7) a	11) e	15) a	19) c
4) b	8) e	12) d	16) d	20) c

Short Answer Questions

1. The new classical theory of the labor market assumes that the quantity of labor demanded depends on the actual real wage rate; the quantity of labor supplied depends on the expected real wage rate; and the average money wage rate continually adjusts to achieve labor market equilibrium.

2. These three approaches are indivisible labor; sectoral reallocation, and job creation and job destruction.

3. The job destruction rate is the number of jobs that disappear in a given time period expressed as a percentage of the total number of jobs.

4. New classical macroeconomics is not a body of established empirical regularities with a classical interpretation for them. Rather, by using a particular theoretical approach, it is an attempt to explain the allocation of resources across different activities, space, and time and fluctuations over time.

5. The Kydland-Prescott model was tested by checking its ability to produce growth and fluctuations in consumption, investment, the capital stock, and employment and then comparing the growth and variability produced in the model economy with their counterparts in the real economy.
Kydland and Prescott concluded that their model economy behaved in a way very similar to the actual U.S. economy, although they did not present any statistical tests of the closeness of fit with reality.

6. The policy ineffectiveness proposition is that anticipated changes in monetary policy have no effect on real variables, such as real GDP, employment and unemployment. Anticipated policy affects nominal variables only, such as the price level and money wage rate. Their ineffectiveness arises from the fact that although the policy changes the aggregate demand curve, anticipated policy also shifts the short-run aggregate supply curve.

7. There are two main ways: (1) labor is indivisible because of startup costs and shutdown costs and (2) job creation and job destruction are not uniform phenomena. Startup costs and shutdown costs make it inefficient for firms to vary the average hours worked rather than the number of workers. When a technology shock hits the economy, labor needs to reallocated between sector and industries, but job creation and job destruction rates vary between sectors and industries.

8. The new classical labor market is always in equilibrium, but the equilibrium is only at full employment when the expected price level turns out to be correct. If the actual price level exceeds the expected price level, the actual real wage is below its full-employment level and employment exceeds its full-employment level. And as a result, real GDP exceeds its full-employment level. That is, the Lucas aggregate supply curve slopes upward.

9. An output-inflation tradeoff is generated along the Lucas aggregate supply curve as aggregate demand fluctuates around its expected level. If fluctuations in expected aggregate demand are small relative to fluctuations in actual aggregate demand, there remains a positive correlation between the price level and real GDP fluctuations.

Problems

1. (a) $36
   (b) 36
   (c) 24
   (d) 190

2. (a) $10.90
   (b) 10.90
   (c) 9.90
   (d) 54.55

3. (a) 2.75
   (b) 3

4. (a) 1.4
   (b) 1,058.77

5. $n^d = 250 - 2.5(W/P)$

6. $17.41, 221.42

7. 12,336.73

8. $y = 12,500 - 2,000/(2 - P)^2$

9. $y = 110n - 0.22n^2$

10. $10 - 0.04n$

11. $n^d = 250 - 2.27(W/P)$

CHAPTER 21

New Keynesian Macroeconomics

Perspective and Focus

This chapter looks at the microeconomic foundations of short-run aggregate supply arising from the research program of the new Keynesian school of macroeconomists. These economists emphasize co-ordination failure as the source of macroeconomic problems. Thus the chapter focuses on a variety of alternative potential sources as co-ordination failure. Most of these occur in the labor market, but more recently economists have turned their attention to co-ordination failure in the markets for goods and services.

Learning Objectives

After studying this chapter, you will be able to:

- Describe some key facts about wages and long term wage contracts
- Explain the new Keynesian theory of the labor market
- Explain the new Keynesian interpretation of differences in performance in the North American and Japanese economies
- Explain the new Keynesian theory of price determination
- Explain the new Keynesian interpretation of price markups and cost changes
- Review and explain some models of real wage rigidity
- Explain how aggregate fluctuations arise according to new Keynesian theory
- Describe the policy implications of the new Keynesian theory

Increasing Your Productivity

The key to understanding the new Keynesian theory of the labor market is to maintain a sharp distinction between the time at which wages are set and the time at which employment is determined. Wages are set on the basis of expectations about the demand for and supply of labor. Employment is determined after wages have been set and based on the actual state of the economy at the time the labor demand decision. Keep this distinction in your mind and you will have no trouble understanding the new Keynesian theory. This labor market is set out in section 21.2.

To reinforce your understanding of both the new Keynesian and the Lucas (new classical) theory of short-run aggregate supply, it is worth spending a good deal of time studying the differences between the two approaches. This material is described on pages 601-603.

If you are studying microeconomics at the same time as macroeconomics, here is another good opportunity for cross fertilization between the parts of the subjects that you are studying in different courses. The material in section 21.4 on price setting and menu costs is a twist on a theory of monopoly and monopolistic competition that you encounter in your microeconomics course. Use your understanding of this material from your microeconomics course to enrich your appreciation of this aspect of the new Keynesian research program.

Self Test

Concept Review

1. The cost of the resources used to change a price is called a
_____.

2. Price minus cost, expressed as a percentage of cost is the
_____.

3. Dimensions of an employment contract that are not written in the contract are _____.

4. Marginal cost is the _____
in _____
resulting from producing the _____ unit of the good or service.

5. The wage above the market wage that is paid to workers while the firm holds a threat over them—to hire them if they shirk—is called
_____.

6. Economic analysis of one part of the economy, given the rest of the economy, is called _____
_____.

7. Marginal revenue is the _____
in _____ resulting from _____ one more
_____.

8. A state in which one economic agent knows something of interest but another does not know it and the second agent knows something else of interest that the first agent dos not know is _____.

9. A COLA is a component of a
_____.

10. An agreement to change wages based on changes in the CPI is called a
_____.

True or False

1. New Keynesians view the economy as consisting of a small number of monopolistically competitive firms.

2. Asymmetric information is a situation where each person is asymmetrically informed relative to everyone else.

3. A partial equilibrium analysis is an economic analysis of one part of the economy, taking the rest of the economy as given.

4. The policy ineffectiveness proposition also applies to a new Keynesian model.

5. According to the new Keynesian theory, labor markets act like continuous auction markets, with wages being frequently adjusted to achieve an ongoing equality between the quantities of labor supplied and demanded.

6. *Shunto* translates into English as spring wage defensive.

7. Marginal cost is the increase in total cost resulting from producing the last unit of output.

8. A COLA is an agreement that makes the rate of wage change over the term of a contract depend on the actual inflation rate.

9. Money wages are set in a contract for an agreed period of time before the quantity of labor supplied and demanded is know.

10. The fact that labor market contracts run for a number of years and overlap does not have important implications for the analysis of economic policy.

11. The Lucas aggregate supply curve is steeper than the new Keynesian aggregate supply curve.

12. The price level turns out to be 50 percent higher than anticipated when the contract was signed. In such a situation, the demand for labor curve shifts downward by 50 percent.

13. If the actual price level is less than the expected price level, then the actual real wage in a new Keynesian labor market is higher than in a new classical labor market.

14. In the new Keynesian labor market, the economy can never be at full employment.

15. In the new Keynesian labor market, the economy can never have less than the natural rate of unemployment.

16. The economy is initially at full-employment equilibrium. An unanticipated increase in aggregate demand decreases the actual real wage rate and by a larger amount if the labor market is new Keynesian rather than new classical.

17. If wage contracts are overlapping, the new Keynesian aggregate supply curve depends on current price expectations, not past price expectations.

18. If the price level turns out to be less than expected, then actual real wage rate is higher if the labor market is new Keynesian rather than new classical.

19. New Keynesians do not believe in rational expectations.

20. The new Keynesian labor market is always in equilibrium.

Multiple Choice

1. Which of the following represent the three key assumptions in the new Keynesian theory of the labor market?
   (a) Money wages are set on a yearly basis, money wags are set to make the actual quantity of labor demanded equal to the actual quantity of labor supplied, and the level of employment is determined by the actual demand for labor.
   (b) Money wages are set for a fixed contract period, money wages are set to make the expected quantity of labor demanded equal to the expected quantity of labor supplied, and the level of employment is determined the expected demand for labor.
   (c) Money wages are set for a fixed contract period, money wages are set to make the expected quantity of labor demanded equal to the expected quantity of labor supplied, and the level of employment is determined by the actual demand for labor.
   (d) Money wages are set every year, money wages are set to make the expected quantity of labor demanded equal to the actual quantity of labor supplied, and the level of employment is determined by the actual demand for labor.
   (e) Money wages are set for a fixed contract period, money wages are set to make the actual quantity of labor demanded equal to the expected quantity of labor supplied, and the level of employment is determined by the expected demand for labor.

2. *Shunto* translates into English as
   (a) winter wage offensive.
   (b) spring wage offensive.
   (c) summer wage offensive.
   (d) spring wage defensive.
   (e) winter wage defensive.

3. Many forces influence the demand for labor and they can be summarized under two broad headings. These are, the
   (a) price level and the marginal product of labor.
   (b) price level and the average product of labor.
   (c) income level and the average product of labor.
   (d) income level and the total product of labor.
   (e) price level and the total product of labor.

4. Which of the following is an agreement that makes the rate of wage change over the term of a contract depend on the actual inflation rate? The
   (a) consumer price agreement.
   (b) producer price agreement.
   (c) wage-inflation agreement.
   (d) COLA agreement.
   (e) current price-inflation agreement.

5. The new Keynesian theory of price determination implies that price changes and cost changes will be
   (a) different from each other but markups will change very little.
   (b) similar to each other and that markups will change very little.
   (c) similar to each other but markups will change by a large amount.
   (d) different from each other and that markups will change by a large amount.
   (e) different from each other and that markups will not change at all.

6. Choose the best statement.
   (a) Lucas aggregate supply curve is steeper than the new Keynesian aggregate supply curve.
   (b) Lucas aggregate supply curve is less steep than the new Keynesian aggregate supply curve.
   (c) Lucas aggregate supply curve is as steep as the new Keynesian aggregate supply curve.
   (d) new Keynesian aggregate supply curve is steeper than the Lucas aggregate supply curve.
   (e) none of the above.

7. The new Keynesian theory of money wages implies a new
   (a) classical theory of aggregate supply.
   (b) monetarist theory of aggregate supply.
   (c) Keynesian theory of aggregate supply.
   (d) rational expectations theory of aggregate supply.
   (e) none of the above.

8. The key difference in the behavior of the growth rate of real wages and the employment rate in the United States and Japan is that in the United States,
   (a) real wage growth has been countercyclical and in Japan it has been procyclical.
   (b) real wage growth has been procyclical and in Japan is has been countercyclical.
   (c) real wage growth has been both countercyclical and procyclical whereas in Japan it has been only countercyclical.
   (d) real wage growth has been both countercyclical and procyclical whereas in Japan it has only been procyclical.
   (e) none of the above.

9. In the new Keynesian labor market, the money wage is set so as to achieve
   (a) full employment.
   (b) expected labor market equilibrium.
   (c) actual labor market equilibrium.
   (d) both (a) and (c).
   (e) all the above.

10. Which of the following theories explain real wage stickiness on the basis of unionized insiders setting wages at level that best serve their interests, with no concern for the interest of the unemployed outsiders?
    (a) Asymmetric information theories.
    (b) Efficiency wage theories.
    (c) Insider-outsider theories.
    (d) Implicit contracts theories.
    (e) Explicit contracts theories.

11. The cost of changing a price is known as the
    (a) adaption cost.
    (b) menu cost.
    (c) markup cost.
    (d) wholesale cost.
    (e) retail cost.

Fact 21.1 Consider an economy with a new Keynesian labor market. The production function, demand for labor, and supply of labor curves are

$$y = 75 + 13n - 0.1n^2$$
$$n^d = 65 - 5 (W/P)$$
$$n^s = 15 + 7(W/P).$$

The expected price level is 1.

12. Use Fact 21.1. Full-employment output is
    (a) less than 100.
    (b) between 101 and 200.
    (c) between 201 and 300.
    (d) between 301 and 400.
    (e) more than 400.

13. Use Fact 21.1. Full-employment level of employment is
    (a) less than 15.
    (b) between 16 and 25.
    (c) between 26 and 35.
    (d) between 36 and 45.
    (e) more than 45.

14. Use Fact 21.1. The contracted money wage rate is
    (a) less than $1.00.
    (b) between $1.10 and $3.00.
    (c) between $3.10 and $4.50.
    (d) between $4.51 and $5.50.
    (e) more than $5.50.

15. Use Fact 21.1. The actual price level turns out to be 2. Employment is
    (a) less than 20.
    (b) between 21 and 36.
    (c) between 37 and 51.
    (d) between 52 and 56.
    (e) more than 56.

16. Use Fact 21.1. The actual price level turns out to be 2. The actual real wage paid is
    (a) less than 5.
    (b) between 6 and 11.
    (c) between 12 and 15.
    (d) between 16 and 20.
    (e) more than 20.

17. Use Fact 21.1. The actual price level turns out to be 2. The expected real wage is
    (a) less than 3.
    (b) between 4 and 6.
    (c) between 7 and 11.
    (d) between 12 and 15.
    (e) more than 15.

18. Use Fact 21.1. The actual price level turns out to be 0.5. Employment is
    (a) less than 20.
    (b) between 21 and 26.
    (c) between 27 and 31.
    (d) between 32 and 35.
    (e) more than 35.

19. Use Fact 21.1. The actual price level turns out to be 0.5. The actual real wage paid is
    (a) less than 5.
    (b) between 6 and 11.
    (c) between 12 and 15.
    (d) between 16 and 20.
    (e) more than 20.

20. Use Fact 21.1. The actual price level turns out to be 0.5. The expected real wage is
    (a) less than 5.
    (b) between 6 and 11.
    (c) between 12 and 15.
    (d) between 16 and 20.
    (e) more than 20.

Short Answers Questions

1. What are the three key assumptions in the new Keynesian theory of the labor market?

2. Why is the Lucas aggregate supply curve steeper than the new Keynesian supply curve?

3. What are the four main approaches to explaining real wage rigidities as consequences of efficient labor market arrangements?

4. There has been a lively debate concerning the efficiency of the labor contracts that new Keynesian economists use in their theory of aggregate supply. Who is involved in the argument?

5. Based on what idea is Assar Lindbeck's and Dennis Snower's labor market model based?

6. What are menu costs?

7. Explain an efficiency wage.

8. What is meant by partial equilibrium analysis?

9. There has been a lively debate concerning the efficiency of the labor contracts that new Keynesian economists use in their theory of aggregate supply. What do the new classical economists, such as Robert Barro, have to say about the efficiency of labor contracts?

10. Does the policy ineffectiveness proposition apply to the new Keynesian model.

Problem Solving

How does it go?

Sunny Island has a new Keynesian labor market, as described by the following equations:

$$n^d = 200 - 2.5(W/P)$$
$$n^s = 100 + 2.5(W/P).$$

The actual price level is 1 and the expected price level is 0.5.

(a) Calculate the money wage rate.

The contract money wage rate (W) is determined by the expected demand for and supply of labor. That is, it is the money wage rate determined at the intersection of:

$$n^d = 200 - 2.5(W/P^e) \quad (21.1)$$
$$n^s = 100 + 2.5(W/P^e), \quad (21.2)$$

where P^e is the expected price level.

But the expected price level is 0.5. Substituting this value into Equations (21.1) and (21.2) gives

$$n^d = 200 - 2.5(W/0.5) \quad (21.3)$$
$$n^s = 100 + 2.5(W/0.5), \quad (21.4)$$

Solving Equations (21.3) and (21.4) gives

$$W = \$10.$$

(b) Calculate the number of people employed when the price level is 1.

To calculate the number of people employed (n), substitute 10 for W in the actual demand for labor curve. That is,

$$n^d = 200 - 2.5(W/P)$$

$$n^d = 200 - 2.5(10)$$
$$= 175.$$

(c) Calculate the expected real wage rate.

The expected real wage rate equals the money wage rate divided by the expected price level. That is,

$$\text{Expected real wage rate} = W/P^e$$
$$= \$10/0.5$$
$$= 20.$$

Now try these

Fact 21.2 Assuming an economy with the following new Keynesian labor market where the demand for labor and the supply of labor are

$$n^d = 200 - 2.5(W/P)$$
$$n^s = 100 + 2.5(W/P).$$

The expected price level is 1.

1. Use Fact 21.2. Calculate the
   (a) contract money wage.
   (b) expected real wage.

2. Use Fact 21.2. The price level turns out to be 1.5. Calculate the employment level.

3. Use Fact 21.2. The economy has the following production function:

$$y = 100n - 0.2n^2.$$

What is the equation to the new Keynesian aggregate supply curve?

Fact 21.2 Sandy Island has a new Keynesian labor market. It production function is

$$y = 100n - 0.2n^2.$$

Its supply of labor is

$$n^s = 200 + 2.5(W/P).$$

The expected price level is 2.

4. Use Fact 21.2. What is the equation to the demand for labor curve?

5. Use Fact 21.2. Calculate money wage rate and the level of employment if the actual price level is 1.5.

6. Use Fact 21.2. Calculate real GDP if the actual price level is 1.5.

7. Use Fact 21.2. What is the equation to the short-run aggregate supply curve?

8. Use Fact 21.2. Sandy Island is hit by a technology shock that shifts the production function upward by 10 percent. What is the equation to the new production function?

9. In problem 8, what is the increase in labor productivity?

10. In problem 8, what is the equation to the new demand for labor?

✓ Answers

Concept Review

1) menu cost
2) markup
3) implicit contracts
4) increase, total cost, last
5) efficiency wage
6) partial equilibrium analysis
7) increase, total revenue, selling, unit of the good or service
8) asymmetric information
9) wage agreement
10) COLA

True or False

1) F	5) F	9) T	13) F	17) F
2) T	6) F	10) F	14) T	18) T
3) T	7) T	11) T	15) F	19) F
4) F	8) T	12) F	16) T	20) F

Multiple Choice

1) c	5) b	9) b	13) d	17) b
2) b	6) a	10) c	14) c	18) b
3) a	7) c	11) b	15) d	19) b
4) d	8) b	12) e	16) a	20) a

Short Answer Questions

1. The three key assumptions in the new Keynesian theory of the labor market are money wages are set for a fixed contract period; money wages are set to make the expected quantity of labor demanded equal to the expected quantity of labor supplied; and the level of employment is determined by the actual demand for labor.

2. The Lucas aggregate supply curve is steeper than the new Keynesian supply curve because in the new classical model money wages adjust to clear the labor market while in the new Keynesian model money wages are fixed by contracts.

3. The four main approaches to explaining real wage rigidities as consequences of efficient labor market arrangements are implicit contracts, asymmetric information, insider-outsider interests, and efficiency wages.

4. New classical economists such as Robert Barro insist that such contracts are inefficient and cannot be rationalized as the types of contracts that rational profit-maximizing and utility-maximizing agents would enter into.

5. It is based on the idea that wages are determined by unions representing those who already have jobs, so called insiders. But the labor market also consists of those who do not have jobs, the unemployed, who, according to this model are the outsiders.
    Insiders represented by the union set wages at a level so that it is too high for the outsiders to get in. As a result, high and persistent unemployment can occur even if aggregate demand increases.

6. The menu cost is the cost of changing a price.

7. The presence of asymmetric information in labor markets often means that workers are better informed about how hard they, individually, are working than their managers. One way of coping with this situation is to pay workers a wage above the market wage but hold over them the threat of being fired if they are found to be shirking. Such a higher wage is called an efficiency wage. The name stems from the idea that the higher wage is paid to induce a more efficient effort on the part of the worker.

8. A partial equilibrium analysis is an economic analysis of one part of the economy, taking the rest of the economy is given.

9. New classical economists, such as Robert Barro, insist that such contracts are inefficient and cannot be rationalized as the kinds of contracts that rational profit-maximizing and utility-maximizing agents would enter into.

10. The policy ineffectiveness proposition does not apply to a new Keynesian model because a change in aggregate demand occurring after the wage contract has been signed but before all existing contracts come up for renewal can be reacted to with a policy change in aggregate demand that will take the economy back toward full employment.

Problems

1. (a) $30
   (b) 30

2. 200

3. $y = 2,500 - 225/P$

4. $n^d = 250 - 2.5(W/P)$

5. $20, 216.67

6. 12,277.78

7. $y = 12,500 - 500/P$

8. $y = 110n - 0.22n^2$

9. $10 - 0.04n$

10. $n^d = 250 - 2.27(W/P)$